D0501644

Locality in Linguistic Theory

Locality in
Linguistic Theory

PETER W. CULICOVER

School of Social Sciences
University of California
Irvine, California

WENDY K. WILKINS

Centro de Estudios Lingüísticos y Literarios
El Colegio de México
México D.F., México

1984

ACADEMIC PRESS, INC.

(Harcourt Brace Jovanovich, Publishers)

Orlando   San Diego   San Francisco   New York   London
Toronto   Montreal   Sydney   Tokyo   São Paulo

ACADEMIC PRESS, INC.
Orlando, Florida 32887

United Kingdom Edition published by
ACADEMIC PRESS, INC. (LONDON) LTD.
24/28 Oval Road, London NW1   7DX

Library of Congress Cataloging in Publication Data

Culicover, Peter W.
   Locality in linguistic theory.

   Bibliography: p.
   Includes index.
   1. Grammar, Comparative and general--Syntax.
2. Generative grammar. I. Wilkins, Wendy K.
II. Title.
P291.C78 1983   415   83-8814
ISBN 0-12-199280-2

PRINTED IN THE UNITED STATES OF AMERICA

84 85 86 87   9 8 7 6 5 4 3 2 1

Contents

Preface

This book explores the implications of a generalized Locality Condition in linguistic theory. The notion that rules of grammar and fundamental relations on linguistic structures are local has been a persistent one in the Extended Standard Theory. We suggest here that locality is in fact a universal constraint that should be abstracted from particular rules and relations and incorporated into the linguistic theory itself.

Chapter 1 sketches the general theoretical framework that is assumed throughout, focusing particularly on the system of thematic and grammatical relations that is central to the later chapters. Size limitations on the book have prevented us from doing justice to many of the interesting and important questions that current research in linguistic theory has been concerned with, especially those having to do with scope, anaphora, and coreference. Nevertheless, we have attempted to provide sufficient discussion to suggest that the framework adopted here can, with appropriate refinement, accommodate new theoretical developments as needed.

Chapter 2 focuses on the phenomenon of predication. We show that there are two coindexing rules of predication, one for infinitival complements and one for other predicates. Both rules are local in a sense that we make precise. We show in this chapter how this approach to predication makes it possible to dispense with the assumption that infinitival complements have underlying sentential structures with controlled PRO subjects. This reduction of control to predication is supported by considerable syntactic evidence.

Chapter 3 discusses NP Movement, the transformation implicated in current analyses of the passive construction and the raising to subject construction. If NP Movement is in fact a transformation, we show that it satisfies the Locality Condition on movement. However, many of the local properties of NP Movement can be explained if raising to subject is a case of predication and if the passive construction is derived through a lexical rule, as suggested by a number of researchers. We adopt a base analysis for the raising construction and pursue the theoretical and empirical implications of both a movement analysis and a lexical analysis for the passive.

Chapter 4 takes up *Wh* Movement, showing how this rule, while apparently unbounded, in fact is subject to the Locality Condition. The well-known extraction constraints follow from the Locality Condition, given a particular formal statement of this rule.

Chapter 5 is concerned with the learnability question. Recent work in learnability theory has shown that in principle a locality constraint may be intimately related to the requirement that the class of grammars proposed for human languages must be learnable. For such a class, we would like to be able to show that a language learner is capable of selecting a descriptively adequate grammar of any language to be learned from relatively simple data from that language. Chapter 5 explores the learnability consequences of the locality condition with the goal of ultimately demonstrating that maximally simple sentences (those of "degree-0," that is, with no embedding) may provide sufficient data for the language learner to acquire grammar.

In the course of writing this book we have received generous support from the National Science Foundation and the Sloan Foundation, and we express our gratitude to them. We have benefited from discussion with friends and colleagues and from their encouragement and helpful criticism, and we thank them here: Hagit Borer, Beatriz Garza Cuarón, Julia Horvath, Leah Larkey, Ed Matthei, Bruna Radelli, Michael Rochemont, and Eric Wehrli. Many of the ideas that are explored or mentioned in passing in this book were directly or indirectly stimulated by the thinking of others, in particular, Joan Bresnan, Noam Chomsky, James Higgenbotham, Alec Marantz, and Edwin Williams. We especially appreciate the contribution of Kenneth Wexler, whose work on learnability theory provided the fundamental framework for Chapter 5. A version of Chapter 2 of the book was commented on by referees for *Linguistic Inquiry,* and we acknowledge here the contribution that their comments have made to the improvement of that chapter. James Valender's hospitality made it possible to work on the book at a crucial early stage, and we thank him here. Finally, we thank our friends and families, namely David Barkin, Benjamin Barkin-Wilkins, and Diane Oye, as well as each other, for support and forbearance, especially during those difficult months when completion of the book seemed to be slipping rapidly away from us.

Locality in Linguistic Theory

CHAPTER 1

The Grammatical Theory

Our goal in this book is to develop the implications of a particular grammatical framework within the general outlines of the Extended Standard Theory of transformational grammar. We will also examine in some detail the relationship between the theory of grammar and the mechanism by which humans acquire linguistic competence upon exposure to linguistic data.

The intimate relationship between the theory of grammar and language acquisition was first recognized by Chomsky (1965). A theory of grammar is a formal characterization of the universals of human language, both absolute and contingent. A central problem in the theory of language acquisition is to explain the fact that the language learner invariably converges upon a descriptively adequate hypothesis about the language to which he or she is exposed. Chomsky suggested that it is most reasonable to assume that the learner is guided in this task by knowledge of the linguistic universals.[1] The theory of grammar characterizes the notion "possible human language" for the scientist; the language acquisition mechanism characterizes the notion "possible human language" for the language learner. Investigation of one is thus an investigation of the other.

---

[1]It is logically possible that the learner is guided not by knowledge of linguistic universals, but by more general principles that are not specific to language. However, no one has demonstrated that there are nonspecific procedures that can acquire language. To do so, it would be necessary to argue that universals of human language are special cases of more general universals of human knowledge (whatever these might be). It seems more reasonable to us to assume a priori that to the extent to which we understand the ways in which other aspects of the external world are organized internally into what we informally refer to as "knowledge about the world," different principles may govern different domains. If two distinct domains share the same principles, this would then be a matter of empirical fact. For elaboration of this view, see Chomsky (1972).

In the precise sense in which some aspects of the theory of grammar can be tied directly to properties of the language acquisition mechanism, we may view this association to be an "explanation" of the aspects of the theory of grammar in question.

In this investigation we explore properties of both the theory of grammar and the theory of language learning. More precisely, we elaborate the language learnability theory of Wexler and Culicover (1980) in the context of recent developments in the Extended Standard Theory. As we will discuss in some detail in Chapter 5, the language learnability theory was formulated in terms of a more "classical" linguistic theory, that of Chomsky (1965). The explanations of linguistic theory that have emerged from the study of language learnability must therefore be reexamined in the context of the later, significantly different linguistic theory.

Language learnability theory seeks to explain linguistic universals directly in terms of the task facing the language learner, that of choosing accurately from among a set of competing hypotheses. In the Extended Standard Theory the notion of the range of such hypotheses is significantly different from that provided by Chomsky (1965). One of the questions that we will be concerned with, then, is the extent to which properties of the Extended Standard Theory can be explained through the investigation of language learnability.

Although we will be assuming much of the general point of view of recent work in the Extended Standard Theory, and especially the Government–Binding Theory of Chomsky (1981), this work will not be the basis for our investigation of language learnability. Rather, drawing from recent insights in a variety of theoretical frameworks, we will sketch a theory of grammar in which we believe we can investigate the problem of language learnability most productively. That is, we will idealize the theory of grammar so that it takes into account a wide range of linguistic relations that linguists have argued for. However, to approach language learnability given a class of grammars that express these linguistic relations, we will not attempt to address the full range of current problems that have resulted in current elaborations of the theory of grammar.

Of course, to the extent that it turns out that we can actually solve certain linguistic problems without appealing to additional mechanisms, the simplification of the theory of grammar that we have assumed for expediency may also be preferred on empirical grounds. In general, we will not attempt to pursue this line of argument; there are so many interesting problems in linguistic theory and linguistic description for which intriguing and complex solutions have been suggested that we could not begin to do justice to them within the limitations of this single book. We will attempt to show, however, that in investigating language learnability in the general context of the Extended Standard Theory we can arrive at constraints that adequately address some important problems with which any linguistic theory must be concerned.

More precisely, we will suggest that a plausible generalization of the locality condition of Wilkins (1977) forms an explanatory bridge between the theory of language learnability and linguistic theory. Imposing restrictive conditions on the learnability theory leads us to impose a condition of locality on all rules of grammar; the precise instantiation of this condition depends on the formal properties of the particular rules. The empirical evidence also suggests that rules of grammar are local, and that the descriptively correct expression of this locality property may in fact be the Locality Condition that we will propose here.

We have organized this book as follows. The remainder of this chapter outlines the theory of grammar that we will assume throughout. In general, the justification of particular assumptions is left to the sections of the book where they can be most productively discussed. In Chapter 2 we provide a first statement of the Locality Condition, and then demonstrate its function in constraining the interpretive rule of Predication. In Chapter 3 we look at the rule of NP Movement. We suggest that the Locality Condition applies to rules of movement as well as to rules of interpretation. In Chapter 4 we discuss the relationship between the Locality Condition and *Wh* Movement. We show how the Locality Condition allows us to derive many of the familiar constraints on *Wh* Movement while allowing it to be unbounded. Finally, in Chapter 5 we discuss the language learnability theory and show how certain plausible assumptions about language acquisition motivate the Locality Condition, and therefore may explain the empirically motivated constraints on rules that we observe in earlier chapters.

1. Overview of the Theory

The general view of the theory of grammar that we will assume here is a "modular" one, in the sense that different (although perhaps related) properties of sentences are accounted for by formally distinct components of the grammar. Similarly, related aspects of syntactic and semantic representation need not be expressed in the same formal level of representation.

We will assume that the relevant levels of syntactic representation are Deep Structure, NP Structure (see van Riemsdijk and Williams 1982), S-Structure (see Chomsky 1981), and Surface Structure. The first and last correspond for the most part to the traditional levels of representation within the Extended Standard Theory, the level of NP Structure is the output of NP Movement, and the level of S-Structure is the output of *Wh*

Movement. We will investigate the possibility that Deep Structure as such does not exist, and that the deepest level of syntactic representation is that of NP Structure.

As far as interpretation is concerned, we will not focus here on the precise properties of levels of "semantic representation" or "logical form"; in general, it is irrelevant for our purposes whether such levels of representation exist as distinct levels with their own particular properties. For practical reasons we will assume that each facet of the interpretation of a sentence is expressed in terms of a distinct module. Tentatively, the relevant modules are the following: Quantifier Structure, Negative Structure, Deep Grammatical Relations, Surface Grammatical Relations, Bound Coreference, Anaphoric Coreference, Focus Structure, and Role Structure. Each of these modules is related to some level or levels of syntactic representation, and it is possible that some can be reduced to others, or even all to one.

We adopt the following general picture: The various modules are formally related not only to the syntactic representation, but also to one another, in that there are restrictions that determine the possible mappings between them. Such restrictions are of the following general form: **For any sentence of language L, X is the case in module M_i if and only if Y is the case in module M_j.** Expressing facts about the language in this way allows us to avoid the sorts of a priori commitments that arise when all (or at least many) important aspects of the interpretation of a sentence have to be expressed in the form of a single phrase marker.

We assume of course that the various modules are universal. This means that the primitives and well-formedness conditions that define the form of statements about a language in each module are universal. So, if we assume that there is a module called Deep Grammatical Relations, then the relations subject, object, indirect object, and so on will be defined in Universal Grammar for every language in terms of the available levels of syntactic representation, and related perhaps to other aspects of the representation of a sentence.

Figure 1.1 illustrates our working hypothesis about the modules of a grammar and the possible relationships among them.

2. Levels of Syntactic Representation

We will assume a view of the syntactic component of the grammar along the lines of Figure 1.2. As suggested in Figure 1.1, each level of syntactic representation plays a role in semantic interpretation.

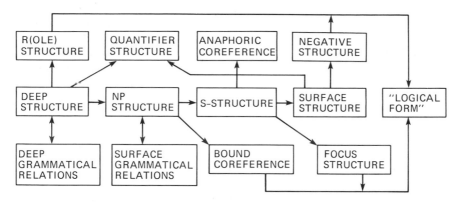

Figure 1.1   Components of the grammar.

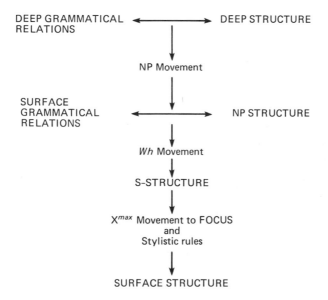

Figure 1.2   Levels of syntactic representation.

2.1. Deep Grammatical Relations

The Deep Grammatical Relations (DGRs) are the familiar notions of subject, object, and indirect object.[2] The representation of the Deep Grammatical Relations is the Deep Structure, in which the DGRs are associated with the relevant NPs. In a configurational language the Deep Structure expresses the DGRs in terms of particular configurations; in a nonconfigurational language the DGRs are expressed in terms of inflectional features on the NPs which have particular phonological realizations in Surface Structure. We will sketch out a few of the details in what follows.

It is traditional to think of the DGRs as the "logical" grammatical relations. However, in current linguistic theory the *by*-phrase of the passive is not the Deep Structure subject, although it is in some sense the logical subject. We capture the similarity between the *by*-phrase and the subject of the active by assigning them the same thematic interpretation.

It is Deep Structure, we assume, that determines the subject–predicate relation, truth (or more generally, satisfaction) conditions, and certain other logical properties that sentences express.[3]

We treat the DGRs as primitives that have a universally limited range of syntactic realization. To assume, as Marantz (1981) does, that there is a universal configurational expression of the DGRs is to suggest that a superficial configurational expression of the underlying grammatical relations, the DGRs, has a certain priority over nonconfigurational realization of these relations. For example, the definition of object as the closest sister to the verb in a verb phrase (Marantz 1981) raises the question of why not all languages appear to have syntactic verb phrases. It is certainly not the case, to our knowledge, that a language with a syntactic verb phrase is "unmarked" in any sense, and yet such a markedness opposition might appear to follow from the configurational definition of DGRs.

If, on the other hand, the DGRs are taken to be syntactic primitives, as in Relational Grammar (Johnson 1979, Perlmutter and Postal 1978),

---

[2]Our view of the DGRs owes much to the ideas of Marantz (1981), which we have borrowed from freely and in some instances adapted considerably. It should be noted that in a theory in which there is no NP Movement and thus no level of Deep Structure distinct from NP Structure (an alternative we in fact consider to be very plausible) the existence of a universal set of Deep Grammatical Relations is problematic. It is possible that the generalizations captured by positing DGRs can be relegated to some other level of representation, such as the lexicon. We will not pursue this complex question here.

[3]We distinguish between the truth conditions that bear strictly on the argument structure of the sentence and those that have to do with logical operators such as negation, quantifiers, and the like. In essence, the Deep Structure determines the structure of the expression which may turn out to be an "open sentence," should one or more of its arguments be quantificational for example.

and syntactic transformations are expressed in terms of grammatical relations rather than configurational notions, then the role of syntactic structure will be to express the grammatical relations at every stage of a derivation. For example, if subject is expressed as [NP, S] (NP immediately dominated by S) as in *Aspects*, a rule that has the effect of moving NP into subject position will actually assign the relation "subject" to this NP; the syntactic realization of this NP in subject position will thus be a secondary effect of the rule.

One virtue of formulating rules of grammar in terms of grammatical relations is that it is possible to ignore those aspects of syntactic structure that must be taken account of in syntactic transformations but that are in fact not crucially involved in these rules. For example, the traditional rule of Passive uses the context X V___Y to restrict movement to the direct object NP only. Yet the relationship between V and the NP appears to be an artifact of the configurational expression of grammatical relations in English. In languages with freer constituent order, although Passive "promotes" a direct object into a subject, as in English, nonetheless there is no overt syntactic structure designating which NP is to be made a subject.

We pursue a point of view here that is intermediate between that of Relational Grammar and more traditional transformational approaches. We will assume that the Deep Grammatical Relations are in fact primitives at a level that is mapped into Deep Structure. In other words, they are not universally defined configurationally, but may be expressed configurationally in a particular language. The DGRs are mapped into Deep Structure by a mapping that we will call Syntactic Realization, or **SR**. We will assume that Universal Grammar makes available a restricted set of devices for the expression of grammatical relations. Word Order–Immediate Domination, Case Marking, and Verbal Agreement may well exhaust the inventory. Syntactic Realization is a mapping from DGRs to particular syntactic devices.

Subsequent levels of syntactic representation are derived by transformations of the restricted form "move α." The extent to which such rules can involve context is an issue that we will not pursue at this point. In general, the syntactic realization of "move NP" is "assign to NP the grammatical relation of some other NP." In a configurational language, this amounts to assigning to one NP the configuration of another. Structure preservation requires that this other NP be empty. In a nonconfigurational language, reassignment of a grammatical relation to an NP means assignment of the case or agreement features associated with the empty NP.

Thus in this approach, the laws of Relational Grammar governing the sequences of grammatical relations that a particular NP may move through in a derivation will be theorems, and not fundamental principles. We will make no systematic point-by-point comparison between the "move NP" approach and Relational Grammar. At the very least, we believe that characterizing matters in more traditional transformational terms (for con-figurational languages at least) allows us to pursue the question of learn-ability more fruitfully, and it is unclear to us at this point how to pursue the question in a substantially different descriptive framework such as Relational Grammar.[4]

Let us consider more formally the mapping from DGRs to syntactic structures. Suppose that γ is a Deep Grammatical Relation and μ is a syntactic mechanism, for example, a grammatical relation as defined in Chomsky (1965) or a morphological case mark. Let **SR** be the cross-product $G \times M$ for G the set of all possible γ and M the set of all possible μ. Then for any language L, $SR_L \in$ **SR**, for **SR** the set of pairs $<\gamma,\mu>$.

Languages do not employ "opaque" subsets of **SR**. Suppose that a language expresses its subjects as "the NP immediately dominated by S," which we may represent by the mapping (1).

(1) $<$subject, [NP, S]$> \in$ **SR**

That language will not also contain the mapping (2).

(2) $<$subject, [NP, VP]$> \in$ **SR**

Generally, we may assume that languages obey a condition of Transparency, a condition that ensures that the language learner is not faced with a systematic ambiguity that pervades virtually every sentence of the language. If (1) and (2) are mappings for a single language, we can show that the class of languages of which this language is a member is not learnable with respect to a plausible learning criterion. We will return to the question of learnability in Chapter 5; at this point we will assume Transparency.[5]

2.2. Deep Structure

As indicated earlier, Deep Structure is the level of representation at which the Deep Grammatical Relations are expressed syntactically. We will argue in Chapter 2 that predication is defined at this level, by a rule

[4]If some formal equivalences between Relational Grammar and Transformational Grammar could be demonstrated, then it should be possible to reduce the learnability properties of the former to those of the latter, which are better understood. The investigation of what these formal equivalences might be is unfortunately beyond the scope of this book.

[5]Transparency restricts the possible subsets of **SR** that are valid for natural language to those that are one–many mappings: No syntactic mechanism expresses more than one grammatical relation, although many syntactic mechanisms may express a single grammatical relation.

of coindexing between NPs and predicates and dependents.[6]

The formal properties of Deep Structure are determined by a theory of the base. For a configurational language like English, the Deep Structure is that level of syntactic representation specified by the context-free phrase structure rules of the base. The theory of such rules is assumed to be something along the lines of the X-bar Theory (see Jackendoff 1977). For a nonconfigurational language, we must assume that there are options for the generation of phrase structures other than the most restrictive instantiation of the X-bar Theory, perhaps along the lines of (3), where $(N^{max})^*$ indicates a sequence of NPs.

(3)   a. $S \rightarrow (N^{max})^* \; V \; (N^{max})^*$
       b. $S \rightarrow V \; (N^{max})^*$
       c. $S \rightarrow (N^{max})^* \; V$

Expansion (3a) defines a language in which the order of arguments of a verb are completely free within S, (3b) defines a verb-initial language, and (3c) defines a verb-final language. Expression of grammatical relations is then carried out in one of two ways, case marking or agreement. We may schematize these two devices as follows:

(4)   a. $N^{max} \rightarrow N^{max} - \text{case}_i$
       b. i. $V \rightarrow \# \cdots + AGR_i + \cdots + \text{root} + \cdots \#$
           ii. $V \rightarrow \# \cdots + \text{root} + \cdots + AGR_i + \cdots \#$

Morphosyntactic devices such as case_i and AGR_i are related to Deep Grammatical Relations by the mappings in the set **SR** discussed in the preceding section.[7]

2.3. NP Structure

Following a suggestion in van Riemsdijk and Williams (1982), we assume that there is a level of NP Structure that is the output of the rule of NP

---

[6]Our account of predication draws heavily on Williams (1980), but differs in certain important respects, including the level of representation at which the coindexing referred to applies and the nature of the constituents to be coindexed.

[7]For languages in which a DGR is expressed simultaneously by more than one device (e.g., by word order and case marking), we might extend our notion of **SR** to allow mappings from DGRs into **sets** of syntactic devices. It is not clear to us that Surface Structure evidence requires us to identify word order with case except in languages like English where the case marking is a vestige of a formerly productive system. For such languages, we could say that case marking is carried out in Surface Structure, whereas for languages with systematic and functional case marking, like Finnish, Russian, and Latin, we could treat case marking as a Deep Structure phenomenon, crucially involved in **SR**.

Movement, applied to Deep Structure.[8] Rules that bind anaphors (e.g., [e]) apply at this level, as does the assignment of Surface Grammatical Relations.

The view of Deep Structure that we considered in Section 2.2 assumed that (morphological) case marking is assigned directly by the mapping from Deep Grammatical Relations to syntactic structures. This appears to imply that languages that have case marking must lack the rule of NP Movement, a rule that assigns to NPs Surface Grammatical Relations that are different from their Deep Grammatical Relations (as in the case of the English passive). But as a matter of empirical fact, case marking languages often have passive (or antipassive) constructions, and other constructions that fall under the NP Movement generalization.

Contrary to immediate appearances, a schema such as (4a) allows us to mark case on an NP in Deep Structure but to realize this case on a different NP in Surface Structure. The key is to interpret NP Movement as a rule reassigning a grammatical relation to an NP. In a language with free constituent order, the effect of NP Movement is to assign the case mark of a dummy NP to the NP that is "moved," as illustrated in (5).[9]

(5)   Deep Structure: $\cdots [e] + \text{case}_i \cdots \text{NP}_j \cdots$
        NP Movement: $\cdots [\text{NP}_j] + \text{case}_i \cdots \emptyset \cdots$

Consider next the counterpart to this account of NP Movement in a language that expresses grammatical relations in terms of agreement markers on verbs. In such languages, the agreement marker AGR_i occupies a designated position in the verbal complex. The form of AGR_i determines which NP will be interpreted as bearing the corresponding grammatical relation. In a language that expresses grammatical relations in this way (e.g., Malagasy) the active–passive opposition might be schematized as follows:

---

[8]Assuming, of course, that there is a rule of NP Movement. Throughout we will make this assumption, but we will always keep in the background the possibility that the relationships captured in current work by NP Movement may be expressed in alternative ways, for example, by lexical rules. See especially our discussion in Section 3 of Chapter 3.

The strong arguments for the existence of a level of NP Structure are of course consistent with the assumption that this level is the only deep level of syntactic representation; what is at issue, then, becomes whether there is independent motivation for a level of Deep Structure. We provide such motivation in Chapter 2, in our discussion of predication, but the phenomena that motivate this level of representation are not so compelling as to effectively preclude the possibility that they can be captured at NP Structure in an alternative approach. We return to this question in Chapters 2 and 3.

[9]It seems to us that this view of case marking is a natural one, at least insofar as it captures what is going on at the interface between syntax and morphology: The syntactic component specifies the cases of a set of NPs without spelling them out; the morphology specifies the actual form of nouns and adjectives (and perhaps other categories) in case paradigms.

(6)   a.   Active: $NP_i\ NP_j\ \#\ \cdots\ AGR_i^{subj} + AGR_j^{obj} + \text{root} + \cdots \#$
       b.   Passive: $(\text{obl}+)NP_i\ NP_j\ \#\ \cdots\ AGR_j^{subj} + \text{root}$
             $+\ \text{Passive} \cdots \#$

In the passive, the underlying subject is marked with an oblique marker, say a preposition, and the underlying object agrees with the subject marker. Since for this language we are mapping from Deep Grammatical Relations to syntactic representations that contain agreement markers, the Deep Structure for the passive in (6b) will be (7).

(7) $[e]_k\ (\text{obl}+)NP_i\ NP_j\ \#\ \cdots\ AGR_k^{subj} + AGR_j^{obj} + \text{root}$
       $+\ \text{Passive} \cdots \#$

Introducing $[e]$ into (7) represents the fact that there is a grammatical relation that is not expressed by any lexical NP in Deep Structure. The syntactic device for expressing a grammatical relation on some NP_x in such a language is the following: "assign to the verb an agreement marker agreeing with NP_x." Thus NP Movement has the following form: "assign to the verb the agreement marker of $[e]$ (in this case, AGR_k^{subj}) with the agreement features of NP_x (in this case, NP_j, yielding AGR_j^{subj}) and eliminate the original agreement marker of NP_x (in this case AGR_j^{obj})." The derived structure of (7) will then be (6b).[10]

---

[10]Although there may be nothing technically wrong with this account, it does suggest that we consider alternatives. A lexical passive in such a language avoids the need to posit empty NPs: The verb is marked with the passive morphology, and NP_j is generated in Deep Structure as the subject. Thus (6b) is the underlying structure.

(6b) $(\text{obl}+)NP_i\ NP_j\ \#\ \cdots\ AGR_j^{subj} + \text{root} + \text{Passive} \cdots \#$

The lexical rule for the passive verb says in effect "assign to the subject of the passive the thematic role(s) that the verb assigns to its object in the active."

More generally, a lexical rule may have the following form: "assign to the subject of the verb marked with the morpheme m the thematic role(s) that the verb assigns to the NP with property (or relation) X in the active." Here, X is some designated NP argument. Malagasy is a language in which this extended type of passive is required (Keenan 1976, Keenan and Ochs 1981). It seems to us that an NP Movement analysis for such a language, although technically workable, lacks the elegance of an NP Movement analysis of the passive in a strict configurational language such as English.

Consider, for example, the Malagasy passive of the instrumental. Normally the instrumental is marked with a preposition. If the verb is marked "instrumental passive," then the subject is interpreted as the instrumental. It cannot be supposed that this verb form "absorbs Case" (in the sense of Chomsky 1981) on the instrumental NP, since Case is normally assigned to this NP not by the verb, but by the preposition. Furthermore, in the instrumental passive the preposition is absent, which raises the question of what the underlying argument position of the instrumental is in these cases. We could suppose that there is a deep preposition that (a) is prevented from assigning Case by the passive verb and (b) is deleted after NP Movement. The technical apparatus required by such an analysis appears to us to be far more complex than the problem requires.

2.4. S-Structure

We assume that NP Structure is mapped into a level of S-Structure by the nonstylistic transformational rules of the grammar, such as *Wh* Movement. Adapting work by Culicover and Rochemont (1983), we assume that these rules leave syntactic traces at the level of S-Structure that are relevant for Focus Interpretation.

In Chapter 4 we will develop an analysis of *Wh* Movement that treats it as an unbounded rule. Evidence that has often been employed to demonstrate that *Wh* Movement is successive cyclic will be explained in terms of the Locality Condition. A consequence of the fact that *Wh* Movement is unbounded, along with the assumption that it applies to NP Structure and before Surface Structure, is that *Wh* Movement can be applied simultaneously to all levels of a phrase marker "across the board."[11] We thus rule out complex interactions of successive applications of *Wh* Movement.

Given across-the-board unbounded movement of *wh*, there is a natural explanation of the fact that otherwise analyzable phrases which have been moved into COMP are not analyzable by *Wh* Movement. As Postal (1972) noted, rules of extraposition appear to be capable of applying to such phrases.

(8)   a. *Who did you believe [that a picture of] John bought?*
        b. *Which picture did John buy of Sal Mineo?*

Across-the-board application thus avoids problems raised by a successive-cyclic analysis of *Wh* Movement.[12]

2.5. Surface Structure

Surface Structure is the level that determines the phonological form of a sentence, including the phonological expression of sentential stress. Surface Structure is, of course, constrained by S-Structure, but is distinct from it.

[11]We use the term "across the board" here in a more general sense than that of Williams (1978), where it refers to simultaneous application to conjoined structures. Our suggestion is that across-the-board application can be generalized to all phrase markers, including those that lack coordination. It is still necessary to specify independently what the **output** of across-the-board application is in conjoined structures. See Williams (1978).

[12]In Wexler and Culicover (1980) the Freezing Principle is invoked to block extraction from COMP. In that framework, successive-cyclic *Wh* Movement is required because of the Binary Principle. We are not assuming either principle here, and suggest in Chapter 5 how they might be dispensed with.

The rules that map from S-Structure into Surface Structure are the "stylistic" rules. These rules must be viewed differently than is suggested in Rochemont (1978), because they do affect the interpretation of the scope of quantifiers and negation. (See Culicover, 1981, for discussion, and see footnote 9, Chapter 4 concerning the role of Deep Structure in quantification.)[13] We will not be concerned in detail with the properties of the stylistic rules, but in Chapter 5 we will speculate on the ways in which certain assumptions about these rules interact with the learnability theory.

3. Thematic Interpretations

Alongside the logical interpretation, a grammar must represent the differences in the thematic roles assigned to NPs in a sentence. The thematic roles include the notions **agent, patient, source, goal, theme, instrument, locus,** etc. We will assume that the thematic roles are derived by a mapping involving Deep Grammatical Relations and lexical entries, along the following lines:

(9)   *Role Assignment*
  (i) *Assign lexically idiosyncratic roles.*
  (ii) *Assign **theme** to the object if there is one. Otherwise assign **theme** to the subject.*[14]
  (iii) *(a) Assign **goal** to subject or (b) assign **patient** to object and **agent** to subject or (c) **instrument** to subject or . . . depending on the governing verb or preposition.*

We will presume that the sort of fact expressed in (iii) about a lexical item is one that is not predictable from any other grammatical facts, but rather is an idiosyncrasy of lexical items that must be explicitly represented in the lexical entries. For simplicity we will not in general represent the particular thematic role assigned to an NP. Rather, we will generalize over the set of thematic roles assigned to transitive direct objects and intransitive subjects by using the notation **A,** and we will refer to the set assigned to subjects of transitives by using the notation **E.** This notational device allows us to capture directly the assignment of **theme;** in general, A abbreviates at least **theme,** and may also be realized as other roles as determined by the governing verb.

Thus we may restate (9) as (9').

---

[13]For Rochemont's more recent views, see Rochemont (in press).
[14]This is Anderson's (1977) Theme Rule.

(9')   ***Generalized Role Assignment***
  (i) *Assign A to object if there is one. Otherwise assign A to subject. Assign E to subject if nothing has been assigned to it.*
  (ii) *Realize A as **theme**.*
  (iii) *Realize A as **patient** and E as **agent**, or A as **patient** and E as **instrument**, or . . . depending on the governing verb or preposition.*

Generalizing over the thematic roles allows us to express certain relations in terms of the general categories. For example, the *by*-phrase in the English passive may be assigned **E**, which will be realized as whatever role would normally be assigned to the subject in the active.[15]

Let us consider some simple examples to illustrate the assignment of thematic roles.

(10)   a. *John fell.*
                A
         b. *John was eating.*
                A
         c. *John hit Mary.*
                E   A
         d. *John saw Mary.*
                E   A
         e. *John gave a book to Susan.*
                E A_{give} A_{to}
         f. *John got a book from Susan.*
                E A_{get} A_{from}

[15]The notation involving **A** and **E** is inspired by the well-known typological difference between "accusative" and "ergative" languages. It is clear that the accusative type of case marking is most naturally formulated in terms of the grammatical relations subject and object, whereas an ergative type of case marking does not appear to have such a natural basis in linguistic structure. In fact, it has been traditional to view ergative case marking as in some sense secondary, marked, or derivative of accusative case marking (although there are other views expressed in the literature; see the articles in Plank 1979).

In ergative constructions, the object of a transitive forms a natural class with the subject of the intransitive. Few languages are pure accusative or pure ergative types. More commonly, a language will show both types of marking in different parts of the grammar. It may be that the ergative pattern is in fact a reflection of a subsystem of the grammar that is parallel to the subsystem of Deep Grammatical Relations. Languages would then differ according to the extent to which one or the other subsystem is expressed syntactically or is parasitic on the other. In a language like English, for example, the grammatical relations are expressed syntactically, whereas the thematic roles are computed from the grammatical relations. It is not difficult to reverse a mapping such as that in (9) [or (9')] so as to have a language in which the thematic roles are expressed syntactically, and the grammatical relations determined by their distribution.

In (10a), *John* is the **theme.** As falling is not a volitional act, the lexical representation for *fall* does not relate subject and **agent.** Here, one might also argue that *John* is an **instrument.**

In (10b) *John* is the **theme** and the **agent** as well, due to the lexical specification of *eat.* In (10c), the lexical entry for *hit* must state that the subject is an **agent.** Thus, *John* is both **source** and **agent,** while *Mary* is both **theme** and **patient.** In (10d), on the other hand, *John* is the subject of *see* and hence is an **experiencer,** while *Mary* is again **theme.**

In (10e) *John* is an **agent** and a **source** while *a book* is the **theme.** The object of the preposition is a **goal.**[16] In (10f) *John* is a **goal** and *Susan* is a **source.** As in (10e), *a book* is the **theme.**

4. Binding

Binding is a coindexing relation that holds between a referring NP and an empty NP. We do not assume the "Binding Theory" of Chomsky (1981). Rather, we derive a condition on empty categories, which we will call the Binding Condition, from independent constraints on the assignment of thematic roles.

The crucial property of any NP with respect to the assignment of thematic roles is that it have a referent. An empty category can only get a referent (in a language like English) by virtue of being coindexed with a referring NP. Although on this approach, the thematic ill-formedness that results from an unbound empty category is not a syntactic one, it correlates with something that can be expressed syntactically, and for convenience we will formulate the Binding Condition as a condition on empty categories, as follows:

(11)   **Binding Condition:** *[e]

In other words, an empty category must be coindexed.[17] We assume that this condition applies at the surface, after thematic interpretations

---

[16]The object of the preposition is thus thematically distinguished from the indirect object in the double object construction; the latter is a **recipient.** See Culicover (1976b), Oehrle (1975), and Stowell (1981) for discussion.

[17]Ellipsis is an exception to the Binding Condition stated as a syntactic condition, but not if it is a condition on interpretations. In some languages (e.g., Chinese), it is possible to have an unbound empty NP in an argument position if its referent is determined by the context. If Wasow's (1979) and Williams's (1977) analysis of VP Ellipsis is on the right track, NPs contained within elliptical VPs are unbound empty categories. Again, in such a case the referent is supplied contextually. What needs to be determined, of course, is why some languages allow freer ellipsis than others, given that the resources of context are equally available in all languages.

have been assigned; it is in fact a superficial syntactic reflex of a condition on the assignment of roles to the referents of referring expressions (Chapter 3, Sections 1 and 2).

We assume in its essence the distinction made in the Government–Binding (GB) framework between pronouns, anaphors, and names. The intuition that this distinction captures is that a name provides its own reference and does not inherit it from the syntactic structure. A nonreflexive pronoun has the important property of being similar to a name. That is, for the purposes of a particular discourse, it can be used to refer to some contextually defined individual; it "stands for" the name of that individual. However, a pronoun may also have its reference determined by the sentence in which it appears. A reflexive pronoun in fact must have its reference determined in the sentence. Shortly we will discuss a formal mechanism for expressing these intuitions.

We will assume throughout that the empty category, which we represent as [e], is an anaphor; that is, its reference is determined grammatically. We depart from current thinking by classifying reflexives as pronouns. Reflexive pronouns are distinguished by the fact that they are insulated against the application of Disjoint Reference. The formalism that expresses this property of reflexives requires them to be coindexed with some NP in the same sentence.

Government–Binding Theory formalizes the foregoing in terms of the notion "governing category," making the further claim that within the domain of a sentence there are subdomains of binding pertaining to different pronouns and anaphors. Let us pursue here some of the implications of the conceptually simpler formulation that the only relevant domain for binding is the entire sentence.[18]

Let us assume first that the scope of a referential element is the domain of the sentence c-commanded by it, bounded from below by nodes that dominate embedded roots. Suppose that there is an index-assigning procedure that randomly assigns referential indices to all NPs except [e].

We must guarantee that lexical NPs and contextually referential pronouns, that is, "names," are not bound anywhere in a sentence. Following standard practice, we will say that β is bound by α if and only if β is within the scope of α. As noted in Footnote 18, the definition of scope must be sensitive to the distribution of "root" sentences.[19]

---

[18]More precisely, the domains in which the coindexing possibilities are valid are precisely those in which "scope" is defined. Other things being equal, such a domain is defined by c-command, and is not bounded from below. So the domain of a subject NP is the entire S that it c-commands. Islands, such as relative clauses and embedded roots, constrain scope somewhat, as we note in what follows.

[19]The definition of "root" originated with Emonds (1970), and has been discussed in the literature by Hooper and Thompson (1973), Grimshaw (1979b), and others.

A diagnostic for roots is that Subject-Aux Inversion must apply in them after *Wh* Movement. For example, we have standard examples like those in (12) and nonstandard examples like those in (13).

(12) a. *What did John see? (*What John saw?)*
      b. *Where did you go? (*Where you went?)*
      c. *Why should Mary do that? (*Why Mary should do that?)*
      d. *Where did you go and what did you do?*

(13) a. *We won't talk to John because what did John really see?*
      b. *I don't want you to tell me much, although where did you go last week, if you don't mind telling me?*
      c. *I don't think that Mary is going to call the cops, because why should Mary do that?*[20]

We do not consider it accidental that in the nonstandard examples in (13) we not only find inversion, but also coreferential lexical NPs. As is well known, normally a lexical NP cannot be c-commanded by a coreferential NP, a fact that motivates the constraint in the Binding Theory that a name cannot be bound.

(14) **John$_i$ says that* $\left\{ \begin{array}{l} \textit{John}_i \textit{ will leave.} \\ \textit{no one likes John}_i. \\ \textit{the woman who saw John}_i \textit{ left.} \end{array} \right\}$

Because pronouns can be bound, it must be possible to assign to a pronoun the index of another NP in the same sentence. This result will occur if indices are assigned freely. If a pronoun is bound, then it will not be eligible for interpretation as a name. The fact that an NP cannot be a name if it is bound is independently required in case a pronoun is assigned the index of an NP that it c-commands, in order to rule out examples like the following.

(15) **He$_i$ says that John$_i$ is a fink.*

We may now reduce the Binding Theory to the following principles.

(16) **Binding Principles**
      (i) *If α is bound it is not a name.*
      (ii) *A reflexive cannot be a name.*

It follows that names cannot be bound, that pronouns may be bound but need not be, and that reflexives must be bound. A lexical NP must be interpreted as a name (unless it is an epithet), and if it is bound a semantic

---

[20]Examples like these were pointed out to us by Richard Oehrle.

violation must result.[21] The conditions on the distribution of [e] follow independently from conditions on thematic interpretations; essentially, if [e] is not coindexed then there is a thematic role that is assigned to a nonreferring NP, an ill-formed interpretation.[22]

Let us consider some examples by way of illustration. Next to each NP are the possible relevant indices.

(17)   a.   *John$_i$ saw him$_{i,j}$.*
         b.   *John$_i$ said that Mary likes him$_{i,j}$.*
         c.   *He$_{i,j}$ said that Mary likes John$_i$.*
         d.   *His$_{i,j}$ mother likes John$_i$.*
         e.   *His$_{i,j}$ mother said that Mary likes John$_i$.*
         f.   *He$_{i,j}$ came in and then John$_i$ fainted.*
         g.   *I hit him$_{i,j}$ before John$_i$ stood up.*
         h.   *I hit him$_{i,j}$ because John$_i$ was obnoxious.*

By the first Binding Principle a name cannot be bound. Thus the pronoun in examples (c) and (g) cannot be assigned the index i. It might be expected that the same would hold for example (h), but the evidence we have discussed suggests that the *because*-clause is a root, and therefore not within the scope of the pronoun. Therefore *John* is not bound in (h), and either index can be assigned to the pronoun.[23]

Example (a) violates Disjoint Reference if i is assigned to the pronoun, which we will take up in more detail in the next section. The lexical noun phrase in (d), (e), and (f) is not c-commanded by the pronoun, and so they may be coreferential.

The real problem with binding and coreference arises when examples involving *Wh* Movement and Topicalization are introduced. Classical cases of "cross over" that must be dealt with in any framework include the following:

(18)   a.   **Who$_i$ does he$_i$ think Mary likes t$_i$?*
         b.   *[Who who he$_i$ likes]$_j$ does John$_i$ want to talk to t$_j$?*
         c.   *[Who who John$_i$ likes]$_j$ does he$_i$ want to talk to t$_j$?*
         d.   **He$_i$ wants to talk to [someone who John$_i$ likes]$_j$.*

---

[21]It is not clear how to make this result follow from other principles. We could assume that a lexical NP has an "inherent" reference that prevents it from being used as a coreferential element, but this just seems to be another way of saying that a name cannot be bound.

[22]We assume that there is a rule of Binding which copies an index that has been assigned to some NP onto [e]. This rule results in a well-formed interpretation only in the *tough* construction (a matter that we will discuss in Chapter 3).

[23]Similar examples are discussed in Culicover (1976a). There it was suggested that perhaps the syntactic structures were different, so that *him* would not c-command the *because*-clause. We do not rule out this possibility here.

If we maintain the strict assumption that the Binding Principles are relevant on domains in which NPs have scope, we must analyze examples like these accordingly. Assuming that the Binding Principles are relevant after *Wh* Movement, we may say that a nonargument NP β is in the scope of another NP α if the trace of β is in the scope of α. Thus example (a) is ruled out. In examples (b) and (c), the application of *Wh* Movement leaves a trace, but it is the trace of the NP with the index j, while *John* has the index i. In (d), again, $John_i$ is in the scope of he_i and thus the Binding Principles apply.[24]

5. Reflexives

We elaborate the function of reflexive pronouns in terms of the thematic roles. Let an **R-structure** R be a set of triples $<i, t, k>$ such that i is the index of an NP, t the thematic roles assigned to i, and k the domain on which t is defined. For practical purposes we may replace k by the verb that defines the domain, so that $<i,$ **theme**, *fall*$>$ would mean that NP_i is the **theme** of *fall*.

The fact that NPs in a sentence may be coreferential means that in R-Structure it may be the case that a particular referential index participates in triples involving more than one domain index. For example, the expression $\{<i,$ **agent**, *say*$>, <i,$ **patient**, *hit*$>, \ldots \}$ means that the set of individuals i is the **agent** of saying that someone hit i. What we are calling a "set of individuals" in R-Structure is, of course, not a set of individuals, but a representation of a set of individuals.

The R-structure is not a configuration of objects in the physical world. Rather, it is a representation of part of the linguistic content of some expression. Consequently an R-structure will be constrained in ways that are not conceptual but linguistic. The Disjoint Reference constraint is one such condition.

The function of a reflexive pronoun is to produce an R-structure in which the index of a particular NP appears in two triples expressing different thematic roles with respect to the same domain. The familiar principle of Disjoint Reference,[25] expressed in terms of thematic roles, stipulates that two triples in the R-structure cannot have the same index and the same domain:

(19)   Disjoint Reference: *$\{<i, t, k>, <i, t', k>, \ldots \}$

[24]The preceding discussion is an adaptation of a more elaborate treatment by J. Higgenbotham (Sloan lectures, University of California, Irvine, Spring 1982).

[25]See Chomsky (1973).

We are assuming that in the mapping from syntactic structure into R-Structure, the referents of NPs are expressed by the indices assigned to the NPs by the procedure discussed in the preceding section. Suppose that the referent of a pronominal NP with index i is i in R-Structure, and so sentences like *John saw him* cannot mean the same as *John saw himself.* Although in principle *him* may be assigned the same index as *John,* it cannot if the two are arguments of the same verb, because of Disjoint Reference.

We suppose therefore that the referent of a reflexive is expressed as (i) rather than simply as i. If we replace (i) by (x), x arbitrary, then we have a representation in R-Structure of "the self" or "oneself."[26] Thus the point of extending the notational system for reference is that in the R-Structure it must be specified that a particular thematic role is reflexive even in cases where the reflexive pronoun is not bound in the syntax.

A reflexive will be assigned an index in the same way as any pronoun. If the index is that of another NP, either that NP c-commands the reflexive or it does not. If it does, then the reflexive is "bound"; that is, it does not have the interpretation of a name. If the reflexive is not bound, then it would have to allow interpretation as a name, but a reflexive cannot be a name, and therefore cannot designate a set of individuals in R-Structure. Thus an unbound reflexive will lead to thematic ill-formedness.[27]

We suppose further that (i) is not subject to Disjoint Reference: A reflexive that is coindexed with some NP in the same domain will insulate the argument position that it occupies. This view of reflexives is consistent with certain facts that cannot be dealt with naturally in terms of standard approaches to coindexing. Consider, for example, the following sentences, in which the pronoun is not coindexed with an NP in the same domain.[28]

(20)   a. *John$_i$ demanded that all messages to him$_i$ be placed in the envelope outside of the door.*
          b. *John$_i$ demanded that all messages to himself$_i$ be placed in the envelope outside of the door.*

An example like (20b) presents two problems for standard approaches to reflexives. First of all, it should not be possible to coindex *himself* with an NP in a higher sentence. Assuming that there is a PRO in the NP that coindexes the reflexive is not a possible option, because PRO cannot be

---

[26]In other words, the proform *one* inherently has the index x or, if we prefer, *arb.*

[27]The exceptions are indexical: *as for myself/yourself/*himself.* Indexical pronouns can always function as names because their reference is determined extragrammatically, as is the reference of proper nouns.

[28]These examples were pointed out to us by Ed Matthei, and much of this discussion was arrived at in the course of discussions with him about these sorts of examples.

governed, but is governed in the NP (the noun is a governor). Second of all, standard approaches to reflexives cannot capture the fact that in (20b), *John$_i$* must be the **source** of the messages, whereas in (20a) he cannot be.

The R-structures of these two examples allow us to capture the observed difference in interpretation. We sketch them out in (21). *Message* defines a domain of thematic relations.

(21) a. $\{<x, \textbf{source}, \textit{message}>, <i, \textbf{goal}, \textit{message}>, \dots \}$
      b. $\{<x, \textbf{source}, \textit{message}>, <(i), \textbf{goal}, \textit{message}>, \dots \}$

Let us say that reflexives in R-Structure trigger the replacement of x by i in **the same thematic domain**. Call this rule Rep. Thus (21b) will be replaced by (22), which is the same partial R-Structure as John's messages to himself.

(22) $\{<i, \textbf{source}, \textit{message}>, <(i), \textbf{goal}, \textit{message}>, \dots \}$

By the use of Rep we are able to eliminate PRO in subjectless infinitives, a point that we discuss in considerable detail in Chapter 2.[29]

If some head noun in an NP does not implicate a network of thematic roles, then coreference will still hold. Suppose we replace *messages* in (20) with *pictures* as in (23).

(23) a. *John$_i$ demanded that all pictures of him$_i$ be placed in the envelope outside of the door.*
      b. *John$_i$ demanded that all pictures of himself$_i$ be placed in the envelope outside of the door.*

In this case, since *picture* does not imply a particular act, in contrast to *message,* we get essentially the same reading regardless of whether the pronoun is reflexive or not.

Importantly, the examples of (23) are grammatical with either a pronoun or a reflexive as in neither case is there a violation of the Binding Principles. In contrast, consider (24).

(24) **John saw a snake near himself.*

This example (to which we return in Chapter 2) illustrates the importance of defining the reflexive relation on R-Structure (rather than simply in terms of syntactic structure). The important point here is that (by predi-

---

[29]It appears that the replacement of x by an index in R-Structure [for examples like (20b)] is required in addition to rules of coindexing that yield interpretations of referential and bound anaphora. We see no way to reduce coindexing in the syntax to index replacement in R-Structure without recapitulating much of the Binding Theory of Chomsky (1981) in a much less general treatment of the phenomena.

cation) *near himself* is coindexed with *a snake*. In other words, the R-structure is $\{<snake_i,$ **theme**, *near*$>$, $<himself_i,$ **location**, *near*$>$, ... $\}$ and not $\{<John_i,$ **theme**, *near*$>$, $<himself_i,$ **location**, *near*$>$ ... $\}$. The thematic structure necessary for a reflexive interpretation is not met in (24).

It follows from our treatment of reflexives that a reflexive will be ungrammatical in subject position. Consider the examples in (25) and (26).

(25)   *$Himself_{i,j}$ shaved $John_j$.

(26) $John_i$ believes that $\left\{ \begin{array}{l} he_i \\ he_j \\ {}^*himself_i \end{array} \right\}$ *will win the race.*

In (25), if *himself* has index i it is functioning as a name, which is impossible for reflexives, by the second Binding Principle. If *himself* has index j then *John* is bound, which is impossible for a lexically specified NP. In (26), the reflexive pronoun is bound by $John_i$, but cannot be assigned the correct interpretation in R-Structure, because *John* and *himself* are not grammatical arguments of the same verb, and hence are not arguments in the same predicational domain.[30]

This concludes our sketch of the grammatical theory that will serve as background to the rest of this book. Our treatment of reflexives as designated elements in the syntax and in R-Structure allows a non-PRO analysis of predication, as the discussion in the next chapter will show. The introduction of R-Structure as a significant level of representation appears to allow a radical reduction in theoretical machinery, as compared with alternative approaches in the Government–Binding framework.

---

[30]The notion that reflexives are well formed only within basic or derived predicational domains suggests an analysis of examples like *John took the book with him(*self)*, where we may say that the *with*-phrase is predicated of *the book* and therefore does not contain a reflexive. Crucially, the entire sentence consists of two predicational domains, not one. Some additional examples that suggest a similar approach are *this sheet has a hole in it(*self)*, *John found a parasite on him(*self)*. The class of PPs that allow for this predicational interpretation appears to be composed of those that do not assign an obligatory thematic role to their complements; compare *John put a blanket under himself/*him*, **John put a blanket* and *John found a blanket under ?himself/him, John found a blanket*.

Our account does not explain examples like $John_i$ *thinks that* $Bill_j$ *bought a picture of* $himself_{*i,j}/him_{i,*j}$. It is possible, as E. Williams suggests, that the conditions on reflexives may be reformulated in terms of a generalized notion of predicational domain. We will not pursue the complexities of the reflexive here.

CHAPTER 2

Deep Structure Coindexing

As discussed in Chapter 1, we assume that R-Structure is read off of Deep Structure after the assignment of arguments to their verbal domains. In this chapter we will discuss the mechanism by which the constituents that do not enter into the system of DGRs are assigned a domain. In many instances an S will contain constituents which will receive no thematic role or DGR by the system we have already discussed. These constituents are assigned a function in the sentence by a system of coindexing for predication (as discussed in the important work by Williams [1980]). Without some sort of rule of predication the constituent *hot* in a sentence like (1) would receive no interpretation as it would have no DGR or thematic role of its own and as it is not part of a constituent that has been assigned such relations.

(1)   *The boy drinks the coffee hot.*

We will concern ourselves with the rule(s) which assure that in an example like (1) *hot* is interpreted as being "predicated of" *the coffee*. We will consider also the assignment of an antecedent to verbal constituents that have no subjects, as *to leave* in (2):

(2)   *John wants (Bill)* $_{VP}$[*to leave*].

We begin our discussion of the grammar of English with a consideration of predication because it turns out to be a key issue in deciding the overall structure of the theory of grammar. Our discussion of predication will lead us to defend exactly the four distinct levels of syntactic representation we have already mentioned, namely, Deep Structure, NP Structure, S-Structure, and Surface Structure. This means that we will argue against the necessity of postulating a syntactic level of Predicate Structure (PS) with its own particular properties, as proposed in Williams (1980). We will argue that it is possible to construct an adequate theory of predication without a separate level of PS, by distinguishing between "predicates" and "dependents," and by determining the predication relation on Deep Structure by means of the two simple coindexing procedures to be proposed in what follows. The determination that predication is a Deep Structure phenomenon gives evidence for the existence of a movement rule of NP Preposing (discussed in Chapter 3) which in turn provides the evidence for a level of NP Structure.[1]

1. Introduction to the Deep Structure Theory of Predication

Our proposal is that coindexing is a Deep Structure phenomenon. Coindexing is relevant for two similar, yet distinct, processes: (*a*) true predication and (*b*) control of dependent complements.[2] The terms "predicate" and "dependent complement" (henceforth "dependent,") are defined as follows:

(3)   A **predicate** is any nonpropositional major category X^{max}, immediately dominated by V^n, that bears neither a DGR nor a thematic role.

A **dependent** is any nonpropositional major category X^{max}, immediately dominated by V^n, that does not bear a DGR but that does bear a thematic role.

Informally, a predicate is any major phrasal category (NP, VP, AP, PP) immediately dominated by a projection of V, which is not the subject,

---

[1]See van Riemsdijk and Williams (1982) where the level of NP Structure is discussed in detail. We differ from their proposed analysis by not identifying "Predicate Structure" with NP Structure. Our analyses make crucially different assumptions with respect to the existence of the element PRO. As we assume no PRO, we can determine the predication relation on Deep Structure. As will be pointed out in the course of the discussion of predication in this chapter and in the discussion of NP Movement in the chapter that follows, the assumption that there is no element PRO turns out to complement a lexical analysis of passives. If there turns out to be no movement rule for NPs, then of course there would be no need for a level of NP- structure. For the purposes of this book we continue to discuss certain issues in terms of NP-movement because it greatly facilitates the account of control. In a theory containing lexical passives there remains much work to be done for an explanation of predication and the control of infinitival complements.

[2]Although it is possible to state these two processes as one, as in Wilkins (1981b), this actually obscures an important distinction. Additionally, it leads to no simple way of defining constituents that must be controlled.

direct object, or indirect object, and which has no role in the system of thematic roles.[3] A dependent is structurally identical to a predicate. It differs in that it is assigned a thematic role by (i) of the Role Assignment algorithm. In other words, as we shall see, dependents bear lexically determined thematic roles.

As indicated in the definitions, predicates and dependents are nonpropositional. A **proposition** is a verbal element together with its complete argument structure. An S (or S') is a proposition as it contains a verb and all its related thematic roles. The result of coindexing for predication is the creation (or perhaps better, the completion) of a proposition. A VP with no subject is not a proposition; once it is assigned an antecedent (in the ways in which we will subsequently discuss) it becomes a proposition.[4] After coindexing applies, thematic roles are assigned by predicates to their antecedents, or in other words, mapping into R-Structure takes place.

A predicate is assigned an antecedent "locally," by the rule of Predicate Coindexing (P Coindex), in accord with first instantiation of the Locality Condition (LC). These are given in (4).[5]

(4)   a.   *P Coindex: Coindex NP and X where X is a predicate.*
       b.   *Locality Condition: All rules are local.*
             #1. P Coindex affects NP and X where X is bijacent to NP.
             *Definition: X is **bijacent** to NP iff:*
             (a) X is a sister to NP, or
             (b) X is immediately dominated by a sister of NP.

Dependents are assigned an antecedent by the rule of Dependent Coindexing (D Coindex) in accord with the second instantiation of the LC. Dependent Coindexing is essentially the Principle of Minimal Distance of Rosenbaum (1970).

(5)   a.   *D Coindex: Coindex NP and X where X is a dependent.*

[3]As it turns out, VPs in the relevant positions invariably bear thematic roles and therefore are dependents rather than predicates.

[4]The inclusion of "nonpropositional" in the definitions of predicate and dependent assures against the assignment of too many NPs to a single verbal element. For instance, a complement S will never be assigned an antecedent.

[5]The coindexing rule is a natural extension of the Variable Interpretation Convention (VIC) of Wilkins (1977, 1980a, 1981a) which was originally proposed as a condition on movement rules. The definition of "bijacent" owes much to the insight provided by Williams (1980, p. 204, Footnote 1) in his discussion of c- subjacency. We define bijacency here rather than use the notion of "weakly adjacent" from the VIC because this new term avoids the necessity of referring to left–right order. In an earlier paper on which this chapter is based (Wilkins 1981b) the selected antecedent for a predicate was "the leftmost weakly adjacent NP." Although the results are the same, it is clearly preferable to avoid an arbitrary reference to "leftmost."

b. *Locality Condition:* All rules are local.
    #2. D Coindex affects the closest preceding NP to X.

As will become clear when we discuss P Coindex and D Coindex, both coindexing principles select an NP which is in the relevant sense "close" to the constituent to be coindexed. In this way they are both local rules. In other words, the basic organizing principle for the assignment of antecedents is proximity (as Rosenbaum clearly argued). Both of these rules are constrained by the LC. "Closeness" or "locality" for the rule of P Coindex is determined with respect to structure, the bijacency requirement, whereas for D Coindex it is determined strictly by order.

After the coindexing rules apply, the antecedent is assigned the appropriate role depending on the nature of the coindexed constituent. Thus AP, PP, and NP predicates (or dependents) always assign **theme** to their antecedents. A VP dependent (as will become clear, VP complements are always dependents rather than predicates) assigns a role to its antecedent according to the role assignment algorithm.

Before we begin a detailed discussion of our analysis of control (for ease of exposition, where it is not necessary to distinguish between P Coindex and D Coindex, we will refer to them both as "control" or both as "predication"), we must lay out two assumptions about the structure of the base in our theory.

2. Structure of the VP

2.1. V^1 and V^2

First of all it is assumed that there is a certain amount of structure within the VP and (at least) one phrasal node that intervenes between the verb and the maximal VP. The maximal projection of V is the matrix VP, and not S. We assume that S is a projection of M(odal).[6] The base component for English therefore includes the following rules:

(6)   a. $V^2 \rightarrow V^1$ (AP) (PP) (V^2) (S')
       b. $V^1 \rightarrow V$ (NP) (AP) (PP) (V^2) (S')

For transitive verbs V^1 contains at least the verb and the direct object NP. For certain verbs certain other complements are also inside V^1. The constituents occurring inside V^1 are those that are obligatorily strictly subcategorized (as the PP that co-occurs with *put*) and those that are directly assigned thematic roles by the verb. Although a constituent immediately

---

[6]For discussion of S' as M^{max} see Klein (1981); see also suggestions in Chomsky (1981) about S as a projection of INFL.

dominated by V^2 might bear a thematic role, the particular role is not assigned directly by the verb, but rather (at least in English) by a preposition (as in "goal" indirect objects governed by *to* or "benefactive" indirect objects governed by *for*). As we will see in what follows, predicates, which by definition bear no thematic role, may occur either in V^1 or in V^2.

Although the structure of a given VP must be determined by the lexical characteristics of the head V (e.g., the number of arguments it requires), there are several syntactic tests to provide independent motivation for the constituency of V^1 that we propose here.

The first test for V^1 is provided by the VP Rule of Williams (1977). This rule, involved in the examples of (7), deletes part of a VP, but according to Williams cannot delete "too small" a part.

(7) a. *Who sent the letter to who(m)?*
         John did to Mary.
     b. *Who baked the cookies for who(m)?*
         John did for the children.
     c. *Who put the book where?*
         *John did on the table.
     d. *Who promised Mary what?*
         *John did $\left\{ \begin{array}{l} \textit{that Bill would leave.} \\ \textit{to leave.} \end{array} \right\}$
     e. *Who promised that Bill would leave to whom?*
         John did to Mary.
     f. *Who persuaded Mary* $\left\{ \begin{array}{l} \textit{to} \\ \textit{that} \end{array} \right\}$ *what?*
         *John did $\left\{ \begin{array}{l} \textit{that Bill would leave.} \\ \textit{to leave.} \end{array} \right\}$
     g. *Who persuaded Mary to leave where?*
         John did on the train.

In our terms the VP Rule deletes the constituent V^1. In (7a) and (7b), where the PPs are outside of V^1, they may be left after the VP Rule applies. Example (7c) is ungrammatical because only part of the V^1 was deleted. Examples (7d)–(7g) show that by the VP Rule test for V^1, the complements for *promise* and *persuade* are inside V^1, but indirect objects and locative objects for most verbs not of the *put*-class are outside of V^1.

A second syntactic test for V^1 involves the movement of emphatic reflexives away from subject position. According to Baltin (1981), terms move only to "landing sites" that are constituent boundaries. The landing site for subject emphatics is VP-final position. The differences in grammaticality in (8) can therefore be accounted for by use of the constituent

V^1. Emphatics may be attached in V^1-final position, but not internal to V^1. (They may, of course, also be attached in V^2-final position, but this fact is irrelevant here.)

(8)   a. ***John** wrote the letter **himself** to Mary.*
        b. ***John** baked the cake **himself** for the party.*
        c. *****John** put the book **himself** on the table.*
        d. *****Mary** persuaded Bill **herself** to leave.*
        e. *****Mary** promised Bill **herself** to leave.*

In (8a) and (8b) the *himself* is attached at the boundary of V^1 and the sentences are grammatical. In (8c)–(8e) where the emphatic reflexive has moved to a position internal to V^1 the results are ungrammatical.[7]

   A third argument involves the base position for adverbs. Assuming the position of VP adverbs to be V^1 in Deep Structure, the deep structures underlying (9a) and (9b) are (10a) and (10b), respectively.

(9)   a. *John gave the book to Mary carefully.*
        b. *John put the book carefully on the table.*

(10)   a.

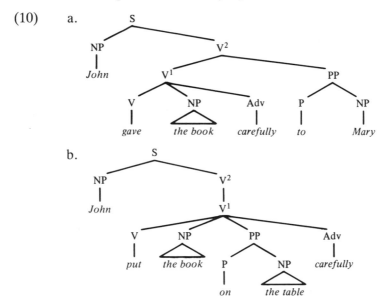

   b.

To derive (9a), *carefully* must be moved to the right. Sentence (9b) must be derived by movement of *carefully* to the left. If we assume that this

---

[7]This account, where the complements to *promise* and *persuade* are involved, is different from, and more accurate than, that in Wilkins (1977). See discussion in de Haan (1979) and Bordelois (1982).

leftward movement adjoins the adverb to the PP, then the resulting structure will be (11). The PP* in (11) indicates a Chomsky-adjunction. Alternatively, there is the possibility that the moved adverb adjoins to the P (see discussion in Culicover 1980).

(11)

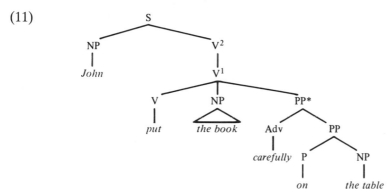

The difference in structure between (10a) and (11), which involves the distinction between V^2- and V^1-PPs can then be used to account for the grammaticality distinction in (12) versus (13), where PP Topicalization is applied.

(12) a. *To Mary, John gave the book carefully.*
      b. **To Mary, John gave the book carefully.*

(13) a. **On the table, John put the book carefully.*
      b. *Carefully on the table, John put the book.*

These grammaticality distinctions are correctly accounted for by the proposed base structures and the theory of adverb movement where the constituency of V^1 is assumed. Sentence (12b) is ungrammatical because *carefully to Mary* is not a constituent and therefore cannot be topicalized. Sentence (13b), on the other hand, is the result of the movement of the PP constituent illustrated in (11). Example (13a) shows that the whole PP must be moved. [Example (13a) must also be prevented as the result of PP Topicalization applying directly to (10b), but this issue is not directly relevant to the constituency of V^1.]

A fourth argument for V^1 involves Gapping. Stillings (1975) notes that the most acceptable cases of Gapping occur when there is exactly one constituent preceding and following the gapped V. Culicover and Wexler (1977) observe that Gapping is preferred when it occurs in a VP that has an NP PP sequence after the verb to when it occurs in a VP with NP NP. Thus we have the following difference:

(14) a. *John gave a book to Mary, and Sam, a magazine to Susan.*

b. *John gave Mary a book, and Sam, Susan a magazine.*

Culicover and Wexler attribute the difference to the fact that the second structure is frozen, and hence the Freezing Principle blocks Gapping.

We suggest an alternative explanation. Assume that in (14a) the indirect object is a constituent of V^2, whereas in (14b) both the direct object and the indirect object are constituents of V^1 after Dative Movement. Gapping is then allowed only where the result is a single constituent in V^1, constituents remaining in V^2 being irrelevant. This account, unlike the use of the Freezing Principle, explains the ungrammaticality of (15c) as compared with (15a) and (15b).

(15)   a.   *John sells trucks on Thursdays, and Mary, cars on Fridays.*
        b.   *John gave a dog to Mary, and Sam, a cat to Susan.*
        c.   **John put Fido in the doghouse, and Sam, Spot in the yard.*

Although the judgments are perhaps subtle, (15c) seems to us worse than the other two. The facts of both (14) and (15) are accounted for by the structures we are assuming utilizing the particular proposed constituency of V^1.

A final test presented here for the internal structure of the V^1 which we are assuming concerns the order of PPs. In general the order of PPs is free, but where there is a VP with a PP in V^1 and one that is outside, the one in V^1 must come first. This is shown in (16). The examples in (17) are the nominalizations related to (16), where a parallel two-level structure is assumed, and where the grammaticality distinction shows up more clearly.

(16)   a.   *John $\left\{ \begin{array}{l} attached \\ fastened \\ nailed \end{array} \right\}$ the handle to the machine for Bill.*

        b.   *?John $\left\{ \begin{array}{l} attached \\ fastened \\ nailed \end{array} \right\}$ the handle for Bill to the machine.*

(17)   a.   *John's $\left\{ \begin{array}{l} attachment \\ fastening \\ nailing \end{array} \right\}$ of the handle to the machine for Bill . . .*

        b.   **John's $\left\{ \begin{array}{l} attachment \\ fastening \\ nailing \end{array} \right\}$ of the handle for Bill to the machine . . .*

The base rule for the V^1 which we have proposed readily accounts for these grammaticality facts.

These five arguments for VP-internal structure are meant to make precise the constituency of V^1 as containing at least the direct object NP, locative PPs for *put*-type verbs (but not indirect object PPs), and the complements of verbs such as *promise* and *persuade*. No claim is made by these tests about constituents that are not daughters of V^1. These might be attached either under V^2 or directly under S. We assume, as will become clear in what follows, that the phrase structure expansion for V^2 is as given in (6a), and the only right sister to V^2 in S is Adverb Phrase.[8]

2.2. VP Complements

A second assumption about the base in our theory is that there are VP complements. In other words, not all surface infinitives are derived from full Ss in the base; certain surface infinitives are base VPs. Verbs can occur with VP complements, or S complements, or they can alternate between the two. Some verbs allow for only VP complements, as in (18).

(18) a. *try:* [___ VP]
      b. *want:* [___ (NP) VP]
      c. *force:*
          compel:
          permit: [___ NP VP]
          pick:
          name:
      d. *be:* [___ VP][9]
      e. *be easy:* [S ___(PP))]
                     [___ (PP) VP]

We take the fact that these verbs can never appear with a following complementized clause to be evidence that they do not subcategorize for full Ss. Presumably COMP is not an optional constituent in the expansion of S' (but see Chomsky 1981). The generation in the base of VP complements where verbs cannot co-occur with any complementizer avoids, of course, the need for filters to delete certain embedded COMPs (cf. Chomsky and Lasnik 1977) or a rule of (sometimes obligatory) S' deletion (Chomsky 1981).

---

[8]This assumption about the VP and AdvP, along with the assumption that S is a projection of M, allows for exceptionless definitions of predicate and dependent and very general coindexing procedures.

[9]This subcategorization frame for *be* is, of course, incomplete. Besides having other constituents which can follow it, *be* can also subcategorize a subject VP (e.g., *To love is to live!*). See Section 6 of this chapter.

Whereas the example verbs in (17) can never co-occur with complementized full Ss, there is a class of verbs whose subcategorizations allow
for a following VP or S.

(19)   a.   *expect:* [__ *that* S]
             believe: [__ NP VP]
         b.   *hope:* [__ *that* S]
             decide: [__ VP]
         c.   *push:* [__ *for* S]
                      [__ NP VP]
         d.   *count:* [__ $_{PP}$[*on* NP] ($\left\{ \begin{array}{c} for \\ that \end{array} \right\}$ S)]
             count on: [__ NP VP][10]
         e.   *appeal:* [__ $_{PP}$[*to* NP] *for* S]
             appeal to: [__ NP VP]
         f.   *depend:* [__ $_{PP}$[*on* NP] *for* S]
             depend on: [__ NP VP]

The constructions in which these verbs do not allow a complementizer are
those where the complement is a VP rather than an S.[11] In the subcategorizations these verbs must specify a particular complementizer and then
S (rather than subcategorizing for S′) because in general the choice of
complementizer is not free.

An important result of the assumption that there are VP complements
in the base is that there is no need for the element PRO. We will return
to this important aspect of the theory in Sections 4 and 5, where we discuss
the coindexing of dependents, and in Section 7, where we discuss proposed
arguments in favor of PRO.

---

[10]It must be the case that certain instances of the sequence P NP, when followed by a VP,
are not actually PP and hence the ungrammaticality of the following sentences:
   (i)**On whom did you count to leave?*
   (ii)**To whom did you appeal to leave?*
   (iii)**On whom did you depend to leave?*
[11]In this framework **not all** surface infinitives are base VPs. Where a complementizer
occurs (e.g., *for* NP *to* VP) or where there is other syntactic evidence, then the complement
is a full S. Criticisms of the VP analysis, such as those of Koster and May (1982), must
therefore be reconsidered in this new light. See Section 7 of this chapter for discussion of
Koster and May.
   Also, it is not necessary for us to distinguish between [+TENSE] and [−TENSE] Ss in the
base. Apparently tenseless Ss occur on the surface only when the structural description for
Subject–Verb Agreement (which determines verb morphology) is not met.

3. The Analysis

With these assumptions about the base, and the definitions of predicate and dependent, we can now return to P Coindex, D Coindex, and the LC (repeated here) to see how they handle certain basic examples.

(20)　　*P Coindex: Coindex NP and X where X is a predicate.*
　　　　D Coindex: Coindex NP and X where X is a dependent.
　　　　Locality Condition: All rules are local.
　　　　　#1. P Coindex affects NP and X where X is bijacent to NP.
　　　　　#2. D Coindex affects the closest preceding NP to X.

The two phrase markers in (21) illustrate the paradigmatic contrast between a predicate that is construed with the object and one that is construed with the subject. (Many examples are borrowed directly from Williams 1980.)

(21)　　a.

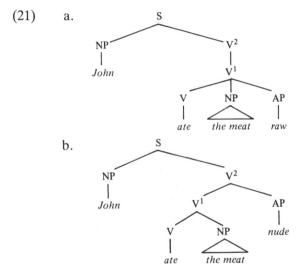

As illustrated here, there are two basic predicate positions: one in V^1, the other sister to V^1 in V^2. We assume that in these examples the APs are not assigned any role (or any DGR). They are therefore predicates and must be assigned an antecedent by P Coindex.

In (21a) *the meat* is the antecedent of *raw* since *raw,* by virtue of being a sister, is bijacent to *the meat. John* would not qualify as a possible antecedent for this predicate because the predicate is not bijacent to it. We assume here that although V^2 does not branch, it is not pruned. If we were to make the opposite assumption about pruning, such that V^2 does prune, then *raw* would be bijacent to both *the meat* and *John*: by being a sister to *the meat* and immediately dominated by a sister of *John*. In this case P Coindex would have to be slightly modified to select the closest NP to which the predicate is bijacent. (As far as we are aware these two possible versions of P Coindex would always select exactly the same NP antecedent.) After it is determined that *the meat* is the antecedent, this NP is assigned the **theme** role of the predicate *raw*.

For (21b) the predicate *nude* is coindexed with *John* by P Coindex and then is assigned **theme**. *Nude* is bijacent to *John* because it is immediately dominated by V^2 which is a sister to *John*. *Nude* is not bijacent to *the meat*.[12]

Another illustrative example of the functioning of coindexing is given in (22) where the constituent in need of an antecedent, *a doctor*, is an NP rather than an AP.

(22)

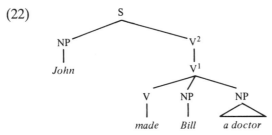

Although in this case P Coindex and D Coindex would give the same results, it is important to point out that, technically, the NP to be controlled here is a dependent. *Make* is a verb that under one reading must lexically determine the assignment of one of its roles. The algorithm for role assignment is repeated here for convenience:

---

[12]It is interesting to point out here that our account, using bijacency and the distinction between V^1 and V^2, avoids a problem of ambiguity which is inherent in the account of Williams (1980). Williams states:

> It can be seen that there will always be a unique antecedent for a predicate. However there may be some ambiguity as to whether the antecedent is thematically or grammatically assigned:
> (24)   a.   John arrived dead.
>   b.   John [arrived]$_{VP}$ dead.
>   c.   John [arrived dead]$_{VP}$.
> In (24b), it is assigned grammatically; in (24c), thematically [p. 208].

For Williams wherever there is a predicate with an intransitive verb there are two possible derivations for the sentence. In our theory (assuming the "no-pruning" hypothesis) Williams's (24b) represents the only possible analysis for the sentence (where VP is understood as V^1) and the problem of ambiguity is resolved.

(23)   **Role Assignment**
          (i) *Assign lexically idiosyncratic roles.*
         (ii) *Assign **theme** to the object if there is one. Otherwise assign*
               ***theme** to the subject.*
        (iii) *(a) Assign **goal** to subject or (b) assign **patient** to object and*
               ***agent** to subject or (c) **instrument** to subject or. . . .*

By (i), *make* assigns **goal** to *a doctor*, the second NP in V^1. **Theme** is then
assigned to the direct object *Bill* by (ii) and **agent** is assigned to the subject
by (iii). Because *a doctor* in this example bears a role, it is a dependent
rather than a predicate. (For an independent analysis of this sense of *make*
where the second NP is also considered the **goal**, see Wasow 1980.) By D
Coindex then, the antecedent of the dependent is *Bill*, which is the closest
NP. *A doctor* is coindexed with *Bill* and *Bill* is assigned **theme** by *a doctor*.
(We return to a discussion of control with the verb *make* in what follows.)

   Although structure (height of attachment) is essentially irrelevant for D
Coindex, much in the P Coindex account of predication depends on the
structural position of the predicate. Because of the requirement of bijacency, a predicate in V^1 will always be coindexed with the object NP if
there is one. A predicate in V^2, however, will be coindexed with the subject
NP. Because structure is so important in this theory, justification for the
postulated structures is necessary. Certain justification comes just from the
fact that the proposed analysis allows for a very general account of the
control phenomena, as will become clear. In this case, however, there is
also independent syntactic evidence that structures such as those proposed
in (21) and (22) are correct.

   The theory predicts (see preceding discussion) that the VP Rule (of
Williams 1977) will apply to include the predicate or dependent where it
is inside the V^1, but that the rule must exclude it where it is outside of
V^1. This prediction seems to be correct:

(24)   a. *Who ate the meat* $\left\{ \begin{array}{l} \textit{in what condition?} \\ \textit{how?} \end{array} \right\}$

        b. *John did* $\left\{ \begin{array}{l} \textit{drunk.} \\ \textit{nude.} \end{array} \right\}$

        c. **John did raw.*

(25)   a. *Who made Bill (a) what?*

        b. **John did* $\left\{ \begin{array}{l} \textit{a doctor.} \\ \textit{angry.} \end{array} \right\}$

   The movement of the emphatic reflexive also supports the structures in
(21) and (22), as does the Gapping test (the other tests for V^1 being
inapplicable here).

(26) a. *__John__ ate the meat __himself__ raw.
　　　b. __John__ ate the meat __himself__ nude.

(27) a. *__John__ made Bill __himself__ a doctor.
　　　b. __John__ made Bill a doctor __himself__.

(28) a. *__John__ ate the meat raw, and Sam, the cauliflower cooked.
　　　b. __John__ ate the meat nude, and Sam, the cauliflower in a tuxedo.

(29) *__John__ made Bill a doctor, and Sam, Paul a nurse.

We assume, therefore, that the structures in (21) and (22) are correct. The examples in (30)–(32) illustrate cases of PP predicates.

(30) a. *John saw a snake near Mary.*

　　　b.

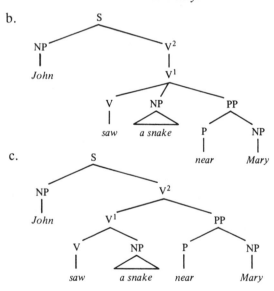

　　　c.

(31) a. *John was beside himself.*

　　　b.

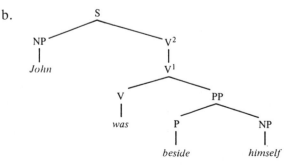

(32)   a.   *John saw a snake near him (*himself).*
         b.

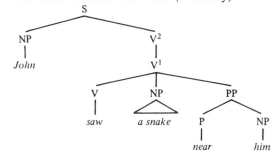

Example (30), as the phrase markers illustrate, is ambiguous. In (30b) the locative PP in V^1 is predicated of the direct object: *near Mary* is predicated of *a snake*. In (30c) *near Mary* is predicated of *John* since it is in V^2 and therefore bijacent to the subject. The examples in (31) and (32) show that predication defines a domain in which reflexivization is possible. In (31) the PP is predicated of *John* and *himself* refers to *John*. In (32) *near him* is predicated of *a snake* but *him* refers to *John*. Were the pronoun to occur in the reflexive in (32) it could only mean that *a snake* were both the antecedent and the object of *near*, a reading presumably out for pragmatic reasons as one cannot be said to be near oneself.

Notice, as the phrase markers here indicate, that although obligatorily subcategorized PPs must occur inside V^1, other PPs optionally may, as long as the result does not lead to ill-formed grammatical or thematic relations. Such ill-formedness would result if, for instance, an indirect object PP, which bears a particular grammatical relation, occurred in the V^1 and therefore could not properly be interpreted as the indirect object.

Next consider the examples in (33), which involve two different senses of the verb *load*.

(33)   a.   *John loaded **the wagon full** with hay.*
         b.   *John loaded **the hay** into the wagon **green**.*
         c.   **John loaded the wagon with **the hay green**.*
         d.   **John loaded the hay into **the wagon full**.*

According to our analysis the Deep Structure phrase markers for (33a) and (33b) would be (34a) and (34b), respectively.

(34)   a.

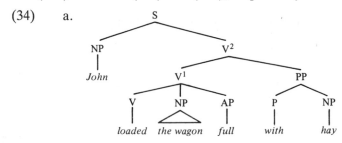

b.

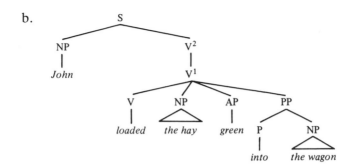

In comparing the structures in (34), it is important to note that there is a difference in the height at which the PPs are attached.[13] The claim is that *load* in the sense of (33b) and (34b) is structurally (and semantically, obviously) similar to the verb *put*, and that the PP is in V^1. Independent justification for the structures in (34) is given by the examples of (35) and (36), using two of the tests from Section 2.1 (the other tests being irrelevant in these cases).

(35)   a.   *Who loaded the wagon with what?*
              John did with hay.
        b.   *Who loaded the hay into what?*
              **John did into the wagon.*

(36)   a.   *John loaded the wagon carefully with hay.*
        b.   *John loaded the hay carefully into the wagon.*
        c.   **Carefully with hay, John loaded the wagon.*
        d.   *Carefully into the wagon, John loaded the hay.*

Example (35b) is ungrammatical because only part of the V^1 has been deleted. Examples (36a) and (36b) differ in that *carefully* is in its Deep Structure position in (36a), but in (36b) it has been moved to the left boundary of the PP from V^1-final position. The PP can be topicalized in (36d), but (36c) is ungrammatical because the preposed phrase is not a constituent PP.

Turning our attention back to the deep structures in (34), we see that the predicates (they are predicates because they surely bear no thematic roles) are both correctly assigned antecedents by the bijacency require-

---

[13]In an earlier version of this chapter the predicate in (34a) was considered to be *full with hay* as a single constituent AP. This phrase, however, does not really function as an AP, as these examples illustrate: **This is the hay full with which John loaded the wagon last night* versus *This is the man very angry at whom Mary must have been last night.*

ment of P Coindex. In both cases the predicate is a sister to its antecedent. Examples such as the ungrammatical (33c) and (33d) are prevented because in such cases the bijacency requirement is violated. Notice that the analysis also accounts for the ungrammaticality of cases like (37) [as compared with (33b)].

(37) a. *John loaded *the wagon* with hay *full*.
      b.

For the predicate *full* to follow the PP in this case it must be in V^2. As such, it is not bijacent to the direct object and (37a) is ungrammatical. The only possible antecedent for *full* in (37b) is *John*, as in *John loaded the wagon with hay full (from a big meal)*.[14]

4. Coindexing at Deep Structure

The examples in (38) and others that follow in this section illustrate the the importance of Deep Structure in our account of predication.

(38)   a. *I presented* **it** *to John* **dead**.
       b. **I presented John with* **it** **dead**.
       c. ?*I presented* **John** *with it* **dead**.

If we assume that the superficial order of constituents in example (38a) directly represents its deep structure, and that the PP *to John* is the indirect object and therefore a daughter of V^2, then we cannot account for the

---

[14]As is obvious throughout this discussion of control (and Williams's as well) no attempt is made to characterize what can and cannot appear as a semantically well-formed predicate. As Bruna Radelli (personal communication) suggests, appropriate selectional restrictions between the antecedent and the predicate are not sufficient. Consider the grammaticality distinction between *John ate the soup hot* and *John ate the soup foul-tasting* when both *John ate the hot soup* and *John ate the foul-tasting soup* are perfectly fine. As Radelli suggests, perhaps the predicate must satisfy not only the selectional requirements of its antecedent, but at the same time those of the V of the VP in which it is contained.

grammaticality of the example: *Dead* would not be bijacent to its ante-cedent *it*. This is illustrated in (39).

(39)

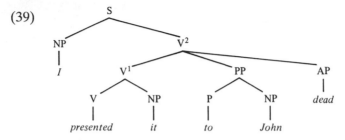

There are two possible alternative analyses. One would be to say that *to John* is actually in V^1, maybe because of some sort of special subcate-gorization for *present*, and that therefore the predicate which follows it is also in V^1. The better alternative analysis is illustrated in (40).

(40)

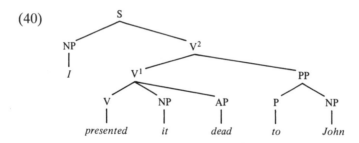

In (40) the PP, like all prepositional indirect objects, is in V^2. The pred-icate, on the other hand, precedes the PP and co-occurs in V^1 with the direct object. *It* and *dead* are coindexed at Deep Structure and then there is an optional reordering of constituents in the VP. Where the reordering does not take place, the sentence is still grammatical: *I presented it dead to John*. Notice that it is not necessary to require that the predicate occur in V^2. If the predicate were in V^2, the sentence would still be grammatical, but the antecedent would be the subject NP because of the bijacency requirement: *I presented it to John dead on my feet*.

Example (38b) presents another interesting case. By our criteria, the PP in this case occurs in V^1. It is obligatorily strictly subcategorized (i.e., **I presented John* in the relevant sense) and probably also receives its the-matic role directly from the verb and not via the preposition *with* (as the meaning of *present* NP *with* NP seems to be quite idiosyncratic). Therefore there are three possible underlying structures for the example.

(41) a.

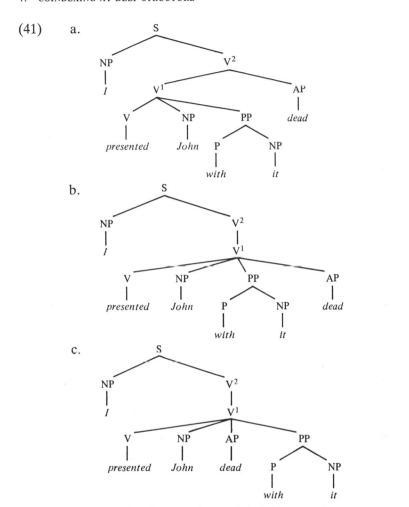

b.

c.

Phrase marker (41a) with the AP in V² can only underlie a sentence where the NP *I* is the antecedent of the predicate; *dead* is not bijacent to any NP in the VP. In neither (41b) nor (41c) is *dead* bijacent to *it*. There is no possible coindexing which would yield (38b), and hence it is ungrammatical.

This brings us to (38c). Given the structure in (41b), our analysis predicts that *John* should be a possible antecedent for the predicate. Although the particular example is marginal, there are others with similar verb subcategorization that are better.

(42) a. *I entrusted **the money** to John **in cash**.*

    b.(?)*I entrusted **John** with the money **drunk**.*
    c.   *He credited **Bill** with the discovery **in his early 20s**.*
    d.(?)*He blamed **Jack** for the fiasco **drunk**.*

Given our analysis of (38a) as involving Deep Structure conindexing and then optional reordering of the predicate, it would seem that structure (41c) would be an alternative analysis for (38c). In order to resolve this ambiguity in the theory, we propose to restrict the base rules to allow predicates in V^1 only in final position. That is, predicates follow the subcategorized and thematic arguments. Thus (41c) is not a possible deep structure.

Another interesting set of examples which provides an argument for Deep Structure as the appropriate level for coindexing is presented in (43).

(43)   a.   *John made **Bill a good friend**.*
           b.   ***John** made **a good friend** for Bill.*
           c.   ***John** made Bill **a good friend**.*

The phrase markers underlying the sentences in (43) are given in (44).

(44)

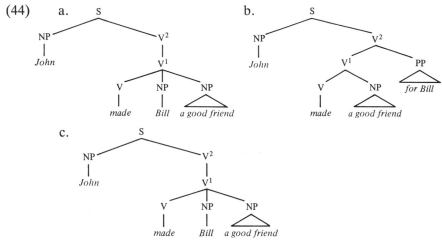

Phase markers (44a) and (44b) both represent deep structures to which D Coindex applies. In (44a) *a good friend* is a dependent as it bears the role **goal**. It is coindexed with *Bill*. In (44b) *a good friend* is not the **goal** as in (44a), since *Bill* is, but rather is assigned **theme** (independent justification for this analysis can be found in Wasow 1980).[15] By D Coindex

---

[15]The **theme** is assigned to *a good friend* in this case by (i) of the algorithm, that is, as a lexical characteristic of the verb. It cannot be assigned by (ii) of the algorithm although it seems to be in position of direct object. This constituent in this case does not bear the DGR direct object because it must be distinguished from the direct object that occurs with the

John is the antecedent of *a good friend*. Phrase marker (44c) illustrates the result of indirect object movement. This movement, of course, applies after D Coindex because the coindexing takes place at Deep Structure. In (44c) *John* remains the antecedent of the dependent. The important thing here is that the two senses of *make* are determined by the thematic role and control facts. There is no need to postulate two different homonymous verbs (as in some traditional grammars), nor is there a necessary difference in phrase structure.[16] The verb *make* has two different senses in the two superficially similar sentences (43a) and (43c) solely because of the difference in thematic roles, the difference in the assignment of antecedent, and the fact that coindexing is accomplished at Deep Structure.

A consideration of predication in passives reveals another advantage of predication at Deep Structure. We consider the examples in (45) (suggested to us by Ellen Kaisse).

(45) a. **John** found Mary **nude.**
      b. **Mary** was found **nude** by John.
      c. **The meat** was eaten **raw** by John.
      d. *The meat* was eaten **nude** by **John.**

Where the predicate is one that is compatible (semantically and pragmatically) with either the active or the passive subject, then the result of predication in both cases is grammatical. Notice, however, that a sentence like *John ate the meat nude* has no passive counterpart, as the ungrammaticality of (45d) illustrates. This fact is readily accounted for if coindexing and selectional restrictions are both determined on the basis of Deep Structure.

The phrase markers in (46) represent the deep structures for the examples of (45).

(46) a.

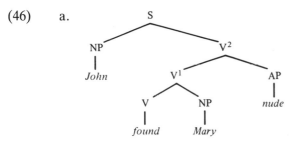

---

unmarked meaning of *make,* as in *John made a good pie for Bill.* In this case the constituent *a good pie* would have both a grammatical relation and a role, both assigned by unmarked instances of the algorithm.

[16]In Williams's theory with a level of PS two different structures would have to be postulated in order to get the predication facts correct.

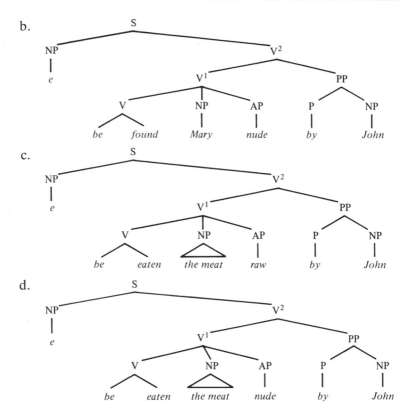

b.

c.

d.

Case (46a) works straightforwardly where P Coindex, as in examples that we discussed earlier, directly coindexes *nude* with *John* at Deep Structure. At the same level selectional compatibility is determined.

In (46b), if the predicate were a daughter of V^2, then the structure would lead to ungrammaticality. We assume that empty nodes cannot be coindexed with predicates (or dependents, as will be discussed in what follows). If some node is an antecedent, then the predicate will assign it some role which is mapped into R-Structure. Thematic roles are assigned only to referring constituents (as we will discuss in detail in Chapter 3, especially with respect to the Principle of Thematic Uniqueness). The assignment, by P Coindex, of the empty NP as the antecedent to the V^2 predicate would lead to ungrammaticality. Given, however, that the predicate is in V^1, it is coindexed with *Mary,* to which it is bijacent. Again, the selectional restrictions are checked at Deep Structure. When *Mary* is then preposed by NP Movement it remains the antecedent of *nude.*

In (46c) P Coindex coindexes *the meat* and *raw,* the selectional restrictions are checked, and then *the meat* is preposed to subject position.

Phrase marker (46d) exemplifies the interesting case. *Nude,* if it were in V^2, could not be coindexed with the subject NP because it is empty. Such coindexing would lead to ungrammaticality. Given that *nude* is in V^1, by P Coindex it can be coindexed with *the meat.* But this is ruled out by the conflict of selectional restrictions. Passivization can take place but the reason for the ungrammaticality of Example (45d) is that *nude* is predicated of *the meat.* This Deep Structure account of selection and predication seems to us simpler than and preferable to an account where predication and/or selection is determined at a post movement level.[17]

Considering further the issue of passive constructions containing simple predicates, we can see that the examples of (47) provide additional evidence for assigning antecedents at Deep Structure.

(47)   a.   *Mary was talked about.*
       b.   **Mary was talked about nude.*
       c.

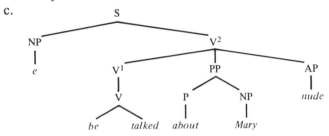

To (47c) NP Movement can readily apply, as the acceptability of (47a) is meant to indicate. The ungrammaticality of (47b) is attributable to the fact that the predicate has an $_{NP}[e]$ as antecedent. There is no conflict of selectional restrictions in this example, it simply illustrates that nonreferring NPs cannot be well-formed antecedents.[18] This fact is expressed as a well-formedness condition on R-Structure. Predicates assign roles which at R-Structure must be borne by individuals. Clearly $_{NP}[e]$ refers to no individual (but see Section 6 of this chapter, where we show that predicates, although they may not be coindexed with [e], may in fact be arbitrary in reference).

We move next to a discussion of VP dependents.

[17]Notice that although there is an argument here against assigning antecedents to predicates after NP Movement, there is really no argument in favor of the movement. The same results for predication and passivization could be obtained in a theory with lexical passives and Deep Structure control. This is important since in Chapter 3 we seriously question the necessity of NP Movement. Certain other facts about passivization and the control of dependents, to be discussed in what follows, are not so readily handled assuming lexical passives. This will be pointed out in the course of the discussion.

[18]Notice that the ungrammaticality of (47b) would be difficult to account for in a theory with lexical rather than movement passives. See Footnote 17.

5. Coindexing of VP Predicates

In our approach there is assumed to be no PRO (see detailed discussion in Section 7, and for an alternative account of control with no PRO see Hasegawa 1981). Constituents that occur on the surface as infinitival VPs without subjects are exactly what they appear to be, namely, VP complements. Consider the cases in (48).

(48)   a.   *John persuaded Bill to leave.*
        b.   *John promised Bill to leave.*
        c.

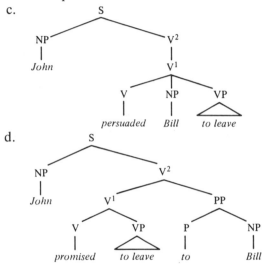

        d.

The phenomenon to be accounted for here, whether or not there is a PRO subject of surface infinitival complements, is the interpretation of the subject, or the antecedent, of the embedded VP. There must be an account of the fact that for *promise* the understood subject of the infinitive is the matrix subject, whereas for *persuade* the understood subject is the matrix object.[19]

In our account the interpretation of the subject of embedded VPs is accomplished by D Coindex; the closest NP serves as subject of the infinitival VP. It is D Coindex, rather than P Coindex, that is relevant in these cases, because VP complements invariably bear thematic roles. Presumably part of the information contained in the lexical entry of any verb is

---

[19]Williams's (1980) innovation is the treatment of the control of PRO as a subcase of predication.

what type of complement it can take, including whether or not it can take a complement with propositional content (e.g., an S'). For the verbs that take embedded propositions there must be some indication of what thematic role the proposition bears as in many cases the assignment of role to this constituent will be idiosyncratic.[20] Verbs that co-occur with embedded S' propositions often also may occur with embedded VP complements. After coindexing assigns an antecedent to the VP it is a full proposition. (Our claim that VP complements bear thematic roles is supported by Wasow 1980.)

Returning to (48), the account of (48c) is straightforward. *To leave* is a dependent which bears the role **goal** with respect to the verb *persuade.* The deep structure (48c) directly represents the surface (48a), and D Coindex assigns the object NP *Bill* the index of the dependent VP. [Although it is not crucial to the determination of control, it is interesting to note that by the relevant syntactic tests the VP complement in (48a) is a part of V^1.] This means that *Bill* is assigned the **theme** of *to leave.* After coindexing, *Bill* is therefore the **theme** of *persuade* and also the **theme** of *leave.*

Consider now the case of *promise,* (48d). The deep structure is as given here, with the complement VP preceding the prepositional indirect object. The embedded VP is assigned **theme** by the verb (and *Bill* is assigned **goal**). The advantages of positing this deep structure for *promise* are several. First of all, the account of control is greatly simplified in that *promise* ceases to be a counterexample in need of some ad hoc feature (as in most accounts of the well-known difference between *promise* and *persuade.*[21] *John* and the VP *to leave* are coindexed by D Coindex because the subject NP is the closest preceding NP to the VP.

Another advantage of the structure (48d) is that it makes obvious the similarity of the grammatical and thematic relations between *promise* with a complement VP and *promise* with a simple NP object. In both cases the subject is the **agent** and the **source**, the immediate right sister to the verb in Deep Structure is the **theme**, and the prepositional object is the **goal.** (Wasow, 1980, gives a very similar thematic analysis of *promise,* and Bach, 1979, assumes a similar analysis of the grammatical relations).

Additional evidence in favor of (48d) and the proposed account of control is the explanation of the passive facts for *promise.* These are illustrated by the examples in (49)–(51).

---

[20]Perhaps there is an algorithm that will take care of such role assignment, similar to that which we have already seen which assigns roles to NPs with grammatical relations. It is not clear to us at this point which would be the unmarked, paradigmatic cases.

[21]For Williams (1980) *promise* is a "worst case" example because the antecedent is the **goal**, not the **theme**.

(49)   a. *John promised a horse to Bill.*
        b. *John promised Bill a horse.*
        c. *?John promised that Mary would leave to Bill.*[22]
        d. *John promised Bill that Mary would leave.*

(50)   a. *A horse was promised to Bill.*
        b. *Bill was promised a horse.*
        c. *That Mary would leave was promised to Bill.*
        d. *Bill was promised that Mary would leave.*

(51)   a. *?John promised to leave to Bill.*   (see Footnote 22)
        b. *John promised Bill to leave.*
        c. **To leave was promised to Bill.*
        d. **Bill was promised to leave.*
        e.

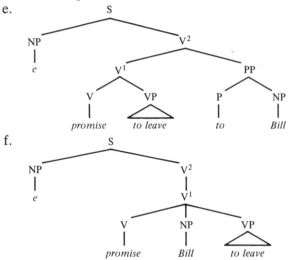

        f.

Sentences (49a) and (49c) directly represent their respective deep structure configurations; (49b) and (49d) are the results of Dative Movement.
Sentences (50a) and (50c) are the results of passivization of the constituent
in deep structure direct object position and (50b) and (50d) are the results
of passivization following Dative Movement.

The phrase marker in (51e) represents a deep structure to which Passive
could apply and (51f) is the result of Dative Movement to which Passive
could also apply. There is nothing to prevent the application of Passive in

---

[22]The marginal status of (49c) seems to be attributable to the "heaviness" of the clausal
direct object. Just as (49d), where Indirect Object Movement has taken place, is better than
(49c), so is *John promised to Bill that Mary would leave* where Complex NP Shift has taken
place. Much better is a sentence like *John promised that Mary would leave to the man that
kept calling on the phone during the weekend.*

either of these cases. The ungrammaticality of (51c) and (51d) is a reflection of the fact that the antecedent which controls the VP *to leave* is an empty NP. At the time at which coindexing takes place, that is, in Deep Structure, the NP to which the dependent is coindexed is $_{NP}[e]$. Although Passive applies properly, either to (51e) or after Indirect Object Movement to (51f), the result is ungrammatical because in both cases a dependent is coindexed with an empty NP. Neither a predicate nor a dependent can be coindexed with an empty NP because the role would have to be assigned to an NP that refers to no individual. To (51e), compare (52b) which is the input to the well-formed (52a).

(52)   a.   *Bill was persuaded to leave.*

      b.

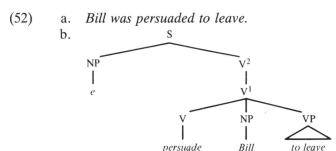

For the *persuade* case the infinitival VP is coindexed at Deep Structure with the direct object. Then Passive applies to move *Bill*. The result is fine because the VP is controlled by an NP with lexical content which is interpreted as the **theme** of *leave* (and of *persuade*). We thus see that in the Deep Structure account of control the case of *promise* is no longer exceptional and additionally there is a coherent explanation of the ungrammaticality of passive examples like (51c) and (51d).[23] It is obviously crucial for this explanation of *promise* that coindexing be accomplished at Deep Structure, and not after transformations have applied.[24]

[23]See Bach (1979) for another account where the ill-formed passive of *promise* is explained by the theory of control. In Williams's (1980) theory the passive facts also follow from the predication facts of *promise,* but the predication facts themselves represent an exception.

[24]Our account here of *promise* makes crucial use of the assumption that the double object construction is the result of a transformation moving indirect objects (but see Baker, 1979, about the nonlearnability of Dative Movement, and cf. Emonds, 1981, where Dative Movement is a subcase of a more general rule of NP-α Inversion, which we assume would be learnable). If there were no such movement then it might have to be stated that dative NPs (in English) never serve as the antecedents of predicates. This may have to be a language-specific restriction since other languages, such as Spanish and French, allow superficial dative antecedents.

In this case of control of the embedded complement of *promise* and the passivization facts, an account involving a rule of NP Movement gives better results than a lexical passive. If we assumed lexical passives, as we will discuss in Chapter 3, then control and passive for *promise* again would become exceptional.

Our analysis of predication in this chapter clearly assumes a movement analysis of passives (discussed at length in Chapter 3). By contrast, the so-called "subject raising" construction is base generated. The embedded infinitive is assigned an antecedent by coindexing. This is illustrated in (53).

(53)   a.   *John seems sad.*
        b.   *John seems to be sad.*
        c.   d.

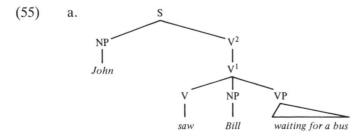

Both (53a) and (53b) directly represent their deep structures. In both cases *seem* is generated with a lexical NP subject that is coindexed with a constituent in the VP, an AP as in (53c) and an infinitival VP as in (53d). We assume that the verb *seem* assigns no thematic role to its subject but that this NP receives a role through coindexing. (The importance of this assumption will be shown in Chapter 3 in the discussion of the well-formedness conditions on R-structures and the Binding Condition.) The advantage of a nonmovement analysis of *seem* is that the similarity of examples like (53a) and (53b) is captured without the necessity of a device such as a rule of *Be*-Deletion to convert a deep structure like (53d) into the surface string (53a). Another case of a VP which must be assigned an antecedent is the gerund, as in (54).

(54)   *John died [waiting for a bus].*

Subjectless gerunds of this type are predicates and as such they can occur in either V^2 or in V^1. They are therefore predictably ambiguous with respect to their antecedent, as shown in (55).

(55)   a.   S

```
          NP              V²
          |               |
         John            V¹
                      ___|___
                     V   NP   VP
                     |   |    ◸
                    saw  Bill  waiting for a bus
```

b.

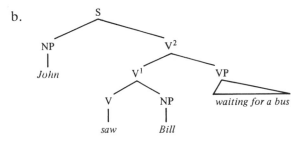

In both cases of (55), since the VPs are predicates, the coindexing is accomplished by P Coindex. In (55a) coindexing may not take place between the subject NP and the predicate because of the bijacency requirement. Coindexing takes place between the predicate and the object NP. In (55b) the VP predicate is bijacent to the subject and coindexing takes place between *John* and the gerund. This correctly accounts for the ambiguity of surface sentences of this type. Importantly, this is a case of predication by P Coindex and not control of a dependent, since if D Coindex were involved, in both (55a) and (55b) the antecedent would be *Bill*.[25]

Before we turn to the issue of arbitrary control, we consider a puzzle which has become very familiar in the literature dealing with control phenomena. This puzzle concerns the verbs *strike* and *regard* and the interpretation of their *as*-clauses:[26]

(56)   a. *John* strikes Bill *as intelligent.*
        b. *John regards* **Bill** *as intelligent.*

Our theory provides a ready account of this control distinction given our two-level VP hypothesis. Consider the structures in (57).

(57)   a.

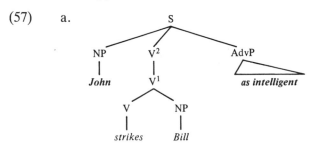

---

[25]An alternative, and perhaps better, account of (55b) would be where the gerund is an AdvP. This could explain why extraction is not allowed: *Which bus did John$_i$ see Bill$_j$ [waiting for t]$_i$.

[26]For Williams (1980) the antecedent of the clause must be the **theme** and the thematic structure of the two verbs differs.

b.

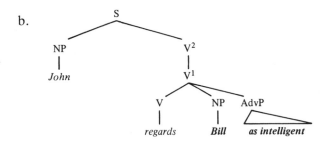

We propose this explanation only tentatively because the different structures are not easy to justify. There is, however, at least some suggestive evidence.

First of all, the thematic structure for *regard* is quite straightforward: subject = **source**, object = **theme**, *as*-clause = **goal**. For *strike* the situation seems to us to be different: subject = **source** and object = **goal**, but the role played by the *as*-clause is unclear (although cf. Wasow 1980).[27] Second, although most of the syntactic tests for V^1 are not relevant, the two that can apply seem to favor slightly the distinction in (57a) and (57b).

(58)   a. *John strikes Bill as intelligent, and Sam, Mary as stupid.*
       b. *?John regards Bill as intelligent and Sam, Mary as stupid.*

(59)   a. *Who strikes Bill* $\left\{ \begin{array}{l} how? \\ as\ what? \end{array} \right\}$
           John does as intelligent.
       b. *Who regards Bill* $\left\{ \begin{array}{l} how? \\ as\ what? \end{array} \right\}$
           ?John does as intelligent.[28]

---

[27]Two complex constructions which function like *strike* are *come across to one* and *present oneself to someone.*

[28]With respect to *strike* versus *regard*, Williams (1980) considers the passive facts of *strike* to be evidence in favor of the **theme** generalization. He says that the ungrammaticality of (i) is due to the fact that the **theme** does not c-command the predicate; the ungrammaticality of (ii) is due to there being no **theme**.

(i)   **Bill was struck by John as stupid.*
(ii) **John was struck as sick.*

He says additionally that (iii) is well-formed because there is no predicate and therefore no problem with predicational structure.

(iii) *John was struck by Bill's pomposity.*

We suggest that (i) and (ii) are ill formed because of certain facts about NP Movement and thematic structure, along the lines of Jackendoff (1972), where the output of Passive

6. "Nonobligatory Control"

Consider the examples in (60)–(63).

(60) a. *To die is no fun.*
      b. *What to do is a mystery.*
      c. *What to do is a mystery to John.*

(61) a. *John wants to win.*
      b. *John wants Bill to win.*
      c. *I* $\left\{ \begin{array}{l} would\ hate \\ would\ prefer \\ arranged \end{array} \right\}$ *(for Bill) to leave.*

(62) a. *I am counting on Bill to perjure himself.*
      b. *I am counting on Bill to get there on time.*
      c. *I am counting on Bill for Mary to get there on time.*

(63) *It is important to John to leave.*

These are all examples which Williams (1980) (the account with which our own must necessarily be compared) analyzes as cases of "nonobligatory control" (NOC) at the postmovement level of Predicate Structure. Where the correct reading is obviously not one of arbitrary or generic control, for example, (61)–(63), there must then be rewriting of *arb* (the index assigned to predicates with "arbitrary" control) to indicate the unique controller. In our Deep Structure account (which unlike Williams's assumes no PRO) a unique controller—that is, the correct antecedent for

---

must not violate the Thematic Hierarchy (see Jackendoff 1972; 43-45). The fact that (iii) is well-formed is not relevant to this issue since it has the peculiarity of not having an active counterpart:

(iv) *Bill's pomposity struck John.*

If the grammaticality of (iii) has something to do with its (lack of) predicational structure, then (iv) is anomalous. Neither of these uses of *strike* exhibits the usual active–passive alternation, regardless of the facts of predicational structure.

To account for the passive facts for *strike* not in terms of predication but rather in terms of conditions on NP Movement amounts to giving up a unitary account of what has been called Visser's generalization (Visser 1963, Bresnan 1976b, Wasow 1980), which says essentially that passive is disallowed in constructions with subject-oriented complements (thanks to Tom Wasow for pointing this out to us). Other examples of Visser's generalization are accounted for here by P Coindex or D Coindex, for example, the case of *promise*. This means that several different phenomena conspire to make up what looks like a unitary phenomenon in the NP Movement analysis.

the embedded VP—is immediately assigned at Deep Structure. This correct assignment is possible in (61)–(63) because the relevant deep structures are as given in (64)–(66).

(64)

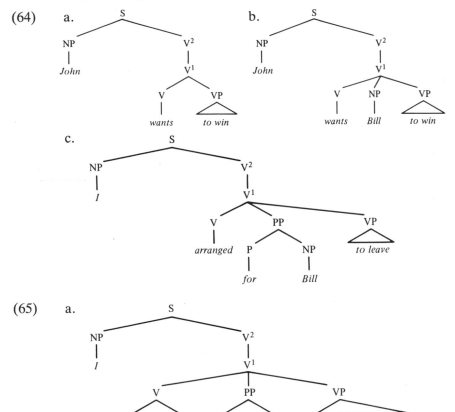

(65)

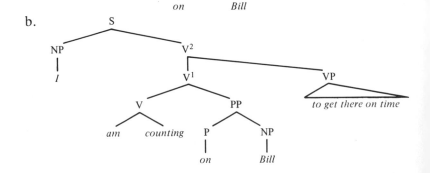

(66)

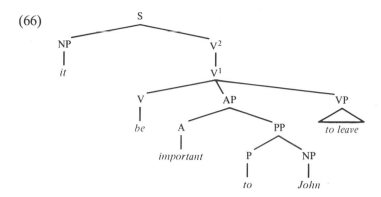

In (64b) and (64c), D Coindex coindexes the VPs with the adjacent NPs, and so *Bill* is the subject of *to win* and *Bill* is the subject of *to leave*. In both of these cases the VP complement is the **goal** and in both cases the dependents assign **theme** to their antecedents. In (64a) the subject, which is the only NP, is also the antecedent of the embedded VP. *John* is the **theme** of *wants* and of *to win*.

Examples (65a) and (65b) illustrate an important contrast. In (65a) the complement VP is coindexed with the preceding NP *Bill* by D Coindex and assigns **agent** to the antecedent (*himself* being the **theme** and **patient**). This VP is a dependent since it bears the role **goal**. In (65b) we believe there to be no thematic role borne by the infinitive VP. (It seems rather to have a "purposive" use, as in *I am counting on Bill in order to get there on time.*) Here P Coindex applies to coindex the VP with *I* and *I* is assigned **theme**.[29]

In (66) again, a VP is coindexed by D Coindex with a strictly adjacent NP (*to leave,* the **goal**, is coindexed with *John*). It is particularly interesting to compare (66) with (67).

(67) a. *It is important to leave.*
       b.

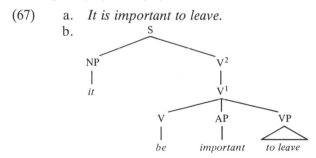

[29]We assume all purpose clauses to be predicates, following Williams (1980, pp. 231–233), except of course we assume no PRO.

The sentence and phrase marker of (67) illustrate one of the ways in which arbitrary interpretation arises in our theory. In this instance the VP *to leave* is coindexed with the antecedent NP *it*. But this NP is semantically empty; it has no referent. The result is therefore an arbitrary reading. Any predicate or dependent coindexed with a nonreferring NP is understood as arbitrary in interpretation. (See section 33.1 of Chapter 3.) This is relevant also for a case like (68).

(68)

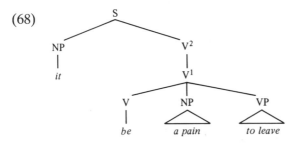

The coindexing of *to leave* with *a pain* yields an arbitrary interpretation for the dependent because *a pain* in this sense does not refer. It is important to note here that coindexing with a nonreferring NP is distinct from coindexing with a lexically empty NP. A predicate or a dependent coindexed with an [*e*] is ill formed.

The other type of case where a VP complement does not have a unique controller is where it is neither a predicate nor a dependent because it is a subject. A subject bears a DGR (along with direct object and indirect object), and any constituent bearing such a relation cannot be predicated of some other constituent (see definitions of predicate and dependent). Any constituent in subject position, no matter what its grammatical category may be, will be an antecedent. This is the case in (60a) where the structure would be as indicated in (69).

(69) $_{VP}$[*to die*] *is no fun.*

In (69) coindexing cannot apply because the complement is the subject. Subjects do not permit antecedents; hence, the traditional distinction between subject and predicate. This is illustrated also in an example like (70):

(70)   *John told Mary that* $_{VP}$[*to leave early*] *was important.*

A VP in subject position does not have an antecedent (controller) and in this sense is arbitrary. It is, however, a subject, like any other subject, in that it will be coindexed as an antecedent with relevant dependents or predicates, as in (71).

(71)   a.   *To leave would be a pleasure.*
         b.   *To leave would be my pleasure.*

Here because *to leave* is the subject, it is the antecedent of the predicate *a pleasure* in (71a) and *my pleasure* in (71b). In both the interpretation of *to leave* is uncontrolled, just as in (69) and (70). The reason that the VP complement in (71b) is apparently controlled by *my* is actually a result of the fact that *my pleasure* is being predicated of *to leave*. A parallel example with a noninfinitival subject is a case like (72).

(72)   *That brown bag on the table is my lunch.*

In (72) the predicate indicates not only that the subject is a *lunch*, but also that it is *mine*; in (71b) *to leave* is not only a *pleasure* but it is also *mine*. *My* is not the antecedent of *to leave*; it is part of what is being predicated.

Although VPs in subject position do not have antecedents, they do have an interpretation at R-Structure which must be correctly represented. Specifically, the infinitive is interpreted precisely as if it had a dummy subject, as shown in examples like the following:

(73)   a.   *To be arrested would bother John.*
         b.   *To be easy to please would be an accomplishment.*

In standard analyses of (73a) an underlying empty object would undergo NP Movement, as illustrated in (74).

(74) $[[e_i]$ to be arrested $[e_j]]$ would bother John$_j$.
         $\Rightarrow [[e_j]$ to be arrested $\emptyset]$ would bother John$_j$.

Similarly in (73b), an empty subject would bind the object of *please*, as shown in (75).

(75) $[[e_i]$ to be easy to please $[e_i]]$ would be an accomplishment.

Analyses such as those in (74) and (75) are impossible in our theory because of our assumption that underlying infinitives are assigned "subjects" by coindexing with antecedents (rather than by the control of PRO subjects). Our proposed explanation works well when antecedents are present in Deep Structure. The problem is how to "project" syntactic subjects of infinitives where there is no overt Deep Structure antecedent, that is, when the infinitive is itself in subject position.

A number of alternative solutions present themselves. First, we could assume the more standard approach that empty (i.e., PRO) subjects appear with all infinitives at Deep Structure. We avoid this revision of our theory for the reasons that are discussed at length in Section 7 of this chapter. Second, we could assume that passives are derived not by NP Movement, but rather by a lexical rule (as in Bresnan 1982, Wasow 1977, etc.). We seriously consider this alternative in Chapter 3 but do not immediately adopt it here because there are certain puzzles about predication which remain to be worked out in such a theory (see Footnotes 1, 19, 20, and 26 in this chapter).

The third alternative is the one we will adopt for now. We suppose that there is a mapping from Deep Structure to an aspect of semantic representation, which we express as R-structure. The first stage in the mapping is a representation in which missing antecedents are supplied by means of a structure-building operation. The construction of this representation is a component of the procedure by which VPs are coindexed with their antecedents, as described in this chapter. Other subcategorized arguments which are not overtly represented must be projected at the same time, for example, unexpressed objects of transitive verbs. It is at this level, an aspect of R-structure, that thematic roles are assigned by the role assignment algorithm (Chapter 1, Section 3).

Owing to the fact that this aspect of R-structure is minimally distinct from Deep Structure, we will not represent the mapping between them systematically in our discussions. Most of the syntactic properties of this structure are also properties of Deep Structure. Crucially, though, it is Deep Structure that is ultimately mapped into Surface Structure, whereas R-structure is a stage in the mapping into the representation of meaning.[30]

We return finally to the remaining examples in (60), (60b), and (60c). Before we discuss these it is necessary to consider briefly the internal structure of noun phrases. The relevant NPs are as in (76) (where the examples are taken from discussion in Jackendoff 1972).

(76)   a.   *Mary received permission to go from Alex.*
         b.   *Mary received from Alex a promise to go.*
         c.   *Mary gave Alex permission to go.*
         d.   *Mary gave Alex her request to go.*

The infinitives in these cases are not subject to the general coindexing procedure because they are noun complements.[31] These infinitives fail to meet the definition of either predicate or dependent and hence are not affected by either coindexing rule. Consider the phrase markers in (77).

---

[30]To return briefly to Example (73a), there is a rule of Universal Passive, which we discuss in detail in Chapter 3, which deletes the role on an antecedent, allowing the well-formedness of this example. The relevant presentation is as in (i).

(i)   [*arb to be arrested* arb] *would bother John.*
         agent ⇒ ∅   theme

An arb with no role has no function, and therefore (i) is not ruled out by Disjoint Reference (as would generally be the case with two NPs with the same index). In contrast, an example like (ii), where Universal Passive cannot apply, is ruled out by Disjoint Reference.

(ii)   [*arb to arrest arb*] *would bother John.*
         agent   theme

[31]For Williams (1980) these are also exceptional and they are treated as cases of "nonobligatory control."

(77)　　a.

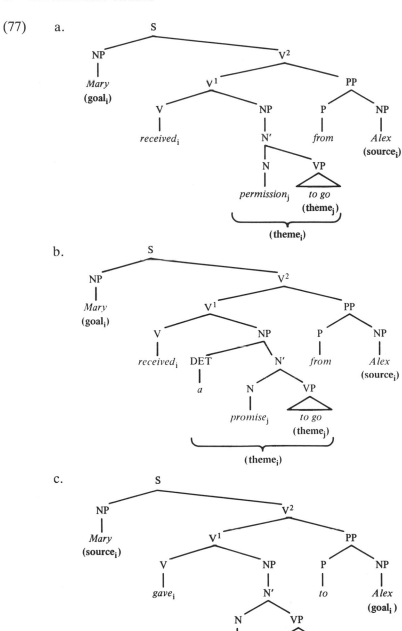

b.

c.

d.

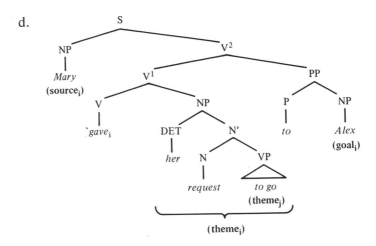

Assuming that bare infinitives in NPs, just like other bare infinitives, are base generated, the phrase markers in (77) represent the deep structures for the examples in (76). As indicated, we assume that both verbs and nominalizations assign thematic roles, as in Jackendoff (1972).[32] But the infinitival VPs qualify neither as predicates nor as dependents since they are not immediately dominated by V^n (but rather by N^n).

These VPs are not subject to control. But they do enter into the determination of the thematic structure of the sentence. The proper construal of these sentences is not determined by any coindexing but by the ordinary interpretation of thematic and grammatical relations which must take into account the interaction of thematic role assignment of the verb and the nominalization and which must also take into account the subjectlike nature of an NP determiner.[33]

---

[32]If nominalizations could not assign thematic roles it would not be possible to distinguish between *give permission* and *give a request.* The "directionality" is not determined by the verb, but rather by the noun. We formalize this in terms of thematic roles.

[33]That these N + VP constructions are indeed NPs is easily demonstrated. Consider (i) as compared to (ii):
  (i)   a. *The promise to go was received (by Mary).*
        b. *The request to go was given to Alex (by Mary).*
        c. *The permission to go was easy (for Mary) to give.*
        d. *It was the request to go that was given to Alex.*
  (ii) a.*The meat raw was eaten (by John).*
        b.*The book open was given to Alex.*
        c.*It was the book open that was given to Alex (by Mary).*
        d.*The meat raw was easy to eat.*

Given this discussion of NPs, we return to Examples (60b) and (60c), repeated here in (78).

(78) a. *What to do is a mystery.*
      b. *What to do is a mystery to John.*

In our theory the subject in these examples cannot be an S (as we make no provision for the element PRO). Nor can it be a VP as in (69) because VPs, having no COMP, do not permit the fronting of *wh*. Our theory here makes an interesting claim: The subjects in (78) are NPs where *Wh* Movement has applied. This is illustrated in (79).

(79) a.

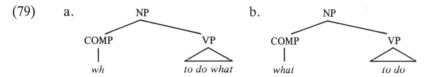

As will be discussed at length in Chapter 4, we assume that *Wh* Movement is the structure-preserving movement of a [+WH] specifier. The landing site for this specifier movement is generally the specifier of the S system, namely COMP. Generalizing the term COMP to include the specifier of any [+v]″ (i.e., V″ or M″), we have an analysis of examples like (78) with no need to postulate the internal structure of the subject as being an S′.

At first glance (79) might seem to provide an implausible analysis since it indicates an NP without a nominal head: an apparent violation of the X-bar Theory. This structure actually results from an instance of the rule schema in (80a), given by Jackendoff (1977) as the basic schema for "deverbalizing" rules (where "af" = affix). Rules (80b) and (80c) are particular instances of the schema which Jackendoff suggests.

(80) a. $X^i \rightarrow af - V^i$
      b. $N'' \rightarrow to - V''$
      c. $N'' \rightarrow ing - V''$

Adapting this analysis slightly, we assume the rules in (81) and (82), whose results are illustrated in (83) and (84), respectively.

(81) a. $N''' \rightarrow SPEC\ V''$
      b. $V'' \rightarrow to - V''$

(82) a. $N''' \rightarrow SPEC\ N''$
      b. $N'' \rightarrow ing - V''$

(83)

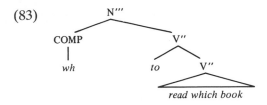

$_{NP}[$*which book to read*$]$

(84)

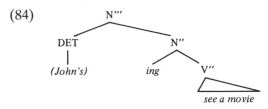

$_{NP}[$*(John's) seeing a movie*$]$

As indicated in the phrase markers, the specifier of V″ is COMP and the specifier of N″ is DET. *Wh* Movement can move a constituent into COMP, but not into DET. Thus we get the right results for infinitival VPs and gerundive VPs inside noun phrases, namely, that the infinitives allow for the fronting of *wh* and that the gerunds occur with determiners. Where no movement takes place in a structure like (83), but there is a [+WH] COMP, the result is *whether* (e.g., $_{NP}[$*whether to read the book*$]$).[34]

Returning to the issue of coindexing, the infinitival VPs in sentences like those in (78) are neither predicates nor dependents. *To do* in these cases does not have a controller, it is part of the subject $_{NP}[$*what to do*$]$. As a subject in both cases of (78), *what to do* is the antecedent of the following predicates.[35] That *what* is understood as the object of *do* is explained by the fact that in Deep Structure it is the object.

In summary, then, with respect to the examples referred to as "non-obligatory control," we provide an account that gives the correct results without the necessity of reassigning improperly assigned arbitrary indices.

[34]We speculate that infinitival constructions such as the subject in *To die is no fun* might in fact also be NPs with [−WH] specifiers and verbal heads. The fact that Topicalization does not apply in infinitival subjects is not a problem for us, because we assume that Topicalization is not movement to COMP, but to FOCUS (= TOPIC). The latter can be restricted to occur only in an S'. See Chapter 5.

[35]In (78b) it is not clear whether *to John* is in itself a predicate, whether it forms a constituent with *a mystery,* or whether it bears some grammatical relation, for instance, similar to indirect object. In any case, the larger predicate *is a mystery to John* has as its grammatical subject *what to do.* This accounts for the fact that *John* might be construed as the apparent controller of *to do.*

Where there is a unique controller it is directly assigned by the coindexing procedures. Where control is arbitrary, this is the result of coindexing with a nonreferring NP or of the absence of any coindexing whatsoever.[36]

7. On the Existence of PRO

We conclude our analysis of predication with some observations on the syntax of infinitival constructions. We have assumed throughout that infinitives in general are not derived from S' complements, and that they lack syntactic subjects. Rather, they are assigned antecedents by coindexing. Most current work, in contrast, assumes that the infinitival is sentential in nature, and that the subject of the infinitive, when it is absent in Surface Structure, is an abstract empty NP, usually referred to as PRO. If it is assumed that there is a PRO, the question still remains of whether infinitivals are S's. If an infinitival is S', it should be possible to find evidence that it contains COMP.[37]

Koster and May (1982) present what they claim is conclusive evidence that in the analysis of infinitival complements it must be assumed that control is effected by the coindexing of an empty PRO, and that in general infinitival complements are S's. In Section 7.1 we will consider some arguments against PRO. In Section 7.2 we will turn to the arguments presented by Koster and May in favor of PRO, and suggest how each can be dealt with in a framework where PRO is not assumed. Our general conclusion is that there are certain constructions where PRO proves to be a useful device, but that the syntactic evidence either fails to support PRO or appears to argue against it. Moreover, there is little direct syntactic evidence to support the view that infinitival constructions contain COMP.[38]

---

[36]Some special stipulation will need to be made in a case like *My intention is to leave* to ensure that *my intention* is not construed as the antecedent of *to leave*. This will be true for all equational sentences. Williams (1980) notes that for cases like *That he is here is the problem* and *To leave is to give up* "no predication is involved. Although *be* typically joins a subject to a predicate, it also has an 'equational' use . . . [p. 224]." It would probably be possible to include these equational VPs into the definition of "proposition" so that they would automatically be excluded from the coindexing procedures.

[37]Current work on this question in general assumes that there are formal reasons not to accept the conclusion that some infinitivals are simple S constituents, without COMP. See Chomsky (1981) and the discussion in what follows.

[38]The position that infinitival complements are S's can of course be supported by considerable indirect evidence that stems from particular theoretical assumptions. We will be concerned here as much as possible with descriptive issues that are relatively independent of the theoretical considerations. This is not to suggest that such considerations are irrelevant, quite the contrary.

7.1. Arguments against PRO and S′

Let us consider first some syntactic arguments against assuming PRO. It should be stressed that we are arguing not against the notion of empty NPs, but against the notion that the subject of a nonfinite clause that lacks an overt subject is in every instance an underlying empty NP. Moreover, if we can show that there is no COMP in an infinitival construction, then we can conclude that there is no PRO, inasmuch as the main theoretical motivation for PRO is that with it we can reduce the set of possible complementation structures from {S′, VP} to S′ alone. It would therefore not be a step forward to conclude simply that S′ and S are possible complements.

7.1.1. GAPPING (I)

The familiar rule of Gapping appears not to be sensitive to the presence of PRO internal to a verbal sequence, although it is clearly sensitive to the presence of a full NP. Thus we have the following, where the material deleted by Gapping appears between square brackets.

(85)   a.   *John tried PRO to leave, and Mary [tried PRO], to stay.*
       b.   *Susan will manage PRO to fix the faucet, and John*
            { *[will manage PRO], to fix the sink.* }
            { *[will manage PRO to fix], the sink.* }
       c.   *Arthur expects PRO to see Mary, and Archie [expects PRO], to go to the circus.*
       d.   *Aristotle wanted PRO to prove Plato's theorem, and*
            Plato { *[wanted PRO], to sit in the sun.* }
                    { *[wanted PRO to prove], Socrates' conjecture.* }
       e.   *John expected PRO to try PRO to leave, and Mary*
            { *[expected PRO to try PRO], to stay.* }
            { *[expected PRO to try], PRO to stay.* }

(86)   a.   *Arthur expects Bill to see Mary, and Archie *[expects Bill], to go to the movies.*
       b.   *Aristotle wanted Socrates to prove Plato's theorem, and Plato *[wanted Socrates] to prove Socrates' conjecture.*

The examples in (86), the general type of which were originally noted in Hankamer (1973), show that an intervening full NP blocks Gapping; the examples in (85) show, in contrast, that PRO does not block Gapping, where PRO appears in various positions in the verbal sequence that is deleted.

Given an analysis involving PRO, one might speculate that if PRO is present, it can be deleted because it is controlled, and therefore uniquely recoverable. The full NP in (86), on the other hand, is not uniquely re-coverable, because, as Hankamer points out, it could be the underlying subject of the infinitive, not of the main clause.

Notice, however, that Gapping is not possible when the gapped material contains a pronoun that is coreferential with another NP in the sentence, or bound by a quantified NP.

(87)   a. *John said that he likes elephants and Mary *[said that she likes], camels.*
         b. *Every man thinks that he is intelligent, and every woman *[thinks that she is], competent.*

Similarly, the trace of *wh*, while bound by the fronted *wh* constituent, cannot be gapped in the same way that PRO can be.

(88)   *Who did John say t ate the cake, and who did Mary *[say t ate], the pie.*[39]

In order to invoke the fact that PRO is controlled, it would be necessary to distinguish controlled PRO from bound anaphoric pronouns, corefer-ence, and bound traces. A simple observation that controlled PRO is re-coverable will not do, because so are the others. Presuming the syntactic reality of all but PRO, the differences in grammaticality between the examples in (85) and those in (87)–(88) follow immediately.[40]

7.1.2. GAPPING (II)

It seems that Gapping cannot apply as shown in (89a), although (89b) is perfectly grammatical.

---

[39]In Wexler and Culicover (1980, p. 287) there is a discussion of an interaction between Wh Fronting and Gapping. It is shown that movement of a *wh* allows Gapping to apply in certain cases by removing from the environment of the verb a **sequence** of complements that would otherwise block it. The examples, which we repeat here, do not determine whether or not the trace of *wh* can be deleted within a sequence that undergoes Gapping because in each case the *t* could be outside of the gapped sequence.
(i)   a. *What will Bill find in Madison Square Garden, and Mary, in Shea Stadium?*
      b. *Where did Mary put the cat and Fred, the goldfish?*
      c. *What did you trade to Susan, and Fred, to Mary?*
[40]We could assume, as is frequently done in the literature, that PRO is "invisible" in the "phonological" component to which "stylistic" rules like Gapping belong. We do not rule out this possibility here. If all the facts discussed in this book can be explained given this assumption, and if there are independent theoretical arguments in favor of PRO, then this section can be taken to be justification of the view that PRO has this particular property of invisibility.

(89) a. $I \begin{Bmatrix} expect \\ want \\ would\ like \\ believe \\ find \end{Bmatrix}$ *Mary to be rich and Bill* $*[\begin{Bmatrix} expects \\ wants \\ would\ like \\ believes \\ finds \end{Bmatrix}]$ $\begin{Bmatrix} Sam \\ Mary \end{Bmatrix}$ *to be poor.*

  b. *John* $\begin{Bmatrix} expects \\ wants \\ would\ like \end{Bmatrix}$ *to eat the beans, and Mary*

  $[[\begin{Bmatrix} expects \\ wants \\ would\ like \end{Bmatrix}]]$ *to eat the potatoes.*

If it is the case that Gapping applies when only one constituent follows (see Stillings 1975), then the data in (89a) can be accounted for by the assumption that the structure of *Sam to be poor* is not $_S$[NP VP], but rather $_{VP}$[. . . NP VP]. Thus (89a) is ungrammatical because two constituents follow the gap. In contrast, (89b) is a case where only one constituent follows the gap, the infinitival VP. If the structure following the gap in (89b) were $_{S'}$[PRO *to eat the potatoes*], it would be difficult to account for the grammaticality distinction between (89a) and (89b) short of saying that Gapping may leave an infinitival S′ only in case it has a PRO subject.

7.1.3. VP TOPICALIZATION

Consider next the rule of VP Topicalization (Culicover 1976b), illustrated in (90) where the fronted VP is enclosed in brackets.

(90) a. *Everyone said that they would leave on time, and [leave on time] they did.*
  b. *John expected Mary to say nothing, and [say nothing] she did.*

The rule of VP Topicalization may apply to an infinitival complement:

(91) a. *They said John would expect to leave, and [leave] John expected to.*
  b. *Mary said we would try to leave, and [leave] we tried to.*
  c. *Everyone suspects that you would want to leave early, and [leave early] you (seem to) want to.*[41]

[41]Some people find . . . *and leave John did expect to* and . . . *leave early you do (seem to) want to* somewhat better than (91a) and (91c), respectively.

When there is an intervening subject, VP Topicalization is blocked.

(92)   a. *They said John would expect Mary to leave, and [leave]
           John expected her to.
        b. *Everyone suspects that Sam would want Alvin to leave early,
           and [leave early] he wants him to.
        c. *They said John would force Mary to leave, and [leave] John
           forced her to.

This blocking of VP Topicalization might appear to be due to the Specified Subject Condition of Chomsky (1973), which blocks movement out
of a clause with a specified (i.e., a lexical or bound) subject. However, in
a theory with traces and COMP, like that of Chomsky (1973), extraction
out of an infinitive is countenanced by the fact that the moved constituent
is moved first to the lowest COMP, where it does not violate the Specified
Subject Condition, and then into higher COMPs. We can see that unbounded movement is also possible for VP Topicalization.

(93)   a. Everyone said that it would be obvious that they would leave
           on time, and [leave on time] it seems to me they did.
        b. John expected Mary to say the wrong thing, and [say the
           wrong thing] we believe she did.
        c. They said John would expect Mary to leave, and [leave]
           John expected she would.

Since the COMP escape route appears to be available for VP Topicalization, it should be possible in the case of the examples in (92).

To block the escape route for VP Topicalization out of infinitives, we
could assume that infinitives, although sentential, lack COMPs. One consequence of doing so would be to eliminate the generalization that "a
clause (S') consists of a complementizer COMP and a propositional component (S)" [Chomsky 1981, p. 19].

It could be stipulated, of course, that VP Topicalization does not operate
over an NP. But then we have a situation in which PRO and lexical NP
are distinguished because in (91) the VP is moved across the PRO. Thus
the stipulation must be reduced to the following: VP Topicalization cannot
function over a lexical NP (or the trace of one).

Moreover, this restriction will be too strong, in view of the grammaticality of the following sentence.

(94)   They expected John to promise Mary not to leave, and [leave] he
        promised her not to.

However, suppose that there is no PRO. The grammatical instances of VP Topicalization are then distinguishable from the ungrammatical ones in the following way: **VP Topicalization cannot move a VP away from an antecedent NP with which it is coindexed (by the assignment of grammatical relations or by predication).** Where the VP has as its antecedent the subject of an embedded S' then it can be moved into the embedded COMP position and still be near its antecedent. This is the case, for instance, in (91a) and (94). In (91a) *leave* is predicated of *John* and after VP Topicalization it is still next to *John*. In (94) *leave* is predicated of *he* and after movement remains next to *he*. In (92a) the predicate has been moved away from its antecedent: *Leave* is predicated of the object *her,* but after movement it is no longer next to *her* (it is next to *John*). This proposed restriction to account for VP Topicalization must, of course, assume that there is no PRO subject of the infinitive in cases like (91a) because otherwise in all cases the infinitive would have PRO as its antecedent.[42]

7.1.4. PSEUDOCLEFTS

It is well known that S' can be the focus of a pseudocleft, as illustrated in (95a)–(95b). To account for the grammaticality distinction between (95c) and (95d) it is sufficient, in a no-PRO analysis, to say that VP can also be the focus of a pseudocleft, but that the sequence NP VP cannot be.

(95)　　a.　*What John expects is that he will be elected President.*
　　　　b.　*What John expects is for Mary to be elected President.*
　　　　c.　*What John expects is to be elected President.*
　　　　d.　**What John expects is Mary to be elected President.*

The assumption that *Mary to be elected President* is an S' in (95d) would make an incorrect prediction, other things being equal. If NP VP is treated as an S constituent, as it is in the theory that includes PRO, examples like (95d) must somehow be ruled out. This could be accomplished in an analysis that makes use of abstract case marking. In a non-pseudocleft, as already noted, the matrix verb assigns (exceptional) case marking to the subject of the infinitive. (For a verb like *expect,* this exceptional abstract case marking must be optional, so that PRO will not be case marked.

---

[42]This restriction on VP Topicalization should follow from more general constraints, but we will not speculate here on what they might be. The obvious solution of ordering Predication after VP Topicalization will not work if Predication applies in Deep Structure as we argue in this chapter. Nor will it work if VP Topicalization leaves a trace that can be coindexed with the predicate.

More generally, we could assume that case marking is always optional.) However, in the pseudocleft, abstract case marking will not apply because *is* is the governing verb, not *expect*. The subject of the infinitive can only be PRO, and not a lexical NP. This would explain the grammaticality of (95c) with PRO subject of the infinitive. (See Chomsky, 1981, for details of the theory of abstract case marking.) Introduction of *for* case marks the lexical subject, so that (95b) is grammatical.[43]

Given the problems inherent in the theory of exceptional case marking (e.g., optional versus obligatory S'-deletion) it seems to us preferable to simply disallow the sequence NP VP in focus position and to analyze (95c) as having a simple VP as focus (see Postal 1974). Assuming that VP is the maximal projection of V, we can then maintain the generalization that the focus constituent in English pseudoclefts is X^{max}, where X ranges over the lexical categories N, V, A, P, and M, the head of S.[44]

7.1.5. APPOSITIVE RELATIVES

In general, full NP allows appositive relatives, whereas PRO does not.

(96)   *John expects Bill, who deserves it, to win the prize.*

(97)   **John expects PRO, who deserves it, to win the prize.*

Sentence (97) cannot be explained simply by disallowing pronominal forms in this position (perhaps for some semantic reason) because reflexives, for instance, are allowed.

(98)   *John expects himself, who deserves it, to win the prize.*

It is not clear how it would be possible to rule out generating appositive relatives on PRO. Emonds (1979) argues that appositives do not form a constituent with the NP. If they do not, it is difficult to see why an appositive cannot appear after a PRO subject, if it can appear after an anaphor like *himself*, as in (98). If Emonds is wrong, and appositives do form

---

[43]In the PRO theory Example (95c) presents a problem because if the focus constituent is an S' with an empty COMP and a PRO subject the PRO subject is either not controlled or is controlled by a non-c-commanding NP. In our predication analysis a similar puzzle arises. We must in some way assure that the antecedent of the infinitive is *John* and not the larger NP *what John expects*. It is not at all clear what definition of "closest" would select, in this case, an NP within a larger NP.

[44]Note that this discussion does not present an argument against PRO, rather it demonstrates that the pseudocleft does not provide an argument in favor of PRO. See discussion of Koster and May (1982) in section 7.2. For discussion of the fact that X^{max} constituents appear as focus in pseudoclefts, see Delahunty (1981).

a constituent with the NP, then the structure in (99) would somehow have to be ruled out.

(99)   NP[PRO S']

A possible solution would be to require exceptional case marking of the entire subject NP when the appositive is present.[45] The case marking would then transfer onto the head, yielding a violation of the principle that PRO cannot have case. Why an appositive must be attached to a case-marked NP is unclear, especially in view of the fact that appositives can be attached to constituents of various categories without requiring that they be case marked.

(100)   a.   *John is angry, which is not a good thing to be.*
          b.   *John arrived late, which is unusual.*
          c.   *Mary lives in New York, where she grew up.*

Thus the stipulation must be that if an appositive is attached to an NP, the NP must be case marked.

If we do not assume PRO, then the examples that we have noted fall into place. As there is no NP[PRO], either on Emonds's account of appositives or on the account in which the appositive forms a constituent with the NP, there will be no antecedent whatsoever for the appositive in the ungrammatical cases.[46]

---

[45]Note that this analysis cannot work if Emonds's analysis of appositives is correct, as PRO and the appositive would not form a constituent.

[46]Another possible way of ruling out the relevant examples is to adopt the surface structure filter *[e] S'. By doing so we rule out examples where a phrase has been moved away from an appositive, a construction otherwise predicted, it seems, given the Emonds analysis.
  (i)   a.   *I expect that man, who Mary knows, to leave.*
         b.* *That man, I expect [e], who Mary knows, to leave.*
         c.   *That man, who Mary knows, I expect to leave.*
  (ii)   a.   *You think that man, who Mary knows, will leave.*
         b.* *That man, you think [e], who Mary knows, will leave.*
         c.   *That man, who Mary knows, you think will leave.*
  (iii) a.   *You think that I saw that man, who Mary knows.*
         b.*? *That man, you think I saw, who Mary knows.*
         c.   *That man, who Mary knows, you think I saw.*
The generalization expressed by this filter is not quite correct though, because it rules out cases like (ivb).
  (iv)   a.   *I saw that man, who Mary knows.*
         b.   *That man, I saw, who Mary knows.*
         c.   *That man, who Mary knows, I saw.*
If the filter is restricted to the case of [e] S' X, X ≠ ∅, then it would incorrectly rule out (vb).
  (v)   a.   *I saw that man, who Mary knows, washing his car.*
         b.? *That man, I saw, who Mary knows, washing his car.*

7.1.6. TOPICALIZATION

An argument against the notion that infinitives are S' (rather than directly against PRO) has to do with Topicalization. As discussed earlier, if we can argue against the sentential nature of infinitival complements, then the a fortiori case for PRO is considerably weakened.

Assume that the derivation of Topicalization involves movement to COMP. If the structure of an infinitival complement is $_{S'}$[COMP $_S$[NP VP]], we might then expect Topicalization to apply within an infinitival complement, just as it applies within an embedded *that* complement. However, it does not.

(101)   a.   *I admitted that yesterday, I had seen Fred.*
        b.   *It is obvious that Bill, Mary dislikes a lot.*
        c.   *John believes that to Mary, Sam gave the book.*

(102)   a.   **John wants (for) tomorrow, Mary to leave.*
        b.   **John believes (for) to Mary, Sam to have given a book.*

(103)   a.   **John wants tomorrow, to leave.*
        b.   **John claims to Mary, to have given the book.*

It seems that the simplest way to rule out the ungrammatical examples in (102)–(103) is to assume that there is no COMP in either of the infinitival constructions. There are then several other assumptions about the structure which would be consistent. First, it could be that these infinitival constructions are S's that lack COMP. Second, it could be that these infinitival constructions are Ss. Third, it could be that they are not sentential at all. Alternatively, it could be that Topicalization does not involve COMP, but some TOPIC node, and that this TOPIC node does not appear in infinitival constructions.

If there is no COMP in the infinitival construction, then there arise the complications we have already mentioned with respect to defining the structure of the clause (S'). Let us consider, therefore, only the alternative in which COMP is not implicated in Topicalization. Examples like the following suggest that it is possible to have an adverbial topic after a COMP into which *wh* has been moved.

(104)   a.   *This is the man who in 1947 they said we would all vote for.*
        b.   *I met the man that on the train Susan introduced to Fred.*

---

        c.   *That man, who Mary knows, I saw washing his car.*
If (vb) turns out to be ungrammatical, then, of course **[e] S' X, X ≠ 0 would suffice.

Although it is not clear how we would explain the range of grammaticality judgments indicated here, it does not appear that they can be accounted for by a generalized filter that will also rule out the cases of the PRO – S' appositive.

    c.   *Anyone who for no reason at all a lion tries to attack*
       should take shelter in the nearest police station.

If there is a TOPIC node in these constructions, and if this TOPIC is introduced as the sister of S′ as Chomsky (1977) suggests, then it must be the case that the well-formed occurrence of TOPIC in S″ is dependent on whether or not the S it contains is [+TENSE] or [−TENSE]. This is illustrated in (105) where (105a) would be relevant for (104a) and (105b) would be relevant for the ungrammatical (102a).

(105)   a.

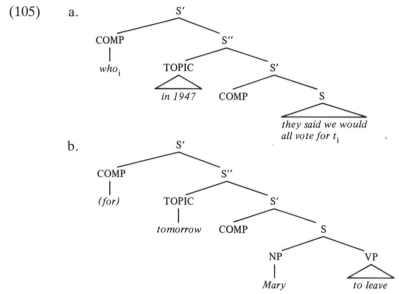

It appears, therefore, that the problem raised by Topicalization in infinitivals cannot be gotten around by assuming that the topicalized constituent moves not into COMP, but into TOPIC.

    The remaining way to block Topicalization in infinitives is therefore to assume that the infinitival complements are not sentential. If, however, they are sentential, they cannot involve S′, hence case marking could not distinguish between PRO and lexical NP. This, however, would mean that we must throw out the core of the theory of abstract case marking, inasmuch as we must now explain why PRO does not appear except in subject position. We may therefore conclude again that there is reason not to assume the existence of PRO.

7.1.7. CONJUNCTION

    If PRO is an NP, we might expect it to conjoin with other NPs. However, as the examples in (106) illustrate, it does not.

(106)   a. *I expect to go to Italy and I expect John to go to Italy.*
         b. **I expect PRO and John to go to Italy.*
         c. **I expect John and PRO to go to Italy.*

Assuming that there is no PRO, these facts follow immediately.[47]

7.1.8. STYLISTIC INVERSION

There is a rule of Stylistic Inversion in English that has the effect of moving a subject into an intransitive VP when a constituent has been extracted from that VP (Culicover 1977, Bowers 1976, Langendoen 1979, Emonds 1976). Stylistic Inversion is illustrated in (108).

(107)   *Into the room walked the President of the United States.*

(108)   *On the stool sat the man in the funny hat.*

It is possible to apply Stylistic Inversion to an infinitive, which might suggest that the infinitive has a syntactic subject and therefore is sentential. In (109b) *the man in the funny hat* has been moved by Stylistic Inversion into the embedded VP as though it had been the subject of *to sit*.

(109)   a. *John expects the man in the funny hat to sit on the stool.*
         b. *?On the stool John expects to sit the man in the funny hat.*

Since, as we suggested earlier, there can be no Topicalization in an infinitival complement, we must predict that the example (109b) does not have an intermediate stage where *on the stool* is inverted to an embedded

---

[47]These facts also follow if the case marking assigned to a conjoined NP is necessarily evenly distributed over the conjuncts. *Expect* case marks the following NP *PRO and John* (because *expect* has S′-deletion). Therefore PRO will get case marked, which is a violation. (If *expect* did not case mark *PRO and John,* then *John* would have no case, which is also a violation.)

Such a straightforward condition on case in conjoined NPs would not work in examples like the following:

(i)   a. *I expect John to leave and Mary to stay.*
       b.*I expect to leave and Mary to stay.*
       c.*I expect Mary to stay and PRO to leave.*

In these examples it is not simply a conjoined NP at issue. Here we are conjoining two sorts of complements of *expect,* NP–*to*–VP and simple VP. If there is no PRO, then we would predict (ib) and (ic) to be bad, because of the lack of parallelism of the complement structures (cf. Chomsky 1957). If there is PRO, then these would be examples of conjoined S′s and we would expect grammaticality as in (ia).

The only way we see to account for (i) in a theory with PRO would be to adopt an across-the-board method for applying abstract case marking to conjoined structures (as suggested for other rules in Williams 1978). *Expect* would then case mark both *Mary* and PRO (or neither), yielding precisely the same sort of violation as discussed in connection with the examples of (106).

position. In other words, we predict examples like those in (110) to be ill formed (although in fact they sound marginal).

(110)   a.(*)*John expects on the stool to sit the man in the funny hat.*
           b.(*)*John believes in this room to have slept a President of the United States.*

Our analysis is that Stylistic Inversion inverts the closest NP to the relevant VP, whether or not that NP happens to be a syntactic subject. Notice that the closest NP to the infinitival VP is the antecedent by predication even though it is not the subject.[48]

On the alternative analysis where the subject of the infinitive is PRO, then we would expect Stylistic Inversion not to apply. This would be the predicted case because the rule does not apply to pronominal NPs, as (111) shows.

(111)   a.   *He sat on the stool.*
           b.   *On the stool sat he.*

What we get in case there is no overt subject of the infinitive is surprising: The subject of the matrix moves into the infinitival VP.

(112)   a.   *The man in the funny hat expects to sit on the stool.*
           b.   *On the stool Ø expects to sit the man in the funny hat.*

Compare (112b) with (113), where the subject of the infinitive is a pronoun.

(113)   a.   *The man in the funny hat expects* $\begin{Bmatrix} him \\ himself \end{Bmatrix}$ *to sit on the stool.*

           b.   **On the stool expects* $\begin{Bmatrix} him \\ himself \end{Bmatrix}$ *to sit the man in the funny hat.*

---

[48]On the assumption that the examples in (110) should be generated, an interesting possibility (suggested by Ken Wexler) is that Topicalization blocks case marking of subjects in infinitives, while Stylistic Inversion of the subject NP puts it into a position where it can be case marked. Thus, in (110b) *a President of the United States* is case marked (somehow), whereas in (i) below it is not. On this view, the examples in (110) are grammatical.
    (i) **John believes in this room a President of the United States to have slept.*
Note, however, that the same Topicalization will block case marking when the subject is PRO, which should render (ii) grammatical.
    (ii) **John claims in this room to have slept.*
It appears, therefore, that the way to sustain the suggested analysis incorporating case marking is to dispense with PRO, but to maintain that *a President to have slept in this room* is an S′ complement. Nothing that we have said in this chapter rules out this possibility, but it is ruled out in the analysis of Chapter 3.

What these examples confirm is that there is in fact no PRO subject of infinitives. Example (112b) is grammatical because the inverted NP is the antecedent (closest NP) of the VP *to sit*. If there was a PRO subject of the embedded infinitive we would expect Stylistic Inversion to be prevented from moving the higher subject into the lower VP. The grammaticality of (112b) suggests not only that there is no PRO but furthermore that the infinitive is not an S' or S, in view of the well-known constraint against lowering constituents (Chomsky 1965, 1973; Wexler and Culicover 1980). The ungrammaticality of the examples in (113b) is due to the fact that the moved subject NP was not the antecedent of the embedded infinitive. Such a movement over the intervening antecedent, whether that antecedent is anaphoric or otherwise, is blocked. This also suggests that there cannot be a PRO NP in (112b).

7.1.9. PARTITIVE FRONTING

Well-known examples such as the following suggest that quantifiers that float can be floated off of PRO.

(114)   a. *The men all tried to leave.*
         b. *The men tried [PRO all to leave].*
         c. *The men tried to all leave.*

(115)   a. *John and Mary both expected to win.*
         b. *John and Mary expected [PRO both to win].*
         c. *John and Mary expected to both win.*

(116)   a. *The men all forced Sam to sing the theme song.*
         b. **The men forced Sam $\left\{ \begin{matrix} to\ all \\ all\ to \end{matrix} \right\}$ sing the theme song.*
         c. *Sam forced the men to all sing the theme song.*

(117)   a. *The men all expected John to win the prize.*
         b. **The men expected John $\left\{ \begin{matrix} to\ all \\ all\ to \end{matrix} \right\}$ win the prize.*

A quantifier cannot float off of the subject of the matrix over an overt subject of an infinitive, as in (116b) and (117b). This suggests that in order for a quantifier to get into an infinitive, as in (114c) and (115c), it must float off of a PRO subject of the infinitive [or be generated on the infinitival subject as in (116c)]. Assuming this analysis, (114b) and (115b) would be the necessary intermediate stages for (114c) and (115c), respectively.

Still assuming this analysis, we might expect that other constituents of a noun phrase containing PRO might be moved out of that phrase, yielding grammaticality just in case the result were an NP exhaustively dominating

PRO in subject position, as in (114c) and (115c). Consider the rule that we will call Partitive Fronting, which yields structures like that in (118b).

(118)   a. *Only Susan of all the women expects to win.*
         b. *Of all the women, only Susan expects to win.*

Suppose that we have the structure illustrated in (119).

(119)   *Only Susan expects [PRO of all the women to win].*

If the infinitival complement is an S′, then we might expect Partitive Fronting to apply as shown in (120).

(120)   **Only Susan expects of all the women PRO to win.*

The ungrammaticality of (120), which would be surprising in the PRO theory, follows directly if we assume that there is no sentential structure for the infinitives and therefore no PRO subjects. Q-Float, as in (114)–(117), would be permitted just in case the Q could be construed with the antecedent of the predicate in which it occurs (see Section 7.2.6.)

7.2. Arguments for PRO

In the preceding discussion we have presented a variety of syntactic arguments that PRO does not exist, and that a fortiori there are infinitival complements that are not sentential. In what follows we will discuss in some detail the most salient arguments of Koster and May (1982) (henceforth K&M) to the contrary. K&M's arguments fall into two categories. First, they argue that to assume that there are nonsentential, bare infinitives causes a complication of the base component. We will note that although under one view this is correct, K&M fail to note that not assuming that there are such complements results in complications elsewhere in the grammar, and that in a different light including VP results in a simplification of the base component.

Second, K&M give a set of grammatical arguments that support the assumption that PRO exists. These arguments, however, do not necessarily have syntactic consequences, and each can be accounted for in a theory that marks the relationship between an infinitive and its subject through the coindexing of a predicate, rather than through control of PRO. Thus, although PRO captures certain generalizations and is consistent with K&M's observations, it is not necessary.[49]

---

[49]K&M's arguments in favor of PRO seem convincing given the VP′ analysis with which they compare their own analysis. A VP′ analysis, to be convincing, must include a coherent theory of predication, such as that which we have already discussed in detail. Following K&M we will here refer to the maximal projection of V as VP′.

7.2.1. COMP IN INFINITIVES

K&M argue that since *wh* infinitives of the following sort must have COMP, they must be S's.

(121)   a. *I wonder what to do.*
         b. *a topic on which to work*

They say: "On the assumption, then, that only S's are introduced by complementizers, such examples provide further evidence that subjectless infinitives are S's [1982, p. 133]." Of course, since they are trying to prove that an infinitival is an S', and since the argument is that it is not ideal to introduce COMP as a constituent of anything other than S', it is not entirely legitimate to take the appearance of COMP as providing evidence that we have S's here. Let us consider the question of whether VP' can introduce COMP on its own merits.

There are two arguments against this position. First, there is the simple fact that COMP is introduced under two nodes. If VP' exists, then presumably part of its characterization in Universal Grammar is that it may take COMP, and thus the fact that COMP can appear in two places is not a problem for the grammar of any particular language. Following K&M's logic, we might question Selkirk's (1977) analysis of NP and AP as both containing DET, an analysis based on examples like *John knows {this/that} man* and *John is {this/that} tall.* But in fact, what Selkirk's observations point to is a generalization: If NP and AP are both analyzed as $[+N]$, DET can be generalized as the specifier of $[+N]$ phrases.

We suppose that VP (or VP') is the maximal projection of V, and that S' is the maximal projection of M (as Chomsky, 1981, and Klein, 1981, suggest). Assuming further that M and V share the feature $[+V]$ (cf. Chomsky 1970), we then have the generalization that COMP is the specifier of $[+V]$ phrases (see Section 6 where relevant examples are discussed).

K&M also argue that the introduction of COMP in both VP' and S' is undesirable given that VP' is not a bounding node with respect to subjacency. They note (1982, p. 135) that the presence of COMP in VP' cannot block configurations like the following [their (79)].

(122)   *$What_2$ does Mary wonder $_{VP'}$[to $whom_3$ [to give e_2 e_3]]

But there are other constraints that will block (122), including the Variable Interpretation Convention of Wilkins (1977, 1980a) and our LC. Additionally, it is not at all obvious that in the framework of Chomsky (1973) VP' could not be treated as a bounding node with respect to subjacency.

So far as we can tell, these are the only two arguments that K&M bring to bear against the notion of COMP in VP' which are relevant in light of our proposed alternative.

7.2.2. DISJUNCTION IN THE BASE RULES

A different source of potential redundancy in the VP′ analysis is the fact that both S′ and VP′ must be introduced in the expansion of VP, NP, AP, and PP, as in (123).

(123)   a. $VP \rightarrow V \left\{ \begin{array}{c} VP' \\ S' \end{array} \right\}$

          b. $NP \rightarrow N \left\{ \begin{array}{c} VP' \\ S' \end{array} \right\}$

          c. $AP \rightarrow A \left\{ \begin{array}{c} VP' \\ S' \end{array} \right\}$

          d. $PP \rightarrow P \left\{ \begin{array}{c} VP' \\ S' \end{array} \right\}$

Of course, there is an immediate generalization here if these rules are correct, as each of these phrases is a maximal projection of a lexical category. So what is really necessary is the following schema:

(124) $X^{max} \rightarrow X \left\{ \begin{array}{c} VP' \\ S' \end{array} \right\}$

If it is in fact correct to treat VP′ and S′ as projections of [+v], then (124) generalizes immediately to (125).

(125) $X^{max} \rightarrow X [+v]^{max}$

On K&M's view, though, the correct elimination of the redundancy in (124) is to eliminate VP′, which we represent in (124′).

(124′) $X^{max} \rightarrow X S'$

K&M also point out that since both VP′ and S′ can be relatives as well as sentential subjects, the same disjunction must appear in the rules in (126).

(126)   a. $NP \rightarrow NP \left\{ \begin{array}{c} VP' \\ S' \end{array} \right\}$

          b. $NP \rightarrow \left\{ \begin{array}{c} VP' \\ S' \end{array} \right\}$ or

          c. $TOPIC \rightarrow \left\{ \begin{array}{c} VP' \\ S' \end{array} \right\}$ (in the framework of Koster 1978)

This redundancy is avoided if VP′ is everywhere eliminated in favor of S′, as K&M propose. Note that the redundancy is also avoided if VP′ and S′ are expressed as projections of [+v], as we have suggested:

(127)   a. $NP \rightarrow NP [+v]^{max}$

b. $NP \rightarrow [+v]^{max}$

Although these points about the base are of interest, K&M have glossed over some additional complexities that are important to take note of. First of all, suppose that (127b) is a base rule. That is, suppose that infinitivals and *that*-clauses may be exhaustively dominated by NP. Then in the expansion of the phrasal categories given in (123), we see that VP' and S' will be introduced whenever NP is introduced. So, for example, we have the unproblematic rules of (128) in the base component of English.

(128)   a.   VP → V PP
          b.   NP → N PP
          c.   AP → A PP
          d.   PP → P PP

Since PP expands as P NP, these rules along with (127) will derive essentially the same configurations as those in (123). However, in the case of (127b), there will be a preposition before each S' or VP', as in (129).

(129)   a.   *John approved of that Mary had left on time.
          b.   *John's anger at that Fred was incompetent was unseemly.
          c.   *I was angry at that you hadn't solved the problem.
          d.   *Until after that Bill leaves . . .

These examples can all be improved by deleting the subcategorized preposition [in (129a)–(129c)] or *that*. Notice that since the lexical items *approve, anger,* and *angry* all govern PPs and S's, if the grammatical examples corresponding to (129) are not derived by deletion of P, each will have to have a more complex lexical entry.

On the one hand we have (127), (128), and a rule for deleting preposition. On the other hand (in K&M's approach) we have (128) and (124') [i.e., (124) with S' only] and a considerably more complex lexicon, in which every lexical item that takes a PP complement can take an S' complement. This redundancy is explained by (127), but would only be stipulated if we added a redundancy rule to the lexicon.

Having formulated matters in this way, we see that the apparent redundancy of (124) (i.e., in the posthead complements) can be eliminated by introducing (127b). Let us consider now (127a). In the case of relatives, it turns out that K&M have not taken note of the full range of post-nominal modifiers in English. Along with (130a)–(130b), we also have (130c)–(130h).

(130)   a.   *the man* s'[*that you saw*]
          b.   *the man* s[*you saw*]
          c.   *the man* vp'[*to whom to give the book*]

    d.   *the man* $_{VP}$[*to give the book to*]
    e.   *the man* $_{PP}$[*in the street*]
    f.   *the man* $_{VP}$[*arrested by the police*]
    g.   *the man* $_{VP}$[*running for the bus*]
    h.   *the man* $_{AP}$[*angry at Mary*]

Quite possibly the postnominal complements constitute a natural class, which could be expressed in terms of a unique syntactic feature configuration. We will not pursue here the question of what these features might be.[50] In any case, it appears that the apparent redundancy claimed by K&M disappears when the full range of constructions is considered, as the full range of complements is in fact not restricted to S' and VP'.[51]

One might try to eliminate the redundancy noted by K&M by arguing that the modifiers in (130b)–(130h) are reduced relative clauses. It would of course be possible to assign to these phrases an abstract structure of the form $_{S'}$[$_S$[$_{NP}$[*e*]$_{VP}$[$_V$[*e*] XP]]], but it is entirely unclear what such a move would accomplish beyond forcing every complement into a uniform abstract S' configuration.

As we have seen, K&M's arguments against the VP' analysis are based on considerations of phrase structure.[52] In addition, K&M present a number of arguments not directly against the VP', but rather in favor of the S' analysis. Such arguments, they claim, pose serious problems for the VP' analysis.

---

[50]It might be profitable to pursue the hypothesis that [+v] relatives may be maximal projections (i.e., S' and VP') and maximal − 1 projections (i.e., S and VP). Thus, the fact that the complementizer *that* need not appear in the relative clause would follow automatically, without the need for a rule to delete it.

[51]Actually it is not obvious that K&M's assumption that the VP' analysis requires both VP' and S' complements in the base rules really represents a complication. Complements to all the lexical categories already must include S, AP, and PP. The real complication for any theory is to explain the distribution of NP as a complement. In other words, the determination of the possible complement types for any major category does not turn solely on the VP' versus S' issue. Perhaps the unmarked base rule is XP → X Complements where the Complements are all XPs (all the major categories) including VP. A complication would then be any deviation from this generalization, for example, *AP → A NP.

[52]K&M have one further argument against the VP' analysis, based on *tough* constructions. They argue that all of the properties explained by the VP' analysis in connection with this construction can be accounted for equally well by the assumption that *Wh* Movement applies to it, as in (i) [their (135) in 1982; p. 126]:
   (i) *John is easy* $_{PP}$[*for Bill*]$_{S'}$[*wh*$_2$ $_S$[*PRO to please e*$_2$]]
[The analysis illustrated in (i) is due to Chomsky (1977).]
   K&M's argument is not really against the VP' analysis, but simply in favor of the view that there is an alternative analysis which does not assume VP' that can do as well. As it is not our concern here to criticize in detail the *Wh* Movement analysis of the *tough* construction, we will not pursue here a comparison of the two analyses in this regard.

7.2.3. PSEUDOCLEFTS

K&M argue that the grammar can be simplified if there is no VP′, because then it only has to be stated that S′ can be focus of a pseudocleft, as in (131) versus (132) [(64) versus (65) in K&M 1982, p. 132].

(131) a. *What he wanted was (for Bill) to see Monument Valley.*
       b. *What he suspected was that Bill saw Monument Valley.*

(132) a. **What he wanted for Bill was to see Monument Valley.*
       b. **What he suspected that Bill was saw Monument Valley.*

As was discussed in Section 7.1.4, all that need be said about pseudoclefts is that both S′ and VP′ can be the focus. The fact that a tensed VP cannot be the focus, as in (132b), follows from an analysis of tense which says that it is overtly expressed only in the environment of a subject, that is, never in VP′ (see Footnote 58 in Chapter 3). There are, of course, other sorts of constituents that can be focus in a pseudocleft, so the fact S′ and VP′ can be foci does not in itself constitute a loss of generalization.

K&M fail to note sentences like the following, which suggest that VP **can** function as a focus as long as it is not tensed.

(133) a. *What he did was feed the ducks.*
       b. *What he wanted to do was feed the ducks.*

Compare the examples in (133) with those in (134).

(134) a. **What John did was that John fed the ducks.*
       b. **What John did was for him to feed the ducks.*
       c. **What John wanted Mary to do was for her to feed the ducks.*

It turns out that the only real point is that tensed VP cannot be a focus, a fact that has little to do with whether there is a VP′ constituent.

7.2.4. EXTRAPOSITION

K&M note that both infinitives and sentences extrapose.

(135) a. *A book which we didn't like appeared.*
       b. *A book appeared which we didn't like.*

(136) a. *A book on which to work appeared.*
       b. *A book appeared on which to work.*

(137) a. *A problem to work on is on the table.*
       b. *A problem is on the table to work on.*

As APs and PPs can also be extraposed, it is not clear what degree of generality is lost by allowing both VP′ and S′ to extrapose.

(138)   a.   *A book bound in leather was on the table.*
         b.   *A book was on the table bound in leather.*

(139)   a.   *A book about armadillos has just appeared.*
         b.   *A book has just appeared about armadillos.*

In fact, it appears that the true generalization is not "extrapose S' from
NP" but "extrapose from NP" or, more generally, "move α to FOCUS,"
as we discuss in Section 8 of Chapter 5.

7.2.5. CONJUNCTION

K&M claim that the infinitival complements conjoin with sentential
complements, from which they conclude that the two are of the same
category. They give the following examples (1982, p. 133).

(140)   a.   *To write a novel and for the world to give it critical acclaim
              is John's dream.*
         b.   *John expected to write a novel but that it would be a critical
              disaster.*

It is not at all obvious that these examples are grammatical; in fact we
find them not to be. Other similar sorts of examples consistently fall short
of grammaticality.

(141)   a.   **John hopes for Mary to leave and that he will be elected
              President.*
         b.   **John expects that he will win or to be given a consolation
              prize.*

However, let us suppose for the sake of argument that these sentences
are well formed. Then the same logic leads to the conclusion that the
complements are all PPs or NPs, because *for–to* complements can be conjoined with PP, and *that* complements can be conjoined with NP, as in
(142).

(142)   a.   *John hopes for Mary to leave and for a miracle.*
         b.   *John planned both for a picnic and for Mary to be invited.*
         c.   *I believe your answer, and that you believe what you are
              saying.*
         d.   *That you were here last night, and John's reaction when
              you told him, surprised no one.*
         e.   *The look on your face, the way you were dressed, and that
              you couldn't speak French, indicated to us that you were
              not a native.*

There is no problem with the notion that all of these complements are NPs, assuming a base rule that expands NP as S' or VP'. However, presumably K&M would not share this view (see Koster 1978a). So the argument from conjunction used in (140) to show that VP' is the same category as S' would lead to the conclusion that in (142) S' is NP.[53]

7.2.6. EVIDENCE FOR SUBJECTS IN SUBJECTLESS CLAUSES[54]

What we find to be the most compelling evidence for subjects in superficially subjectless clauses has to do with anaphora and coreference. K&M point out several facts that can be explained if these clauses contain a PRO subject.

One argument has to do with Q-Float, which we discussed in Section 7.1.9. Sentences like (143) suggest that the infinitive has a PRO subject with which the quantifier is construed.

(143)   *The men expect to all leave.*

Notice, however, that once it is established that *to leave* is coindexed with *the men* (in a predicational theory), the subject of the infinitive is known. Hence the construal of *all* is not a problem, if it is expressed in terms of the controlling NP. Thus we get *The men promised Mary to all leave* but not *The men forced Mary to all leave*. In the first case the whole VP [*to all leave*] has *the men* as the antecedent. In the second case [*to all leave*] is predicated of *Mary* and *all* has no well-formed antecedent because *Mary* is not plural (compare: *The men forced the women to all leave*). Such a view of Q-Float does not appear to be any more problematic than a transformational one, given that no convincing account of the underlying source of the quantifier has yet been given.[55]

[53]Note incidentally that the grammaticality of (142e) constitutes an argument against the position of Koster (1978a) that sentential subjects are really topics. If they were, then all subjects would have to be topics, at least for examples like (142e). Such an analysis appears to have little independent motivation. See also Bresnan and Grimshaw (1978) for another argument against Koster's proposal.

[54]In K&M the discussion of COMP in infinitival complements is considered in the section on arguments for S'. We have already covered this in our discussion of the base rules and the Subjacency Condition.

[55]A pair of sentences that constitute slight evidence for the predication analysis and against a PRO analysis is the following:

(i)   a. *The men all tried to fit in the car.*
       b. *The men tried to all fit in the car.*

Although it is possible to accommodate such examples in both analyses, the PRO analysis allows for a possibility that does not actually occur, as follows. In the PRO analysis *all* could in principle be coindexed with the closest subject NP. As the examples in (ii) show, *all* would then receive the same index for the two sentences in (i) given that the controller and PRO have the same index.

(ii)   a. *The men$_i$ all$_i$ tried PRO$_i$ to fit in the car.*

Along these lines, there are sentences like (144) which appear to require a predicational analysis.

(144)   *John, Fred, and Mary have all left. (*All John, Fred, and Mary have left.)*

In (144) there appears to be no well-formed source for a transformational account of *all*.[56]

In a VP′ analysis without a theory of predication there are some problematic cases having to do with reflexives and pronouns. Examples like the following suggest, in the context of the Extended Standard Theory, that there is a PRO subject in a sentential domain. (The star in [145b] refers to the reading in which *Oscar* and *him* are coreferential.)

(145)   a.   *John said it was difficult [PRO to help himself].*
          b.   **[PRO realizing that Oscar was unpopular] did not disturb him.*

In these two cases in (145) PRO acts just like the NP in (146), coreferential with *John* in the (a) examples, and disjoint in reference with *Oscar* in the (b) examples.

(146)   a.   *John said it was difficult for him to shave himself.*
          b.   **Bill's realizing that Oscar was unpopular did not disturb him.*

K&M assume the Binding Theory, which stipulates that anaphors must be bound in their governing category. For an example like (145a), this means that there must be a PRO to bind *himself* in the embedded S (the governing category).[57] The reasoning that leads K&M to the conclusion that there is a PRO in infinitivals and in gerunds means that there must

---

b.   *The men$_i$ tried PRO$_i$ to all$_i$ fit in the car.*

But this analysis fails to account for the difference in interpretation between (ia) and (ib). In the first the men could be trying to fit in as a group or each one individually. In the second the interpretation is that the group of men were trying to fit into the car together. This difference in interpretation can be associated with the different embedded predicates. In the first case *all* is part of the predicate *all try*, whereas in the second it is part of the predicate *all fit*. In a theory without PRO, this predication analysis is the only possible one, and the difference between (ia) and (ib) follows directly.

The difference illustrated in (i) was noted by Baltin (1978).

[56]In French, the corresponding rule of R-*Tous* applies in constructions where it cannot have a source, suggesting that that rule is one of construal. See Ruwet (1982) for discussion.

[57]The account of (146b) is somewhat more complicated as it requires a theory of control of PRO the discussion of which is beyond the scope of our presentation. See Koster and May (1982; p. 138).

also be a PRO in the determiner of NPs, as NP, along with S, is a governing category. Consider the following examples.

(147)   a.   *John stipulated that (all/no/every . . .) message(s)*
             $to \left\{ \begin{array}{l} him \\ himself \end{array} \right\}$ *be put in the envelope outside the door.*[58]

        b.   *Mary said that it was clear that it was important for there to be a picture of herself hanging outside the door.*
        c.   *The realization that Oscar was unpopular did not bother him.*
        d.   *Mary admitted that self-help would be difficult.*

In (147a), when the pronoun is reflexive, the NP *messages to himself* must have the interpretation "messages from John to himself," while when the pronoun is not reflexive, the NP *messages to him* has the interpretation "messages from someone to John." In the theory that K&M assume, these NPs must contain a PRO, given that NP is the relevant governing category. A similar conclusion seems to hold for *a picture of herself* in (147b).

In (147c), the NP *the realization . . .* behaves just like *realizing. . . .* In fact, if the realizer is taken in either case to be other than *Oscar*, coreference between *Oscar* and *him* is grammatical. In (147c), the realization cannot be Oscar's realization, on the coreferential reading. In (147d), *self-help* must contain a PRO as well, since *self* must be bound within its governing category, which is NP.

These conclusions lead us to speculate on how PRO could be introduced into NP. As PRO must c-command the anaphor that is coindexed with it, it must be that PRO appears in the specifier of NP, that is, where possessives and determiners appear. Significantly, PRO would be the only NP that can appear in a specifier that contains other elements: Sequences like *the John's book, *every Mary's answer, *Sam's the intuitions, and so on are all ungrammatical, but apparently {every/all/no} PRO, as in (147a); *a PRO,* as in (147b), and *the PRO,* as in (147c), must be possible in underlying structure. But these determiners do not alternate with PRO in gerunds where PRO is argued to appear, as in K&M's **PRO realizing that Oscar was unpopular did not disturb him* (where the asterisk indicates the ungrammaticality of the coreferential reading). Compare *{the/every/any/a} realizing that you would leave made us angry. Thus we might suspect that any attempt to introduce PRO into NPs would be highly artificial at best.

The preceding discussion is not to suggest that the problems noted are not problems for an analysis that does not assume the existence of PRO.

----

[58]See also the discussion in Chapter 1, Section 5.

Indeed, it is not completely clear how to explain the interpretation of anaphors and pronouns in terms of the coindexing of a VP with some NP that is thereby its antecedent, although some suggestive examples were discussed in Section 3 of this chapter (and recall also discussion in Chapter 1, Sections 4 and 5). Nevertheless, it does not appear to us at this point that the approach argued for by K&M is sufficiently unproblematic that we should be led away from the attempt to develop an analysis of binding in an alternative framework.

7.3. Conclusions

K&M point out that in an analysis where the properties of argument structure are characterized in logical representation (Logical Form) and where the structure of logical representations is represented at all grammatical levels, then in order to characterize the "control" phenomenon (i.e., represent the logical subject of infinitives) it is necessary to have a PRO subject for infinitives. "It is thus rather unclear just what is gained by assuming a VP′ structure, since it would seem to play little if any role in fixing the form or interpretation of bare infinitival complement clauses [p. 141]."

Suppose, on the other hand, that our syntactic observations about the nonexistence of PRO (and of $_{S'}$[COMP [PRO . . .]]) are in essence correct. As far as the syntax of English is concerned, at least, it appears that there is something to be gained by assuming a VP′ structure: We do not have to develop elaborate syntactic machinery to explain the apparent inconsequentiality of the hypothesized COMP and PRO in a wide range of cases.

This problem arises because of the attempt to utilize a single level of representation to mediate between phonological form and logical form. If, as assumed by K&M, this level is syntactic (i.e., S-Structure), then a paradox arises when we try to use an abstract PRO to represent a logical argument position in logical form. This PRO lacks syntactic properties, unlike all other abstract constituents expressed at S-Structure, that is, bound $_{NP}[e]$ and the trace of *Wh* Movement. (We will argue in Chapters 3 and 5 that NP Movement does not leave a trace.)

Suppose, however, that logical form is not a syntactic representation that is related transformationally to S-Structure (or to other levels of syntactic representation). There is no particular reason then, why the interpretation of syntactic structures into logical structures should not be able to introduce arguments under conditions of predication.[59] What is gained,

[59]It is necessary to explain why it is that the particular argument that is introduced by this mapping is the subject. Such an explanation will follow from a sufficiently restrictive char-

in fact, is an explanation of the fact that understood subjects, unlike other "invisible" constituents (like trace), have no syntactic or phonological reality.[60]

One might claim that current work on abstract case marking explains the behavior of PRO. Turning the matter upside down, one could also say that the isolation of PRO as a purely **logical** element eliminates the need for an elaborate machinery of abstract case.[61] The question is not simply a terminological one, but one that concerns as well the expressive power of the devices licensed or demanded by the theory. For cxamplc, thc thcory of abstract case marking says that PRO cannot have case; thus it must always be the subject of an infinitive, as all other nonsubject argument positions and the subject of a tensed S are governed and hence receive case. We can imagine that the situation could have been otherwise, or even that the rules for abstract case marking and the treatment of PRO vary from language to language. The expressive power of the theory is thus very much greater than that of a theory in which there is no PRO, except perhaps as a notational by-product of a theory of predication, in which the primitive notion "predicate" entails that of "unexpressed subject," and does not allow for any other unexpressed argument in the absence of a binding relation.

It seems that the correct conclusion to draw from the observations of K&M and those in this chapter is that the levels of syntactic and logical representation should be autonomous and should be founded on distinct primitives and principles. The formal demands of the level of logical representation are met through the mapping from syntactic structure into logical structure, but it does not then follow that every component of logical structure is represented syntactically. In fact, our discussion of PRO suggests that there is at least one component of logical structure, namely, the understood subject of the infinitive, that has no syntactic expression.

---

acterization of the notion "predicate," one that does not allow a subject–verb pair to constitute a "predicate" with respect to the direct object. Thus the fact that PRO must always be a subject is moved into the specification of the primitives of the theory of predication, and does not follow as an accident of the theory of abstract case marking.

[60]For evidence concerning the phonological reality of trace of *wh* see Culicover and Rochemont (1983).

[61]Correctly, those who hypothesize abstract case marking seek to find additional applications for it beyond the phenomena that we have been discussing here. If abstract case marking is eliminated, then one is forced to try to account for these applications in terms of what is left in the theory, surely a welcome result. See Iwakura (1982) for discussion of this point.

CHAPTER 3

NP Movement

In this chapter we examine rules that may informally be classed under the rubric of "move NP." The defining characteristic of such rules is that they relate (by movement or otherwise) one Surface Structure grammatical argument position with a different Deep Structure grammatical argument position. The paradigm instance of NP Movement is, of course, the English passive. In our framework, as in the *Aspects* framework, the Surface Structure subject in the passive construction bears the Deep Structure grammatical relation object; Deep Structure is the level at which the logical grammatical relations are represented.

Note that we are using the term "NP Movement" as a mnemonic, inasmuch as the definition that we have given for this class of rules in principle allows at least three ways other than movement by which the thematic role of an NP that bears a particular underlying grammatical relation may be expressed in Surface Structure in terms of a different grammatical relation:

1. A constituent in position *B* may be deleted under identity with a constituent in position *A* (where *B* but not *A* has a thematic function), and *A* derives its thematic function from its identity with *B*.
2. A constituent in position *A* "binds" or in some other way governs a gap or another constituent in position *B*, and *A* derives its thematic function from *B*.
3. There is a lexical relation between structures such that the same thematic role is assigned to different grammatical relations in the two structures.

In the course of this chapter we will suggest that at least binding is necessary, and that movement in certain cases can be represented as well by a lexical relation.

This chapter is organized into three main sections. Section 1 considers the passive in English as a literal instance of movement of NP. We show that NP Movement is subject to the Locality Condition, which in the case of actual movement takes essentially the form of the Variable Interpretation Convention of Wilkins (1977, 1980a). In this section we introduce the well-formedness conditions on thematic interpretations that determine particular properties of the passive construction.

Section 2 discusses the *tough* construction. We adopt a variant of the view first put forth by Lasnik and Fiengo (1974) that there is no transformation of *Tough* Movement; rather, there is a rule that relates an empty NP argument position to the subject of predicates like *tough, easy,* and so on. Following an alternative suggested but not developed by Lasnik and Fiengo, we formulate this rule not as a deletion but as a binding of the empty node.

Section 3 is concerned with a set of problems that arise in an NP Movement analysis of the passive when PRO is not assumed. This section includes also discussion of the alternation between tensed and nontensed embedded complements and the occurrence of the semantically null formatives *it* and *there.*

Traditionally, NP Movement is invoked in the account of Raising to Subject; for example, [e] seems $_s$[*John to be intelligent*] ⇒ *John seems to be intelligent.* Although such an analysis makes a number of correct predictions given the Locality Condition, our analysis of predication (Chapter 2) provides us with an alternative account of such sentences. A theme that is addressed throughout this chapter is the possibility that NP Movement can be dispensed with entirely, given that it is not needed for Raising to Subject and that in our framework it creates problems in the analysis of the passive construction.

1. Passive

1.1. The Form of NP Movement

The goal of limiting the expressive power of the theory of grammar has been realized, in syntactic theory, by means of a radical impoverishment of the notion "possible structural description of a transformation." The most extreme expression of this impoverished theory is found in Chomsky

(1981), where all transformations are of the form "move α," where α ranges over a restricted set of syntactic categories. The possible surface structure targets of a moved constituent in such a theory are determined by the theory: Cyclic rules must be structure preserving (Emonds 1976), and so movement must be substitution for an empty category of type α (see Chomsky 1981). Alternatively, the theory might be formulated to mark as ill formed certain (illegal) movements as a consequence of the logical forms derived from the output of the movements.[1]

The virtue of such a severe restriction on the expressive power of transformations is clear. There is only a very small number of possible transformations, and hence a restricted range of hypotheses available to the language learner. As Chomsky (1977) suggests, it might be possible in such a framework to permit language-specific idiosyncracies in grammars of natural languages, but only at the cost of considerable complexity in the rules that express these idiosyncracies. It is even conceivable that the task of language acquisition is categorically different with regard to the learning of the severely restricted rules of the class "move α" versus the learning of the less severely restricted rules expressing language-specific idiosyncracies.[2]

In the framework of the Locality Condition, both the constituent to be moved and the category of the target are specified in the rule. This increased expressive power (in comparison with the "move α" theory) in the form of rules allows for a simpler statement of rule conditioning in comparison with other theories of grammar. It is the form of a given rule, in interaction with the general convention of locality, which determines rule applicability.[3]

In keeping with this restriction, the SD of a rule mentions the terms that are affected, but no variables and no contexts. The NP Movement rule that moves NP in the English passive is thus stated as follows:

(1) $_{NP}[e] - NP \Rightarrow 2 - \emptyset$

---

[1]See Chomsky (1981) for a discussion of the possible empirical differences between these alternatives.

[2]For discussion see Wexler (1982).

[3]It is possible that the target does not have to be stated explicitly in the structural description of any rule; it might be strictly determined by the theory itself, perhaps along the lines suggested by Baltin (1978, 1981). The target is nevertheless crucial for determining the domain of application of the rule, and we have therefore chosen to formulate our rules by providing both terms in the structural description. Doing so clarifies the close similarity between movement transformations and rules of interpretation with respect to the Locality Condition, a similarity that is somewhat obscured if "move α" does not specify where "α" is to be moved to.

1.2. The Syntax of NP Movement

Given the severely restricted form of the NP Movement rule in (1), there will be a great deal of overgeneration. The role of the general theory of grammar, which in our case includes the Locality Condition, is therefore to assure that only well-formed results are permitted.

There are two types of ill-formedness that must be prevented. The first is where the wrong NP is selected to be moved, that is, where Rule (1) incorrectly analyzes a phrase marker with respect to term 2 of its SD. This is illustrated by the ungrammatical examples of (2) – (5):

(2) a. *John gave the book to Mary.*
     b. *[e] was given the book to Mary by John.*[4]
     c. *The book was given 0 to Mary by John.*
     d. **Mary was given the book to 0 by John.*
     e. *John gave Mary the book.*
     f. *[e] was given Mary the book by John.*
     g. *Mary was given 0 the book by John.*
     h. **The book was given Mary 0 by John.*

(3) a. *John painted a picture of Mary.*
     b. *[e] was painted a picture of Mary by John.*
     c. *A picture of Mary was painted 0 by John.*
     d. **Mary was painted a picture of 0 by John.*

(4) a. *Mary expected John to leave early.*
     b. *[e] was expected John to leave early (by Mary).*
     c. *John was expected 0 to leave early (by Mary).*
     d. *Mary expected John would leave early.*
     e. *[e] expected John would leave early (by Mary).*
     f. **John was expected 0 would leave early (by Mary).*

(5) a. *John expects [e] to be convinced Bill to praise Mary.*
     b. *John expects Bill to be convinced 0 to praise Mary.*
     c. **John expects Mary to be convinced Bill to praise 0.*

The second way in which ill-formedness can occur is a misanalysis with respect to term 1 of the SD of the preposing rule. In an account of NP Movement that substitutes a moved NP for an empty NP, problems can arise if there is more then one empty NP in Deep Structure. As we assume,

[4]We use the expression [e] to designate empty NP, that is, an NP that does not branch and dominates no lexical item(s).

along with Chomsky (1981) and others, that lexical insertion is optional, there can technically be many empty NPs in a given Deep Structure phrase marker, or an empty NP could be in an inappropriate position with respect to substitution. If a moved NP substitutes for the wrong $_{NP}[e]$, the result is ungrammatical. This is illustrated by (6) and (7):

(6)   a.   *John expects [e] to believe [e] to kiss the elephant.*
        b.   **John expects the elephant to be believed [e] to kiss 0.*

(7)   a.   *John gave [e] to Mary.*

        b.   **John $\left\{ \begin{array}{l} gave \\ was\ given \end{array} \right\}$ Mary to 0.*

By way of review, before presenting our analysis, we indicate next how these problems with NP Movement have been dealt with in various approaches to the grammar of English. We leave for last the approach taken in Wilkins (1977,1980a), as it is in many respects the approach that we will take in this chapter.[5]

1.2.1. THE CONDITIONS FRAMEWORK (CHOMSKY 1973)

To block extraction of NP from another NP [as in (3d)], Chomsky must assume the A-over-A Condition of earlier work (see Chomsky 1964, Ross 1967, and for more recent work, Bresnan 1976a), as formulated in (8).

(8)   *A-over-A Condition: If a transformation applies to a structure of the form*
        $$_{\alpha}[\ \cdots \ _{A}[\ \cdots \ ] \ \cdots \ ]$$
        where α is a cyclic node, then it must be so interpreted as to apply to the maximal phrase of the type A.   [Chomsky 1973, p. 235].

The A-over-A Condition is necessary because the Subjacency Condition, given in (9), cannot block extraction from NP by NP Movement. This is because Subjacency is formulated so as to allow extraction of NP from NP by *Wh* Movement, as in (10).

(9)   *Subjacency Condition: No rule can involve X, Y, X superior to Y, if Y is not subjacent to X. If X is superior to Y in a phrase marker P, then Y is "subjacent" to X if there is at most one cyclic category C $\neq$ Y such that C contains Y and C does not contain X.*   [Chomsky 1973, p. 247].

---

[5]The analyses that we have focused on here appear to us to be the best of the competing explanations; we have not attempted an exhaustive review of the literature.

(10)   *Who did you buy a picture of ∅?*

In the Conditions framework, the requirement that an NP not undergo NP Movement unless it is immediately preceded by a verb [see (2c) and (2d)] must be specified in terms of the structural description of the rule itself; there is no constraint in the theory that will lead to this result. The constraint against extraction out of a tensed S [see (4f)] is taken care of by the Tensed-S Condition.

(11)   **Tensed-S Condition:** *No rule can involve X, Y in the structure*
$$\cdots X \cdots {}_\alpha[\cdots Y \cdots] \cdots$$
         where α is a tensed sentence.   [Chomsky 1977, p. 238].

It is clear that this constraint will prevent movement of the subject NP in the lower clause into the higher clause, ruling out (4f).

Finally, the problem of blocking NP Movement over an intervening NP, (5c), is taken care of by the Specified Subject Condition.

(12)   **Specified Subject Condition:** *No rule can involve X, Y in the structure*
$$\cdots X \cdots {}_\alpha[\cdots Z \cdots -WYV \cdots] \cdots$$
         where Z is the specified subject of –WYV in α.

As the examples in (5) show, the subject of an infinitive, and not another NP below and to the right of it, must be the NP that undergoes NP Movement, as (12) requires. For examples like (13), where there does not appear to be an intervening specified subject, the Conditions framework assumes that there is in fact a PRO subject. The subject of the infinitive, controlled by some term other than that corresponding to X in (12), functions as a specified subject of the infinitive. The PRO subject in (13b), for example, would block the movement or construal of *each*.

(13)   a.   **We persuaded Bill to kill each other.*
         b.   *We each persuaded Bill* [COMP *PRO to kill the other(s)*].   (Chomsky 1977, p. 255).

1.2.2. THE LANGUAGE LEARNABILITY THEORY (WEXLER AND CULICOVER 1980)

There are two main constraints in this framework that are relevant to the problems of NP Movement that have been noted here, the Binary Principle and the Principle of No Bottom Context (NBC). They are formulated as follows, where the term "B-cyclic nodes" refers to the set {S', NP}, and an S-essential transformation is one that involves constituents of more than one S'.

(14)   ***Binary Principle:*** *A transformation may apply no deeper in a phrase marker than the immediate constituents of the next B-cyclic node below the one at which the transformation is applying.*   [Wexler and Culicover, 1980, p. 312–313].

(15)   ***Principle of No Bottom Context:*** *If T is an S-essential transformation, then it may apply only if T is a no-bottom-context raising or deletion transformation. That is, the raising or deletion of a constituent in a lower cyclic domain, when triggered by a constituent in a higher cyclic domain, may not depend on the context in the lower domain.*   [Wexler and Culicover 1980, p. 420].

The Binary Principle blocks extraction out of a tensed S [Example (4f)] because the tensed S constitutes a lower B-cyclic domain. Extraction from an NP is blocked analogously; the dominating NP constitutes a B-cyclic domain, as in (3d).

In the learnability theory, the fact that the NP that undergoes NP Movement must be immediately preceded by a verb must be stipulated as part of the structural description of the rule, as in the Conditions framework, and therefore Examples (2d) and (2h) are prevented. Given this necessary structural description, the NBC is relevant for cases like (5). The NP that is to move must be immediately preceded by a verb, and, as the repetition of (5a) illustrates, in this case the V context is in a lower S.

(5)   a.   *John expects* $_S$[[*e*] *to be convinced Bill* $_S$[*to praise Mary*]].

Given that NP Movement contains the context predicate V, in order for *Mary* to move into [*e*] in the higher S, the rule would have to apply in the higher S, and hence the verb *praise* would constitute a bottom context. This would be a violation of NBC. There is a slight indeterminacy in the theory as a consequence of this application of NBC, because of the fact that for the Binary Principle S' is a B-cyclic node, whereas for NBC the node S constitutes a lower domain. See Wexler and Culicover (1980, Chapter 7) for discussion.

In the learnability framework, Example (6b) is subject to NBC.

(6)   b.   **John expects* $_S$[*the elephant to be believed* $_S$[[*e*] *to kiss* $\emptyset$]].

The operative domain for NBC is S. In (6b), the verb in the lower S, namely *kiss,* cannot satisfy the SD for NP Movement into an empty NP in the next S up. In the learnability framework, the SD of NP Movement requires that the moved NP be immediately to the right of the verb. As for Example (7b), it is also ruled out by the SD of NP Movement, since the moved NP does not immediately follow the verb here either.

(7)   b. *John $\left\{ \begin{matrix} gave \\ was\ given \end{matrix} \right\}$ *Mary to 0.*

1.2.3. GOVERNMENT–BINDING THEORY (CHOMSKY 1981)

In the Government–Binding (GB) Theory, the locality property is imposed on NP Movement through the interaction of Abstract Case Assignment, Θ-Role Assignment, a filter for Case, a filter for Θ-role assignment (the "Θ-Criterion") and government. In this analysis, a locality condition is built into the definition of "governs." In a structure such as (16), Abstract Case is not assigned to the NP immediately following the verb but is assigned to the empty subject, while no Θ-role is assigned to the empty subject. Moreover, NP_i cannot be assigned Case by another V, because no other V can govern it, given a local definition of government.[6]

(16) $_{NP}[e]$ Passive $+$ V NP_i $\cdots$ NP_j $\cdots$

If NP Movement does not apply, or if it applies to NP_j but not to NP_i, then NP_i lacks Case at S-Structure and so (16) is filtered out. If (16) is generated with a full NP in subject position, NP Movement is blocked, and NP_i again has no Case in S-Structure. Furthermore, if a passive is generated with a fully specified NP in Deep Structure subject position (and $[e]$ in object position), this NP does not have a Θ-role assigned to it directly, which violates the part of the Θ-Criterion that requires every NP argument to have a Θ-role.

Consider once again the ungrammatical examples in (2)–(7).

(2)   d. *Mary was given the book to 0 by John.
       h. *The book was given Mary 0 by John.

(3)   d. *Mary was painted a picture of 0 by John.

(4)   f. *John was expected 0 would leave early (by Mary).

(5)   c. *John expects Mary to be convinced Bill to praise 0.

(6)   b. *John expects the elephant to be believed [e] to kiss 0.

(7)   a. John gave [e] to Mary.
       b. *John gave Mary to 0.

[6]A typical definition of "governs" that illustrates the locality property is the following, from Chomsky (1981, p. 163):

α governs β if and only if

(i) $\alpha = X^0$
(ii) α c-commands β and if γ c-commands β then γ either c-commands α or is c-commanded by β.

In Examples (2d), (2h), (3d), and (5c) there is a passive verb with a direct object in its original position. As a passive verb "absorbs case" in the GB framework, these examples are ruled out by the Case Filter, which requires that case be assigned to every lexical NP.

Example (4f) is ruled out because the trace of NP Movement is not bound in its governing category. Example (6b) is ruled out because the empty category [e] is not bound at all. (See the discussion of the Empty Category Principle in Chomsky 1981.) The active example in (7b), *John gave Mary to,* is ruled out because *John,* which is assigned a Θ-role by *to,* is assigned a conflicting Θ-role in the derived subject position, in violation of the Projection Principle. In the structure NP *gave* NP *to* NP, both objects have Θ-roles at Deep (or D-) Structure, and this distribution of Θ-roles must be preserved after NP Movement. Next, consider again Examples (7a)–(7b), where an NP is moved from an argument position to a nonsubject position in the absence of passive morphology.

(7)   a. *John gave [e] to Mary.*
       b. **John gave Mary to ∅.*

This problem does not arise in any variant of the Standard Theory because (7a) would not satisfy the SD for NP Movement. In a theory such as GB Theory that contains the generalized rule Move α, (7b) becomes a possibility which must be ruled out if it is generated, because contextual elements play no role in structural descriptions except in marked cases. As noted earlier, an example like (7b) is ruled out in GB Theory because it does not satisfy the Projection Principle.

1.2.4. THE LOCALITY CONDITION AND THE VARIABLE INTERPRETATION CONVENTION (WILKINS 1977, 1980a, 1981a)

The Locality Condition as it applies to NP Movement is essentially the Variable Interpretation Convention (VIC). Effectively, the VIC requires that NP Movement move an NP to an "adjacent" empty NP position, where by "adjacent" is meant that there is no other NP that the preposed NP moves over.

To illustrate, let us consider the four problems with NP Movement discussed earlier. We repeat the crucial examples.

(17)   a. **Mary was given the book to ∅ by John.*
       b. **The book was given Mary ∅ by John.*
       c. **Mary was painted a picture of ∅ by John.*
       d. **John was expected ∅ would leave early (by Mary).*
       e. **John expects Mary to convince Bill to praise ∅.*
       f. **John expects the elephant to be believed [e] to kiss ∅.*

In Examples (17a), (17b), and (17e) the moved NP has been reordered over some other intervening NP, *the book* in (17a), *Mary* in (17b), and *Bill* in (17e).[7] Example (17c) is ungrammatical because the VIC is actually stated in terms of categories or their heads and in this case an NP, *Mary,* was reordered over an N, *picture*, which is the head of an NP.

Examples (17d) and (17f) are ungrammatical not by virtue of the VIC per se, but rather by two corollary principles. The problem with (17d) is that there is subject–verb agreement in the absence of a subject, and the problem in (17f) is that there is a violation of the prohibition against unbound empty nodes.[8] There is no way for the remaining $_{NP}[e]$ to be lexically filled.

1.3. Passives and Thematic Relations

In the preceding section we looked at a variety of formal devices that have the effect of allowing just the direct object of a verb (or, more generally, the NP immediately following the verb) to move into subject position when the verb is morphologically marked as a passive. Drawing from the insights of the work reviewed, we will investigate here the minimal framework that will accomplish this task. In particular, we will

1. Assume a version of the Locality Condition, generalizing it to all grammatical processes and relations (including government, binding, and movement).
2. Eliminate Abstract Case and assume thematic roles along the lines outlined in Chapter 1, Section 3.
3. Formulate a set of conditions on the distribution of thematic roles over conceptual entities in a semantic representation that has many of the effects of the Θ-Criterion and the Projection Principle of GB Theory, but which seems to us more perspicuous in certain respects.

We consider first the problem of relating the passive to its corresponding active in such a way that they are given essentially the same interpretation although they are derived from different underlying structures. We begin with certain assumptions about the base, then discuss the system of thematic roles which was presented in Chapter 1. In the next section we move on to the movement rule itself and the precise sense in which it is local.

---

[7]Actually this is somewhat more complicated because the "grossest constituent analysis," plus the SD of the Passive rule, which in Wilkins (1977) includes the V, must be taken into account.

[8]See Chapter 1, Section 4. As indicated there, the Binding Condition is a constraint against unbound [e] at the level of representation at which NPs are assigned thematic roles.

1.3.1. UNIVERSAL PASSIVE

In line with the goal of reducing the expressive power of transformations, we assume that the morphology that marks the passive in English is generated in base structures and is not transformationally introduced. The phrase structure analysis that we assume here is given as the set of rules in (18).

(18)   a. $S' \rightarrow$ COMP S
          b. $S \rightarrow$ NP M V^2
          c. $V^2 \rightarrow V^1$ (AP) (PP) (V^2) (S')
          d. $V^1 \rightarrow$ V (NP) (AP) (PP) (V^i) (S')

Following in its general outlines the analysis of the English auxiliary of Lapointe (1980), we may assume that the passive *be* functions as the main verb of a VP. It subcategorizes a complement VP that bears a feature that indicates that it displays the passive morphology. The underlying structure for a typical passive sentence is shown in (19).

(19)   a.

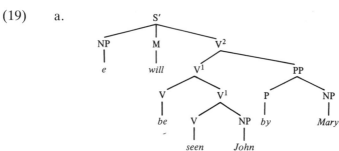

        b.   *John will be seen by Mary.*

The preliminary formulation of the schema for assigning thematic roles is the following, which we take from Chapter 1.

(20)   ***Role Assignment***
        (i) Assign lexically idiosyncratic roles.
        *(ii) Assign **theme** to the object if there is one. Otherwise assign*
          ***theme** to the subject.*
        *(iii)(a) Assign **goal** to subject or (b) assign **patient** to object and*
          ***agent** to subject or (c) **instrument** to subject or . . . .*

This schema is in part language specific. In certain languages, there are different correlations between the roles assigned to arguments than there are in English. In English, for example, a **theme** is a **patient** only if it is an object (or the subject of a passive). In Maninka on the other hand (see Bird and Shopen 1979), it appears that if a verb assigns the **patient** role, it assigns it to its **theme**, regardless of whether **theme** is object or subject. Thus in Maninka, a sentence that translates literally as *John drinks* does not have the interpretation that *John* is an **agent**, in contrast to English. Rather, it has the interpretation that *John* is being consumed by someone's drinking, which entails that *John* is a liquid.

As discussed in Chapter 1, we will for convenience represent the class of thematic roles that correlate with **theme** by A, and the class of thematic roles that correlate with subjects in transitive sentences by E. Thus A will be assigned to the subject of an intransitive and the object of a transitive. Use of the notation A and E has a mnemonic function, in that it recalls the fact that in ergative languages the absolutive case is assigned to the object of a transitive and the subject of an intransitive, while the ergative case is assigned to the subject of a transitive.

A characterization of thematic role assignment for English and Maninka in terms of the mnemonic A would be as follows: Given that in any language a verb that expresses the concept of drinking assigns the **patient** role, the lexicon must specify to what. For English, the general rule is as follows: $<$A, object$>$ $\Rightarrow$ **patient**; in Maninka, the rule would be $<$A$>$ $\Rightarrow$ **patient**. Assignment of roles for the underlying structure in (19) functions in essentially the same way as it does for the corresponding active. The verb *see* is unmarked with respect to Role Assignment. Taking first the active, shown in (21), A is assigned to the direct object and E is assigned to the subject:

(21)   *Mary will see John.*
         E   A

Example (22) illustrates basic Role Assignment for the passive:

(22) $_{NP}[e]$ *will be seen John by Mary.*
         E   A

It seems reasonable to assume in the case of (22) that the function of *by* is to assign E to the NP that it governs. The object of the preposition *by* is assigned the role E_{by}, which is interpreted in the same way as the E of the main verb, given that a prepositional phrase is in the domain of thematic role assignment governed by the verb.[9] The result of Role Assignment for (22) is therefore (23).

---

[9]Much the same sort of process is involved in the interpretation of the object of the *to*-phrase in the dative construction as the indirect object of a verb like *give*. (We will discuss the details of how the role assigned by a preposition is associated with a verb in Section 1.3.2.)

(23) $_{NP}[e]$ *will be seen John by Mary.*
          E   **A**   **E**

This brings us to the rule that we will refer to as "Universal Passive," or UP—a universal rule that performs an operation on a set of roles after they have been assigned as, for example, in (23). Intuitively, UP expresses the basic characteristic of the passive construction: No NP is directly assigned the role(s) that is(are) assigned to the subject in the corresponding active sentence.[10] This is accomplished formally in the following way: UP erases the role that has been assigned to the NP that bears the grammatical relation subject in Deep Structure. Crucially, if UP fails to apply, the empty NP will have a role but, because it is an empty NP, it will have no referent. If NP Movement fails to apply, the grammar will assign a thematic role to a nonreferring NP, which will lead to semantic ill-formedness. If UP fails to apply and NP Movement moves an object which already has a role assigned to it into the empty NP, then the moved NP will end up with two roles, again an ill-formed result.

The most general form of UP would be "delete role." It would be interesting if general and independently motivated principles of the theory of grammar would render well formed only those instances of deletion of roles that were associated with the passive morphology.[11] Taking a more conservative approach here, however, let us formulate UP as follows.

(24)   ***Universal Passive:*** *Delete the role of the antecedent of a VP with designated passive morphology.*

We assume that the notion "passive" is a primitive one in the theory of grammar, and that languages must choose morphological devices to express the passive construction through UP.[12] Notice that we do not restrict

[10]Thus UP corresponds to the stipulation in GB Theory that the subject of a passive is not assigned a Θ-role. In principle the application of UP requires the subject position to be a "dummy" element if the verb has passive morphology, yielding impersonal passives in those languages that have such elements. (See Chomsky 1981, p.125.) The peculiar fact about English is that although it has dummy elements, they cannot in general be used as the subject of the passive. See Section 3.3.

[11]There are languages with "antipassive" constructions as well as or in addition to passives; in such languages, the direct object is not expressed and the verb is appropriately marked. We could express this construction by a rule that specifically deletes the role assigned to the object. It is not clear how to turn the analysis backwards, by deleting roles freely and then characterizing well-formedness in terms of the verb morphology.

[12]A fact that will lead us to ultimately question the NP Movement analysis of passive is that in Malagasy there are several passive constructions corresponding to different arguments of the verb; movement of the direct object into subject position is only one of the passive constructions. Given this, the notion of a unique, universal "passive" that is expressed morphologically in most languages could not be correct. See Footnote 18 for further discussion.

UP to grammatical subjects, as not all empty NPs that will be filled by NP Movement in our framework are syntactically subjects, although they might have predicates predicated of them, and are therefore antecedents.[13]

Our method of assigning and manipulating thematic roles suggests a solution for a well-known problem involving examples like (25)–(26).

(25)   a. *John slept in this bed.*
         b. *This bed was slept in by John.*

(26)   a. *John slept in New York.*
         b. **New York was slept in by John.*

Whereas (25) shows that it is possible to passivize out of a PP, (26) suggests just the opposite.

The literature contains proposals for "restructuring" in cases like (25b), so that the preposition and the verb become a unit. If such restructuring applies in (25) but not (26), the prohibition against NP Movement out of PPs could be maintained. Some additional device would have to be invoked to explain why restructuring only applies in (25) and not in (26). (See Hornstein and Weinberg, 1981, for one proposal for restructuring.)

The suggestion has also been made in the literature that in (25), *sleep in* constitutes a "semantic unit," and that this in some way correlates with the intuition that the bed is affected by John's sleeping in it, but New York (in 26b) is not. We do not believe that restructuring offers the most natural account of the differences between (25) and (26), or for this intuition, mainly because restructuring, although correlated with the "semantic unit" intuition, is not formally dependent on it.

In the current framework, we may extend slightly the notion that a verb assigns thematic roles to its arguments to allow verbs to assign thematic roles to arguments of adjacent PPs. Let us say that *sleep* optionally assigns the **A** (i.e., **theme** and perhaps **patient**) role to the object of the PP. We thus have the following derivations, showing NP Movement and UP for one case where the object of the PP is the **A** of the verb, and one case where it is not.

(27) $[e]$ *was slept$_i$ in$_j$ New York*
                         A$_i$ **location$_j$**
         UP: $\emptyset$
         NP Movement: *New York was slept$_i$ in$_j$ $\emptyset$.*
                         location$_j$

---

[13]As discussed in Chapter 2.

(28)   *[e] was slept$_i$ in$_j$ the bed*
                             E$_i$ **A$_i$**
                                                    location$_j$
            UP: **∅**
            NP Movement: *The bed was slept$_i$ in$_j$ ∅.*
                             A$_i$
                             location$_j$

After UP applies in (27), the verb *slept$_i$* has no arguments in surface structure. We hypothesize that such a situation leads to ill-formedness, by the
Local Argument Principle: **If an NP bears a Surface Structure grammatical
relation with respect to some element, then it must be assigned a thematic
role by that element in Deep Structure.**[14] Thus in (27), *New York* is a
Surface Structure subject of *was slept* but is not assigned a thematic role
by *was slept* in Deep Structure, whereas in (28) it is assigned a role by *was
slept* at Deep Structure and bears a grammatical relation to *was slept* at
Surface Structure.[15] If (27) is assigned thematic roles in the pattern of (28),
then a semantic anomaly results, in which *New York* is interpreted as the
patient of sleeping.

---

[14]Effectively, this principle is a version of the Projection Principle of Chomsky (1981),
reformulated in terms of thematic roles instead of "subcategorization restrictions." The LAP
rules out an NP Movement analysis of Raising to Subject, a consequence that is acceptable
in view of the fact that our theory of predication eliminates the need for such an analysis
anyway. Ultimately, LAP also rules out an NP Movement analysis of complex passives like
John was expected to be arrested, in which the subject of *was expected* is not a Deep Structure
argument, as the structure (i) shows.

(i)   *[e] was expected* $_S$*[[e] to be arrested John]*

We face a choice, therefore, of modifying LAP or of rejecting an NP Movement analysis
for passives in general. As will become increasingly clear during the course of this chapter,
the latter alternative has much to recommend it. In contrast, in the current framework it is
unclear what the appropriate revision of the Projection Principle would be, given that there
is no obvious difference between moving an NP from the domain of a preposition to the
domain of a verb and moving an NP from the domain of a verb to the domain of another
verb.

We could generalize LAP in terms of some notion of "argument," whereby the Deep
Structure arguments are those NPs that are assigned thematic roles by an element and the
Surface Structure arguments are those that bear a grammatical relation to the element. It is
not clear that there is much to be gained by doing this.

[15]A point worth noting is that LAP is a version of the Locality Condition, and it is implicit
in any theory of lexical rules that relate argument positions governed by a verb. Crucially,
a specification of the arguments to which thematic roles are assigned by a verb is by assumption the only information about that verb available in the lexical entry; it follows that
only these arguments can participate in lexical rules for deriving passives and the like.

Returning to the assignment of thematic roles to the object of the prepositional phrase, notice that only the first PP in a series of PPs can undergo this optional assignment.

(29)   a.   *Mary was talked* $\left\{ \begin{array}{l} to. \\ about. \end{array} \right\}$

         b.   *Mary was talked* $\left\{ \begin{array}{l} to\ about\ Fred. \\ *about\ Fred\ to. \end{array} \right\}$

         c.   *Mary was talked* $\left\{ \begin{array}{l} about\ to\ Fred. \\ *to\ Fred\ about. \end{array} \right\}$

There are two ways in which the ungrammatical examples in (29) might be blocked. First, we might formulate the Locality Condition for NP Movement so that the object of a prepositional phrase cannot be moved over the object of another prepositional phrase. Alternatively, we might speculate that these examples are ruled out by LAP. For this sort of analysis, we would have to guarantee that only the first NP could be assigned a thematic role by the verb.

Let us briefly pursue the second alternative. We will use the term "Θ-government" to refer to the domain of assignment of thematic roles to NPs. Suppose that Θ-government is local, in the sense that an NP is not "Θ-governed" by a V unless the V is the minimal V that c-commands it.[16] Suppose that the assignment of thematic roles is simplified to "assign **theme** to a Θ-governed NP." The object of a PP in V^1 is Θ-governed in the appropriate sense. As Role Assignment is optional, **theme** will not necessarily be assigned to the object of a PP; if it is not, the preposition can still assign a role to its object, ensuring that the NP will end up with a thematic role. In contrast, in a sentence that has no prepositional object, **theme** must be assigned to the direct object, as otherwise the direct object would have no role at all.[17]

---

[16]This follows from the following definition of Θ-government: An NP is Θ-governed by a verb iff (*a*) it bears a grammatical relation with respect to the verb or (*b*) it bears a grammatical relation to a preposition that is subcategorized by the verb. Although we rule out the use of subcategorization of the arguments of a verb, it is still necessary to specify for a particular verb that it co-occurs with certain morphological forms, for example, prepositions and complementizers. See Chapter 5, Section 7.6.

[17]This analysis bears a resemblance to the discussion of Case Assignment in Stowell (1981). We have chosen to try to simplify the theory of grammar by eliminating Abstract Case in favor of thematic roles, which are independently required. We would expect to find that many of Stowell's analyses could be translated directly into a thematic role framework. Of particular importance is his notion that the dative object in double object constructions are "clitic" to the verb, thus allowing the verb to directly assign case (or in our analysis, A) to the direct object.

We will return to both alternatives in what follows. In an NP Movement analysis of the passive, the first alternative appears preferable, as the Locality Condition in general constrains the application of the transformation. In a lexical passive, the second alternative proves to be the more natural approach.

1.3.2. WELL-FORMEDNESS CONDITIONS ON R-STRUCTURES

We have expressed passive as a universal rule operating on roles and grammatical relations. This treatment of the passive construction cross-linguistically is not a syntactic one per se, but rather is syntactico-semantic, in that it refers both to grammatical and thematic relations. As we modify this account of the passive and consider alternatives, this basic point of view will be maintained.

The approach suggested here predicts the existence of languages in which the role of an antecedent is eliminated, but there is no movement. Suppose that the role of a dummy, nonreferring subject NP is deleted. No movement takes place, but there is no referring subject NP in such cases. So-called impersonal passives in languages like French, German, and Dutch seem to be passives of this sort, with no movement. We discuss the impersonal passive in more detail in Section 3.3, where we attempt to explain why English generally lacks such a construction.[18]

The result of the application of UP to the roles assigned to (23) is as in (30), where the eliminated role is expressed as ∅.

(30) $_{NP}[e]$ *was seen John by Mary.*
            ∅   A   E

As UP is a very general and unconstrained rule, it could well apply to any underlying structure with an NP antecedent in the environment of passive morphology. It could apply, for instance, in (31).

(31)   *Mary was seen John by Susan.*
            ∅   A   E

---

[18]In languages with relatively free constituent order, there does not appear to be any motivation for deriving the passive construction by NP Movement. In an NP Movement analysis, the passive in such a language would involve the following steps: (i) delete the role assigned to an empty subject; (ii) assign to some other NP the subject grammatical relation; (iii) assign to this NP the appropriate Surface Structure case marking; (iv) the original empty subject, having neither grammatical role nor thematic role, is effectively deleted. Because there is no fixed configuration, a locality condition cannot block the movement of one NP while allowing the movement of the other, as contrasted with English. Hence NPs other than the direct object should be capable of becoming the subject of the passive.

Later in this chapter we consider a different view of the passive for such languages which does not involve NP Movement.

In order to ensure the correct results for cases like (30) and (31) (and myriad other cases, as will soon become evident), we will formulate a condition on the well-formedness of outputs of Role Assignment; this is a condition of "thematic uniqueness." Intuitively, we want the assignment of roles to be "unique," in that there is no assignment of a single role to (the set of individuals designated by) more than one NP. As we will see, thematic uniqueness in fact can be analyzed into a set of conditions on the distribution of roles with respect to NP arguments. Certain restrictions on the assignment of roles to NPs can be shown to follow from well-formedness conditions on the set of thematic roles itself; others, however, appear to be syntactic, in that they bear solely on the assignment of roles to NP arguments expressed in a sentence, and not on the assignment of thematic roles to individuals.[19]

The thematic roles constitute necessary properties possessed by **individuals** (not NPs) involved in some event or state by virtue of their being in that event or state. For example, if by **agent** we mean "one who acts volitionally," then there is an entailment relation between a sentence of the form NP VP-*ed* where NP is an agent and the sentence "NP acted volitionally." As pointed out by Marantz (1981), the precise thematic roles associated with an individual are just those that define the event or state that the individual is said to have participated in.

An individual referred to by an NP may bear more than one thematic role with respect to a situation characterized by a verb or a set of verbs: It may function both as **agent** and **theme** of a single verb (as in *John jumped,* for example), or it may be **patient** of one verb and **agent** of another(as in *Mary forced John to jump*). In standard syntactic analyses, the problem of multiple assignment of thematic roles is in part solved by the introduction of control of PRO, so that strictly speaking the controlling NP is assigned one thematic role and the controlled PRO (which is the subject of another verb) is assigned another. But there remain simple cases where two or more independently characterizable thematic roles are associated with a single, noncontrolling NP (see Jackendoff 1972).

Let us consider the conditions of Completeness, Distributedness, and Argument Isomorphism which, taken together, define the set of well-formed thematic interpretations for a language.

---

[19]We will be adapting and reformulating here parts of the Θ-Criterion of Chomsky (1981), which we believe to be essentially correct. We will be suggesting a more fine-grained analysis of some of the phenomena that are within the scope of the Θ-Criterion of the Government–Binding Theory.

1.3.2.1. *Completeness*

Let us say that the R(ole)-structure of a sentence is the set of thematic roles assigned to the sets of individuals referred to by the NPs in the sentence. The elements of an R-structure are triples of the form $<i, t, k>$, where i is the index of the set of individuals, $\{t\}$ the set of thematic roles, and s the act or state with respect to which the set of individuals is playing a role or roles. In a complex sentence, it is necessary to distinguish not only the roles assigned to different actors, but the acts with respect to which they are actors. Thus for *Mary$_m$ said that John$_n$ jumped,* the partial R-structure is as in (32).

(32) $\{<m, \{\textbf{agent}\}, say>, <n, \{\textbf{agent}, \textbf{theme}\}, jump> \ldots \}$

The requirement of Completeness assures, first of all, that each element of the R-Structure (i.e., each $<i, t, k>$ triple) is complete, and second, that each R-structure includes all of the roles governed by any given verb. Traditionally, subcategorization has been employed to represent the fact that a verb requires that certain arguments be expressed. We depart from this practice by deriving subcategorization restrictions from the Completeness requirement on R-Structure.

Many but not all subcategorization restrictions follow from Completeness. If a verb requires a certain individual to have a certain thematic role (say, **goal**) in R-Structure, then an NP must appear in the sentence in the appropriate position to bear this role. If no such NP appears, the thematic role will not be assigned, and the R-structure will not be complete.

What remains as true linguistic subcategorization is the idiosyncratic morphology that is governed by a verb (or some other type of element). For example, the fact that a verb governs the preposition *at,* when the verb does not govern a thematic role that would be clearly associated with an *at*-phrase, must be expressed by subcategorization restrictions. Selection of complementizers are another case of the same sort.[20]

The Binding Condition that we introduced in Chapter 1 follows from the Completeness requirement. Recall that the Binding Condition stipulates that an empty NP cannot appear in a syntactic structure (at some relevant level) unless it is coindexed with some other NP in the structure.[21] If [e] has a thematic role assigned to it but is not referential, then there is a violation of Completeness. Thematic roles can only appear in R-Struc-

---

[20]Note that in Chomsky (1981) the subcategorization of arguments is extended to all levels of syntactic representation, by the Projection Principle. Our LAP requires merely that a derived argument of some element be an underlying argument.

[21]Since [e] is by definition not a name (in English, at least), it cannot possess its own referential index.

ture in triples $<i, t, k>$ where i is the index of some set of individuals, the referent of some NP. If a thematic role is assigned to a nonreferring NP, it is not expressed in R-Structure, and the triple is incomplete.

The requirement that each triple be complete will also rule out a case like *John slept [e]*, as this would yield an R-structure where even if [e] were somehow coindexed with a referring NP it would lack a role. That is, the R-structure would be $*<n, \emptyset, sleep>$, because *sleep* assigns only a single role, which in this case is associated with the subject *John*.

1.3.2.2. *Distributedness and Argument Isomorphism*

We will say that an R-structure is "distributed" if there is a one-to-one assignment of roles to individuals. The Distributedness requirement has two parts. First of all, it prohibits the assignment of a particular thematic role (relative to a particular act or state) to more than one set of individuals. That is,

(33) $*\{ <i, t, k>, <j, t, k>, \ldots \}$

This restriction is not one of syntax per se. Nor does it pertain to the real world; there is no particular physical reason why two different individuals could not be acting volitionally in different ways to perform two different actions at the same time. Therefore there is no physical reason why there cannot be a verb *haloop*, for example, that takes two arguments such that the subject and the object are agents of the same "complex act" occurring in two places. That is, it is possible to imagine a sentence of the form *John halooped George*, meaning that John and George yelled at the same time. However, we cannot speak of such situations in terms of one verb with several arguments, but rather must indicate the different acts individually, or with the use of conjoined structures.

Note as well that for the purposes of thematic role assignment two distinct NPs that have different grammatical functions cannot together refer to a single set of individuals. Thus, the thematic roles are assigned in terms of single arguments. The formalism for expressing the assignment of thematic roles to sets of individuals must incorporate the principle that a distinct NP argument refers to a distinct set of individuals with a distinct thematic role. We refer to this condition as Argument Isomorphism.[22]

---

[22]By formulating Argument Isomorphism in terms of argument NPs rather than in terms of NPs we allow for the possibility that a sentence will contain referring NPs that do not appear in R-Structure. This possibility may be realized by vocatives, which are not arguments in a sentence, but which certainly refer.

The second aspect of the Distributedness requirement assures that a given verb does not assign more than one role to the same set of individuals.[23] Thus we may not have the following R-Structure:

(34)   *{ $<i, t, k>$, $<i, t', k>$, . . . }

The only way that Distributedness can be violated is if one of the indices i is insulated by virtue of being the index of a reflexive, as we discussed in Section 5 of Chapter 1.

From the Distributedness requirement follows the requirement usually referred to as Disjoint Reference. The latter has traditionally been expressed in terms of NPs in the sentence. We will express it in terms of thematic roles in the R-structure. Given the Completeness requirement, which assures that every referring NP in the sentence has a corresponding role in R-Structure, Distributedness prevents two arguments of the same verb from referring to the same individual(s), which is the Disjoint Reference condition.[24]

The following summarizes the conditions of Completeness and Distributedness.

(35)   **Conditions on R-Structures**
         (i) The R-structure of a sentence and each individual element of it must be complete. (Every required role must be assigned, each role must be assigned to a set of individuals, and each set of individuals must have a role.)
         (ii) The R-structure associated with a sentence must be distributed. A thematic role relative to a particular act or state cannot be assigned to more than one set of individuals and more than one thematic role of the same type cannot be assigned to the same individual or set of individuals. (See Footnote 23.)

1.4. Role Assignment in the Passive

Let us consider now a range of examples where UP and Role Assignment interact. As noted earlier, Role Assignment is relevant at Deep Structure. Thus, (36) is ill formed after the application of UP because

[23]In Section 3.3 of Chapter 5 we distinguish between two classes of thematic roles, intensional and extensional. The proper formulation of Distributedness in terms of these roles is that the same verb cannot assign two roles **of the same class** to the same individual. Alternatively, we could reformulate Distributedness in terms of the mnemonics **A** and **E**, which we can call "Thematic Relations." Distributedness then rules out the assignment of two Thematic Relations to the same NP. By Argument Isomorphism, the corresponding thematic roles would be distributed with respect to the sets of individuals in R-Structure.

[24]A bound empty node must be interpreted as referring to the same individual(s) as the NP that binds it, in order for Distributedness to rule out examples like *John$_i$ hit [e$_i$]*. It is for this reason that reflexives must be insulated from Distributedness.

Mary lacks a role in violation of Completeness. As indicated earlier, we assign the mnemonics **A** and **E** instead of the particular roles governed by the verbs.

(36)   *Mary was seen John by Susan.*
         ∅   **A**   **E**

To avoid this type of violation, subject of a passive must be empty.
   Let us consider next some examples where NP Movement applies.

(37)   a. *[e] was seen John by Mary.*
             E   **A**   **E**
         b. *Mary was seen John.*
             E   **A**

(38)   *John was seen by Mary.*
         A   **E**

In (37a) UP deletes **E**. Subsequently there are two possible outcomes. If NP Movement fails to apply, there will be an empty NP in Surface Structure. If NP Movement does apply, this empty NP will be eliminated as in (38). The Completeness requirement assures that an empty NP in English is coindexed with a lexical NP if it appears in Surface Structure. In (37a) [e] is not bound when NP Movement does not apply and the result is ungrammatical. After UP, the R-structure for the subject NP would be *< ∅, ∅, *see*>, an ill-formed triple. For convenience we may say that such examples are ruled out by the Binding Condition *[e] of Chapter 1 which, as already noted, follows from the Completeness requirement.

   In (37b), the passive has a nonempty Deep Structure subject. The application of UP eliminates the role on this NP, yielding a violation of Completeness. A referring NP must have a role.

   We turn now to somewhat more complicated examples. Since NP Movement is a substitution for [e], we must consider what happens when [e] is the subject of a nonpassive sentence, and what happens when [e] is not the subject. The first case is illustrated in (39).

(39)   a. *[e] see John.*
             E   **A**
         b. *[e] see John by Mary.*
             E   **A**   **E**

In (39a), UP cannot apply, because there is no passive morphology. If NP Movement does not apply, the surface structure contains an unbound empty NP, violating the Binding Condition referred to earlier. If NP Movement does apply, *John* ends up with two roles, in violation of Distributedness. The same considerations rule out NP Movement applying to *John* in (39b).

As NP Movement contains no contexts (such as passive morphology), it can in principle apply to fill any empty NP position. Given that lexical insertion is considered to be optional, there are other types of strings to which the rule could apply. An example is given in (40).

(40)   a.   *John see [e] by Mary.*
                    E   A   E
          b. **John see Mary by 0.*
                    E   E
                          A

The result of applying NP Movement to (40a) would be (40b). In this case there is an NP that bears more than one role. This results because we are making the minimal assumption with respect to movements and roles, namely, that movements have no effect on roles whatsoever. Role Assignment remains constant in the sense that a moved NP continues to bear its role as does the $_{NP}[e]$ into which the NP is moved. The result in the case of (40) is two roles on a single NP, in violation of Distributedness.[25]

1.5. Locality and NP Movement

We thus far have the one well-formed passive, (38), from the underlying structure (37a). This passive is the result of UP applying to the roles and NP Movement applying to the underlying structure. We have seen that, assuming certain conditions on roles, many facts about passivization can be accurately accounted for. There are still certain other strictly syntactic issues that must be addressed. The examples in (41)–(43) present some cases in point.

(41)   a.   *[e] was written Sara a letter.*
          b.   *Sara was written a letter.*
          c. **A letter was written Sara.*
          d. **Sara was written a letter to.*[26]

(42)   a.   *[e] was elected Joan president.*

---

[25]Our analysis assumes crucially here that NP Movement leaves behind no trace.

[26]Example (41d) is included to complete the paradigm. Although the LC could be stated in such a way as to prevent NP Movement from yielding it, we think it is probably better ruled out by an addition to the LAP. The LAP would therefore have a second part that says, "every element that assigns thematic roles in deep structure must have some element which bears a grammatical relation to it in surface structure." In Example (41d), the preposition *to,* which assigns the thematic role **goal** in Deep Structure, occurs in Surface Structure without an argument. Nothing bears a surface grammatical relation to it. Thus LAP would be violated.

As noted elsewhere in this chapter, the LAP is not required if we assume that NP Movement is not a rule of the grammar.

    b.   *Joan was elected president.*
    c.   **President was elected Joan.*

(43)   a.   *[e] was expected [e] be hit John.*
        b.   *John was expected to be hit.*
        c.   **John was expected [e] be hit.*

The ungrammatical cases here do not involve violations of the well-formedness conditions on R-structures. This is illustrated in (44), which in each case shows the result of UP and NP Movement.[27, 28]

(44)   a. *?*A letter was written$_i$ Sara.*
              A$_i$ **goal$_i$**
        b. **President$_j$ was elected$_i$ Joan$_j$.*
                             A$_i$
        c. **John was expected$_i$ [e] be hit$_j$.*
           A$_j$

What the ungrammatical examples (41c) and (42c) illustrate are violations of the local nature of the NP Movement rule. The LC, in the domain of movements, requires that all transformations be local in the sense of affecting only adjacent terms, where the notion of adjacency is relativized to the form of the structural description of the transformation. As the SD of the rule of NP Movement is stated in terms of $_{NP}[e]$ and NP, the movement must affect an $_{NP}[e]$ and an NP that are adjacent in the sense of being the two minimally distant items of these categories in a given phrase marker.[29] More simply, a rule that involves the movement of an NP cannot function over some other NP contained in the variable.[30]

[27]We use the label **goal** for the thematic relation assigned to the indirect object. It is possible that there is a more abstract characterization of this relation, parallel to E and A, which is realized as the thematic role "goal" in certain contexts and as other thematic roles elsewhere. We leave this matter open here.

[28]For some people, sentences like (44a) are not particularly bad. Although they are ruled out by the Locality Condition, they are not ruled out in the account that we sketch out later in this chapter which treats the passive construction as lexical. Therefore, it would be of some interest to explain the relative unacceptability of such examples in other than grammatical terms, if for independent reasons we want the grammar to generate them. Such an explanation is suggested in Chapter 5.

    President is a predicate in (44b), and it is coindexed with *Joan$_j$*. There is no evidence that *President* bears a thematic role in sentences like these. It is possible that there is a restriction against moving predicates into argument positions, which would rule out (44b), but we know of no clear evidence bearing on this possibility.

[29]Rosenbaum (1967) first developed a formal notion of minimal distance.

[30]So far as we can tell, for minimal distance a constituent counts as being "contained" in the variable X between A and B if the constituent is between A and B in the linear order. Thus minimal distance is distinguished from relative adjacency, which makes reference to the relation "c-command" (see Chapter 4). We have been unable to find evidence that would require a structurally more interesting constraint on minimal distance.

In (41c) the NP *a letter* has been reordered over the NP *Sara;* in (42c) the NP *president* has been reordered over the NP *Joan*. These movements did not affect adjacent categories in terms of the NP Movement rule. The well-formed examples (41b) and (42b), on the other hand, are the result of NP Movement properly applied to adjacent terms. Although the affected items were not strictly adjacent, in the sense of being right next to each other, they were adjacent relative to the NP Movement rule: They were the minimally distant instances of $_{NP}[e]$ and NP. This is illustrated in (45).

(45)   a. $_{NP}[e]$ *was written* $_{NP}[Sara]$ $_{NP}[a\ letter]$.
        b. $_{NP}[e]$ *was elected* $_{NP}[Joan]$ $_{NP}[president]$.

Example (44c) presents a case where the $_{NP}[e]$ to which the NP was moved was not the minimally distant $_{NP}[e]$. However, this is not prevented by the LC because empty nodes do not block the application of rules (as will be discussed in Chapter 4). After NP Movement as illustrated in (44c) there would be no way to fill the empty position. This example would therefore be excluded by the Binding Condition.[31]

Passivization (in fact all movement of NP, and all other movement, as we will show) is "relatively" local. The theoretical advantages of such a formulation will become obvious as we develop our thesis that all components of the grammar are subject to the LC. We will leave until Section 3 cases involving NP Movement in passive constructions where there is more than one main verb, and more than one empty NP.[32]

---

[31]If the Binding Condition is to apply after NP Movement, then the mapping from syntactic structure into R-Structure would have to apply at NP-Structure. Clearly, if NP Movement is a rule of grammar, we do not want to rule out all Deep Structure [e]s, which we would do if the Binding Condition applied to deep structures.

We thus face the possibility of a contradiction. To capture the thematic identity of the active and passive, we propose to assign thematic roles on the basis of Deep Structure. But to apply the Binding Condition as a condition on R-structures, we must delay assignment of thematic roles until NP Structure. The obvious solution is to assume that there is no NP Movement; rather, the passive is lexical and the deepest level of syntactic representation is NP Structure.

Alternatively, we could reformulate the Binding Condition as a constraint on the distributional properties of [e] in (derived) syntactic structures, and abandon the notion that it follows from a constraint on R-Structure. The decision will ultimately turn, it seems to us, on the viability of an NP Movement analysis of the passive. In the current framework, at least, assuming no NP Movement turns out to resolve a substantial array of independent problems.

[32]As noted at the beginning of this chapter, we do not formulate the traditional Raising to Subject as NP Movement. The analysis of predication in Chapter 2 subsumes those examples involving verbs like *seem* which do not assign thematic roles to their subjects. We

We can now formalize the LC as it is relevant for syntactic rules. As our main thesis states, syntactic transformations, like all rules of the grammar, must function locally.

(46)   **Locality Condition:** *All rules are local.*
        #1. P Coindex affects an X which is bijacent to NP.
        #2. D Coindex affects the closest preceding NP to X.
        #3. NP Movement affects minimally distant terms.

The notion of "minimally distant terms" can be formally defined as follows:

(47)   **Definition:** *Two terms, A and B, are **minimally distant,** where*
        (a) A and B are constant terms and X a variable of the structural description A X B of an operation which functions on a phrase marker
        (b) X does not contain any instance of an A^i or a B^i,
            $0 \leq i \leq max$

This interpretation of locality, as we have already illustrated, constrains NP Movement for passive. As we will argue in the discussions that follow, it is also correct for all other operations that map phrase markers into phrase markers. Using this notion of locality, we can explain the ungrammatical examples of (41)–(43), examples introduced earlier involving movement of an NP in one PP over another NP in another PP, as well as A-over-A type examples. In (48) we give some typical cases.

(48)   a. **A letter was written Sara.* [= (41c)]
        b. **John was talked to Mary about.*
        c. **Bill was bought a picture of.*

In (48a), as we have already discussed, the NP *a letter* cannot be moved into subject position over the NP *Sara,* as the latter is minimally distant from [e] in subject position. The same restriction holds for (48b), where *Mary* is the NP that is minimally distant from subject position. In this case, it might also be the case that *John* is not Θ-governed by *talked,* because of the Locality Condition on the assignment of thematic role to arguments of PPs, and hence LAP would also rule out the example (see Section 1.3.1). In (48c), the NP *Bill* cannot be moved over the N *picture,* which is the 0-projection of the category N.

---

must then block NP Movement from applying in examples like (i).

(i) [e] *seems* ₛ⁺[*John is intelligent*] ⇒ *John seems* ₛ⁺[0 *is intelligent*]

For cases such as these we stipulate that a tensed verb in English must have a lexical subject to agree with. In (i), there is no subject of *is* after NP Movement, and hence NP Movement yields ill-formedness in this case.

2. The *Tough* Construction

We will consider in this section the traditional rule of *Tough* Movement, which superficially at least falls into the category of NP movement rules.[33] Our approach will be based on a suggestion of Lasnik and Fiengo (1974), wherein there is a binding relationship between a gap in a complement and an NP in higher clause.

2.1. *Tough* Predicates

There are several constructions that share properties of the *tough* construction, some of which are illustrated in (49).

(49)   a.   *Mary is tough to see [e].*
       b.   *Mary is pretty to look at [e].*
       c.   *Mary is ready to visit [e].*
       d.   *Mary is too stubborn to visit [e].*
       e.   *Mary was pleasant to leave [e].*

The most salient characteristic of these examples is that the object of the infinitival complement is functioning as the subject of the matrix. *Tough* and *pleasant* can be distinguished from the other adjectives by the fact that they share the property of allowing an extraposed paraphrase, as in (50).

(50)   a.   *It was tough to see Mary.*
       b.   **It was pretty to look at Mary.*
       c.   **It was ready to visit Mary.*
       d.   **It was too stubborn to visit Mary.*
       e.   *It was pleasant to leave Mary.*

Pleasant can be distinguished from all of the others in that it can be used as the paraphrase of another extraposed construction, illustrated in (51).

(51)   a.   **It was tough of Mary to go away.*
       b.   **It was pretty of Mary to fall.*
       c.   **It was ready of Mary to visit us.*
       d.   **It was too stubborn of Mary to visit us.*
       e.   *It was pleasant of Mary to leave.*

---

[33]As we note later in this section, this construction has also been analyzed as a special case of *Wh* Movement. See Chomsky (1977).

Taking in its essentials the approach of Nanni (1978), we will attribute the ungrammaticality found in (50) and (51) not to syntactic restrictions on the rule that relates the matrix subject with the lower clause, but to semantic restrictions that the matrix adjectives impose on their complements.[34] Nanni argues that the complement verb of a *tough*-class predicate must be understood as "specifying the agent's intentions."[35]

Significantly, this restriction holds just in case the subject of the *tough*-class predicate binds a gap in the lower clause. We will formalize this intuition by imposing three conditions on the complements of a *tough*-class predicate when binding of [e] holds:

1. The set of individuals referred to by the subject of the *tough*-class predicate must be assigned thematic roles by the verb of the complement clause (and thus must bind [e] in the complement).
2. The subject of the complement must be an **agent**.
3. The **benefactee** of the matrix clause must be identical to the **agent** in the complement.

The examples in (52) illustrate.

(52)   a. *The man was hard for Mary to find [e] sick.*   [Nanni 1978, p. 95, (40b)]
        b. *The money was tough for John to lack [e].*   [Nanni 1978, p. 91, (28a)]
        c. *The boss was nice for Bill for Sam to talk to [e].*

Examples (52a) and (52b) are bad because the subject of the complement is not an **agent**. In Example (52c) the **benefactee** is not the **agent** of the complement, and so it is ruled out by Condition (3) (see Nanni 1978). Examples that satisfy Conditions (1) and (2) are the usual well-formed illustrations of *Tough* Movement, such as those in (49).

We assume that binding contributes a referential index to an NP. It does not assign thematic roles to the [e], nor does the binding NP inherit a thematic role from the NP that it binds. Thus an NP with no thematic role cannot bind [e], as such a structure would result in a violation of Completeness.

In (49b), for example, it seems that we must assign the same interpretation to *Mary* as we would in a sentence like *Mary is pretty*. It would be

---

[34]". . . only verbs which can be understood as specifying the agent's intentions can appear in the VP complement in a TM sentence [Nanni 1978, p. 94]."

[35]The notion that a predicate may impose semantic constraints on its complement is not an entirely novel one. Most commonly it is expressed in terms of subcategorization, and is concerned with complementation. See Grimshaw (1979a) for one example.

an error to assume that the subject of *pretty* has no thematic role with respect to *pretty*.

The relationship between the subject of the *pretty* predicate and the gap is one of binding, similar to bound anaphora, along the lines discussed by Lasnik and Fiengo (1974). We will call the rule that relates the subject and the gap **Binding**. In order to rule out a broad class of examples in which Binding is inapplicable, we must assume that its application is restricted to structures that satisfy the particular semantic constraints (2) and (3) noted earlier. The *tough* construction requires that these constraints be met because it requires Binding.

We will focus here on three central aspects of the analysis:

1. Binding applies to underlying structures.
2. Binding is subject to the Locality Condition.
3. The system of roles is instrumental in assigning the correct interpretations to structures to which Binding applies.

2.2. Binding

Consider once again Example (49b).

(49b)   *Mary is pretty to look at [e].*

We suppose that the underlying structure of (49b) is essentially (53), with certain details omitted.

(53)

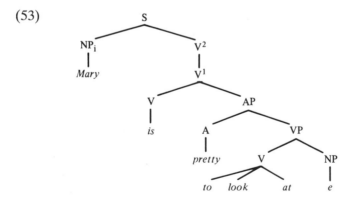

The rule of Binding will assign to the empty NP the index of NP_i. *Mary* is assigned the role **A** by the AP containing *pretty*.

We formulate Binding as a coindexing rule, as follows.

(54)   Binding: NP_i $_{NP}[e]$
                        1   2 $\Rightarrow$ 1 2$_i$
         Condition: 1 c-commands 2.

The structural change indicates that the referential index of NP_i is assigned to the empty NP.[36]

After Binding has applied, (49b) will have the following representation:

(55)   *Mary$_i$ is pretty$_j$ [to look$_k$ at [e$_i$]].*
          A$_j$ **A$_k$**

We assume, following general conventions, that the assignment of the index of the binding NP to the empty NP allows the latter to refer. This avoids the derivation of a surface structure in which an empty NP has no index, which would be ruled out by the Binding Condition *[e]. If the binding NP is an argument of the same verb as [e], then the Distributedness requirement is relevant and examples such as (56) are ruled out.

(56)   *John$_i$ fixed$_j$ [e].*
          E$_j$ **A$_j$**

If **A$_j$** is assigned to [e] and then Binding applies, the result is a set of individuals ({*John*}) with two roles. On the other hand, if no coindexing occurs, (56) would be ruled out by the Completeness requirement, as [e] would have a role but would lack a referent (*<∅, **A**, *fix*>). Failure to assign a role to [e] would also violate the Completeness condition, as *fix* assigns two roles.

Let us extend our analysis now to (49a).

(49a)   *Mary is tough to see.*

We will derive this sentence from the underlying structure in (57).

(57)

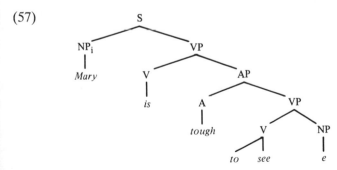

---

[36]This is effectively the rule Coindex of Koster (1978b), although with a somewhat narrower set of applications.

The same rule of Binding applies here as in (49b). In this case, again, *tough* assigns a role to its subject, namely **A**. Possibly a role is assigned to the infinitival complement by the adjective (cf. *This kitchen is tough for cooking in*). The representation of (57) is given as (58) after all of the relevant rules have applied.

(58)   *Mary is tough$_j$ [to see$_k$ [e$_i$]]*.
       A$_j$ **A$_k$**

It will turn out, now, that (58) will have a different assignment of roles from (59) and (60).

(59)   *It is tough to see Mary.*

(60)   *To see Mary is tough.*

In (59) and in (60), *to see Mary* is the only argument of *tough,* and it is assigned the same role in both cases, **A$_j$**, whereas in (58) it is assigned some other role. Thus we have a representation in terms of roles of a subtle difference in meaning: "Mary is tough for seeing" versus "seeing Mary is tough." There is no question, of course, that the two are very close in meaning, but this difference seems to us to be a real one.

In saying that *[to see [e]]* is assigned a role in (58) we leave open the question of what role it might be. We will return to this question in Section 2.3.

Let us consider again the difference between *tough* and *pretty.* As the examples in (49) and (50) show, the main difference is that we cannot attribute the property *pretty* to the propositional argument *to look at Mary.* This fact follows not from any deep fact of grammar, nor from any difference in the lexical representation of the adjectives, but from the fact that *pretty* is an adjective that can be used descriptively only of physical objects (and conceptual objects, like ideas and theories), and not of propositions and events. *Tough* has an "adverbial" sense in that it is descriptive of actions. This distinction presumably forms the basis for the difference between *Mary pleases easily* and **Mary pleases prettily.*[37]

---

[37]We get interpretations similar to those of (59) and (60) for the following examples.

   (i)   *It is tough seeing Mary.*
   (ii) *Seeing Mary is tough.*
A curious fact about these constructions is that (iii) is not possible.
   (iii) **Mary is tough seeing e.*
But we do get (iv), as expected in view of (iii).
   (iv) *Who was it tough seeing?*
Compare this with (v).

Our analysis can now be seen to be an instantiation of the basic position set out in Lasnik and Fiengo (1974), in which essentially the same derivations were argued to hold for *Tough* Movement constructions, where movement is at least plausible, and for Binding, where movement is implausible. We have shown how to reduce both constructions to Binding, and how to get the interpretations to fall out of the assignment of roles. There is no need to assume that the subject of *tough* lacks a role, a conclusion that is consistent with Lasnik and Fiengo's (1974) observations about the interpretation of the *tough* construction.[38]

2.3. Semantic Constraints on Binding

The range of accessible NP positions is subtly different for Binding versus NP Movement. The differences are revealed in the following examples.

(61)   a.   *It is tough to give expensive presents to wealthy people.*
       b.   *Sam gives expensive presents to wealthy people.*

(62)   a.   *Expensive presents are tough to give to wealthy people.*
       b.   *Expensive presents are given by Sam to wealthy people.*

(63)   a.   *Wealthy people are tough to give expensive presents to.*
       b.   **Wealthy people are given expensive presents to by Sam.*

(64)   a.   *It is tough to give wealthy people expensive presents.*
       b.   **Wealthy people are tough to give expensive presents.*

(65)   a.   *Sam gives wealthy people expensive presents.*

(v)   *Who was it tough to talk to?*

It is possible that Nanni's requirements on the *tough* construction will rule out (iii). The gerund must be analyzed as an NP that does not have an arbitrary subject that could be construed as an **agent**. Then the requirement that the **benefactee** and the **agent** be identical cannot be satisfied. For an analysis of gerunds consistent with these observations, see Chapter 2.

Notice that it is possible to have a **benefactee** with the gerund construction.

(vi)   *It was $\left\{ \begin{array}{c} tough \\ nice \end{array} \right\}$ for us seeing Mary.*

But in this case, *Wh* cannot be extracted from the complement.

(vii)   a.*Who was it tough for you seeing?*
        b.*Where was it nice for you seeing Mary?*

We have no explanation for the facts of (vii).

[38]See Chomsky's (1981, pp. 309ff.) discussion of a "paradox of Θ-theory" that arises in the attempt to account for the *tough* construction in GB Theory.

b.   *Wealthy people are given expensive presents by Sam.*

The examples in (62)–(63) show that NP Movement must move the closest NP to the empty NP in subject position, a point elaborated in Section 1.5. In (62b) the closest NP to the subject is moved into subject position, whereas in the ungrammatical (63b) the moved NP is not the closest (but see Footnote 26). In contrast, where there is Binding it is possible for there to be an NP between the binding NP and [*e*], as in (63a). Furthermore, NP Movement may move an indirect object when it immediately follows a verb as in (65b). But there may not be an [*e*] in this position that is bound by a binding NP through the application of Binding, as Example (64b) shows.

We express the contrast between the two types of examples in terms of the fact that NP Movement does not leave a trace.[39] Assuming that the configuration V–[*e*]–NP is ruled out on independent grounds, the difference between Binding and NP Movement follows immediately.

It might be thought that a direct object would appear in the variable in the case of Binding, blocking access to the object of a preposition. Consider the structure in (66). Notice that the direct object is in the variable, but Binding applies.

(66)

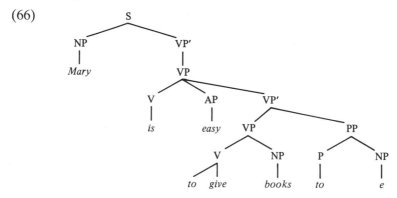

What is crucial to the interaction of the Locality Condition and Binding is not simply the presence of any intervening NP in the variable, but the presence of an NP that could in principle be construed as the binder of the [*e*]. Consider for example the following.

(67)   a.   *John is pleasant to persuade Mary to visit* [*e*].
        b.   *Mary would be tough to get Bill to write about* [*e*].

---

[39]We assume that NP Movement does not leave a trace. See Chapter 1 and Section 8.3 of Chapter 5 for discussion.

In (67a), *Mary* is in the variable, yet Binding is not blocked. If *Mary* and
[e] were coindexed, then there would be a violation of the Distributedness
requirement, as the individual referred to by *Mary* would be both the **A**
and the **E** of *visit*. Similar considerations are relevant for (67b). The obvious conclusion here is that the Locality Condition operates over the class
of "eligible" binding NPs in the *tough* construction, where this class is
determined by the well-formedness conditions on thematic interpretations,
and by the particular requirements of the *tough* construction as adapted
from Nanni (see Section 2.1).

Chomsky (1977) suggests that the *tough* construction can be collapsed
with *Wh* Movement, although more traditional treatments would suggest
that formally, at least, NP Movement would be a closer match. However,
there are two ways in which the traditional *Tough* Movement transformation, which we have reformulated as Binding, differs from other movement rules: First, as we have seen, it may apply to any NP in the verb
phrase, unlike NP Movement, which must apply to the first postverbal
NP;[40] second, unlike *Wh* Movement, *Tough* Movement cannot apply into
sentential complements, as the following examples illustrate.[41]

(68)   a. *Who do you think (that) Mary likes [e]?*
        b. *Who do you think [e] likes Mary?*

(69)   a. *It is nice that Mary likes John.*
        b. **John is nice that Mary likes [e].*
        c. **Mary is nice (that) [e] likes John.*

(70)   a. *It is pleasant to think that Mary likes John.*
        b. **John is pleasant to think (that) Mary likes [e].*
        c. **John is pleasant to think [e] likes Mary.*

Although the assumption that *Tough* Movement is in fact *Wh* Movement
will explain certain facts, it incorrectly predicts that the starred examples
in (69)–(70) will be grammatical.

The starred examples in (69) are ruled out by the conditions on interpretations for the *tough* construction. Recall that the **agent** of the complement must be the **benefactee** of the matrix. In both (69b) and (69c) the

---

[40]Moreover, NP Movement,in the passive at least, relates the thematic roles of one grammatical relation to the thematic roles of another in Surface Structure; such a relationship
does not hold in *Tough* Movement.

[41]These data are cited as support for the Binary Principle in Culicover and Wexler (1977).

benefactee is arbitrary (unspecified), which conflicts with the fact that the **agent** of the complement is *Mary*.[42]

The examples in (70) have been treated in the literature as marginal (Chomsky 1977) and ungrammatical (Culicover and Wexler 1977). In the present framework we have no non-ad-hoc way of ruling out (70b); (70c) may constitute a violation of agreement along the lines suggested in Footnote 42. We will provisionally assume that the unacceptability of (70b) is due to interpretive factors, perhaps an extension of the restrictions on the *tough* construction discussed earlier. We know of no convincing explanation for the ill-formedness of this example other than the Binary Principle of Culicover and Wexler (1977), which we are not assuming here.

In the remainder of this section, we will consider two questions that arise in conjunction with this (or any) analysis. First, how do we explain the fact that not all adjectives allow for the *tough* construction (e.g., *John is eager to talk to*)? Second, what is the explanation for the particular binding relationship that holds when there is more than one way to satisfy the structural description of Binding? We have already suggested that the Locality Condition allows for the resolution of this problem, and we will explore the consequences of the LC in more detail.

2.4. Binding and Locality

We begin with the question of why it is that certain adjectives (and verbs) govern Binding, and others do not. The difference, we suggest, resides in the thematic roles imposed on the infinitival complement by the matrix. In the case of *eager* and an infinitival complement, the infinitive is predicated of the **E** subject of *eager,* necessarily, by predication. Thus we get the following assignment of roles.

(71)   *John is eager$_i$ to talk$_j$ to [e].*
         A_i A_j
         E_j

In such a case, in the domain of *talk,* Binding would result in a violation of the Distributedness requirement. The set of individuals referred to by

[42]In both of the (c) examples of (69)–(70) there is another possible source of violation, which is that the subject of the tensed S is [e]. We may assume that [e] does not allow agreement unless it is the trace of *Wh* Movement. Presumably, this [e] that is a *t* retains the syntactic features necessary for syntactic agreement, whereas a bound [e] has a referential index assigned to it but no syntactic features. Equivalently, we could say that agreement morphology is determined on NP Structure.

John would be both the **E** and the **A** of the verb. Binding in such a case is prohibited.

In the corresponding example with *easy* no predication can take place because it would result in a violation of the requirement that the **agent** of the complement be the **benefactee** of the matrix. As in such a case the **benefactee** of the matrix is *arb*, the interpretation of the antecedent of the VP is also *arb*. This is illustrated in (72).

(72)   *John is easy$_i$ to see$_j$ [e].*
          A$_i$ **A$_j$**

As indicated in (72) there is no coindexing for predication since it would lead to a violation of the semantic well-formedness of the construction. The antecedent *arb* is not represented here as it is an element of the R-structure and not of the syntax per se. Notice that this predication distinction between *easy* and *eager* also predicts the correct results in examples like those in (73).

(73)   a. **John is easy to talk.*
          b. *John is eager to talk.*

Example (73a) is ungrammatical whether or not predication takes place. If there is coindexing then the antecedent of the complement is not the **benefactee.** If there is no coindexing then *John* plays no role in the complement. Both results violate the well-formedness restrictions on the *easy* construction. In (73b) predication simply coindexes the infinitival complement with the matrix subject and the result is fine.

Notice that the antecedent of the embedded complement in the *easy* construction is not always arbitrary. [We indicate **benefactee** in (74) by **B**.]

(74)   *John$_j$ is easy$_i$ for Bill$_k$ to see$_m$ [e$_j$]*
          A$_i$ **B$_i$**   **A$_m$**

In this case the antecedent of the infinitive is the **benefactee** *Bill* and therefore the subject of the matrix is free to bind the [e]. Recall that *Bill* in the variable material between *John* and the [e] does not cause ill-formedness as it is not an eligible binder.

We come now to an important difference between *too* and *easy*. Whereas *easy* seems to require the application of Binding, *too* allows it but does not require it.

(75)   a. *John is too tall to talk to Mary.*
          b. *John is too tall to talk to [e].*
          c. **John is easy to talk to Mary.*
          d. *John is easy to talk to [e].*

We must attribute the difference between *too* and *easy* to a lexical difference. The simplest device to express the difference would be a feature that indicates that *easy* must appear in a structure whose interpretation has the properties that we have already identified as Conditions (1), (2), and (3) on the interpretation of Binding, which we repeat here: (1) the set of individuals referred to by the subject of the *tough*-class predicate must be assigned a thematic role by the verb of the complement clause (and thus must bind [*e*] in the complement); (2) the subject of the complement must be an **agent**; and (3) the **benefactee** of the matrix clause must be identical to the **agent** in the complement. The interpretation specified by Conditions (2) and (3) is possible but not obligatory for *too*.

Thus in (75d) the individual *John* gets a thematic role from *talk to,* and the **agent** subject of the complement must be the same as the unspecified **benefactee** of the matrix, in accord with Condition (3). As there is no binding in (75c), no thematic role of the complement can be associated with *John* in this case; therefore *John* cannot have a role in the complement. In (75a), however, *John* need not have a role in the complement. It is the **theme** of the matrix, and as it binds nothing in the complement, the complement can (and must) be predicated of it. In (75b) *John* must bind [*e*] in the complement, otherwise the Binding Condition would yield a violation. As *John* is the **goal** of *talk to,* it cannot also have the complement predicated of it. Therefore the subject of the complement in (75b) is unspecified.

Of the five examples that initiated our discussion of Binding, only (49c) remains to be considered.

(49)   c.   *Mary is ready to visit.*

As far as *ready* is concerned, we see that, like *too,* it patterns both like *eager* and like *pretty.* On the first reading, *ready* assigns no special interpretation to the complement, Predication applies, and hence there cannot be binding between the matrix subject and an NP in the complement. On the second reading, the *tough* interpretation is assigned to the complement, and therefore binding (but no predication) is allowed.

Let us consider now more complex examples of Binding, in which there is potential interaction between several full NPs and several empty NPs. We will see that in applying Binding, we have to guarantee the following:

1. Where there is more than one potential binding NP, the one closest to the empty NP (in the sense of Locality) is chosen. So, for an underlying structure represented as (76), only the binding indicated in (77a) is well formed.

(76)   *John$_i$ is eager for Sam$_j$ to be easy to please [e].*

(77)   a. *John$_i$ is eager for Sam$_j$ to be easy to please [e$_j$].*
        b. *John$_i$ is eager for Sam$_j$ to be easy to please [e$_i$].*

This follows from the fact that *Sam* would appear in the variable if we attempted to apply Binding to *John* and the empty NP, as illustrated in (78).

(78)

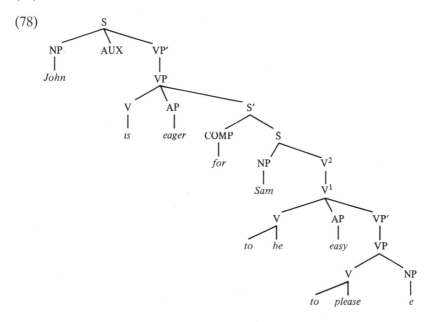

2. Where there is more than one empty NP, the closest one to the binding NP is bound to it. This point can be illustrated by the following example:

(79)   *John$_i$ is easy to convince [e] to try to be pleasant to talk to [e].*

There is no coherent paraphrase of the interpretation in which *John* binds the object of *talk to* (and if there is, it is the wrong one). The reason for this interpretation being impossible is that the object of *convince* would not be coindexed. The Binding Condition rules out the possibility of generating such a configuration.[43]

---

[43]There is a principle implicit here, which is that one NP cannot bind more than one [e]. Binding thus cannot be like the binding of pronominal anaphors, because we can get examples like *Everyone$_i$ tried to convince himself$_i$ to get Bill to be nice to him$_i$.*

In summary, we incorporate into the Locality Condition an instantiation for Binding, given below as #4.

Locality Condition: *All rules are local.*
   #1. P Coindex affects an X which is bijacent to NP.
   #2. D Coindex affects the closest preceding NP to X.
   #3. NP Movement affects minimally distant terms.
   #4. Binding affects the closest eligible NP to [e].

3. Infinitival Complementation

3.1. Differences in Thematic Roles

We consider now a more complex set of examples that test our analysis of Role Assignment and NP Movement. We will see that although the assumption of NP Movement which we used in Chapter 2 allows us to explain certain facts concerning the range of predication possibilities in passives, our assumption that there is no PRO forces us to question whether NP Movement is in fact the correct approach to the passive construction in general.

Of central importance is the treatment of the complements of verbs such as *expect* and *persuade.* It is well known that passivization of the infinitival complement of *expect* has no effect on interpretation, whereas passivization of the infinitival complement of *persuade* does. The following are the classic examples.

(80)   a.   *I expected* $\left\{ \begin{array}{l} \textit{the doctor to examine Mary.} \\ \textit{Mary to be examined by the doctor.} \end{array} \right\}$.

       b.   *I persuaded* $\left\{ \begin{array}{l} \textit{the doctor to examine Mary.} \\ \textit{Mary to be examined by the doctor.} \end{array} \right\}$

There is a vast literature concerning such examples. We will not attempt to review the many alternative analyses that have been proposed, but will assume that the reader is familiar with them. What is common to most analyses is that the complement of *expect* is sentential, whereas the complement of *persuade* is of the form NP S'.

Let us consider the alternative suggested in Chapter 2. Suppose that a possible complement structure of *expect* and of *persuade* is NP VP.[44] Pred-

---

[44]These verbs differ, however, in other complement structures. *Expect* takes NP and S' complements, whereas *persuade* takes NP–of–NP and NP–S' complements. We do not take the position that all verbs that take propositional complements govern a single "subcategorization frame." Thus we allow the possibility that *persuade* may appear in and correctly assign an interpretation to both NP-VP and NP-S'. The question of what the correct interpretations are is taken up further in what follows.

ication (see Chapter 2), extended to VPs, will express the fact that VP is predicated of the NP in such a construction. As we are assuming the same underlying structure for the two verbs, the assignment of grammatical relations will be the same in both cases. We must therefore attribute the observed differences between the two verbs not to any syntactic differences between them (in contrast to traditional analyses), but to the thematic representations that are associated with the structures in which they appear. In other words, there will be lexical differences between *expect* and *persuade* such that the same thematic roles (R-structures) are assigned to the active and passive for *expect,* but different thematic roles are assigned for *persuade*. We repeat the schema given in Chapter 1 for mapping roles and grammatical relations into thematic roles.

(81) **Role Assignment**
    (i)   *Assign lexically idiosyncratic roles.*
    (ii) *Assign **theme** to the object if there is one. Otherwise assign **theme** to the subject.*
    (iii) *(a) Assign **goal** to subject or (b) assign **patient** to object and **agent** to subject or (c) **instrument** to subject or . . . .*

For expository convenience we will, as before, assign **E** and **A**, so that instead of (ii) and (iii) we will actually carry out the following: *Assign A to the object if there is one; otherwise assign A to the subject.*

Let us return to the difference between *expect* and *persuade*. The **A** (i.e., **theme**) of *persuade* is a **patient,** whereas the **A** of *expect* is not. The subject of *persuade* is thus an agent,[45] whereas the subject of *expect* is a **goal.** The crucial difference between the two verbs, then, devolves upon the thematic role assigned to the direct object. The following examples illustrate.

(82)   *I expected$_i$ the doctor [examine$_j$ Mary].*
      E_i E_j A_j
                   A_i

Thematic roles:	*I*	**goal** of *expect*
	the doctor	(i) **theme** of *expect*
		(ii) **agent** of *examine*
	Mary	**patient** of *examine*[46]

---

[45]We assume that general principles of thematic relations stipulate that where there is a **patient**, there is an **agent** or an **instrument**. Such principles are not strictly linguistic, as they have to do with the way in which we perceive events and actions.

[46]*Mary* is also the **theme** of *examine* here, and in the other examples that we will consider. We will omit mention of it where it is not crucial to the example.

(83)   *I persuaded$_i$ the doctor [examine$_j$ Mary].*
     E$_i$ A$_i$ A$_j$
                  E$_j$

Thematic roles: *I*	(i) **source** of *persuade* (ii) **agent** of *persuade*
the doctor	(i) **theme** of *persuade* (ii) **patient** of *persuade* (iii) **agent** of *examine*
Mary	**patient** of *examine*

A crucial assumption of the approach that we are taking here is that it is possible to isolate thematic roles for verbs like *expect* and *persuade* such that the differences between them can be correctly characterized. We represent *expect* as assigning a role to its direct object here, but we will later abandon this assumption for reasons that will be discussed. We will ultimately assume that the **theme** of *expect* is the proposition expressed by predicating the infinitive of the direct object.

Notice that the verb *persuade* can be used with the NP VP construction, NP S′, NP *of* NP, and perhaps NP *into* V-*ing*.

(84)   a.   *John persuaded Mary to leave.*
       b.   *John persuaded Mary that she should leave.*
       c.   *John persuaded Mary of the necessity of leaving.*
       d.   *?John persuaded Mary into leaving.*

The empirical evidence does not support the view that all these uses of *persuade* have the same thematic structure. In (84a) and (84d) Mary is moved to action by the persuasion of the subject, whereas in (84b) and (84c) Mary arrives at a state of mind that agrees with the subject's intentions. As is shown by (85), in (84b) and (84c) it is possible to say that Mary changed her mind after having been persuaded whereas in (84a) and (84d) it is not.

(85)   a.   *?John successfully persuaded Mary to leave but she later changed her mind.*
       b.   *John successfully persuaded Mary that she should leave but she later changed her mind.*
       c.   *John successfully persuaded Mary of the necessity of leaving, but she later changed her mind.*
       d.   *?John successfully persuaded Mary into leaving but she later changed her mind.*

Thus we might distinguish the two groups by saying that in (a) and (d) *Mary* is a **patient** whereas in (b) and (c) *Mary* is a **goal** or **recipient**. In (b) and (c) the **theme** is the complement, either S' or (*of*) NP, whereas in (a) and (d) the **theme** is *Mary* and the complement is the **goal**.

Although the details of this analysis are debatable, the distinction that it expresses seems to be necessary. Notice that a verb like *force* displays only the (a)–(d) pattern. This fact suggests that there are in reality two patterns, as otherwise we would expect all four constructions to be appropriate for *force*.

(86)   a. *John forced Mary to leave.*
         b. **John forced Mary that she should leave.*
         c. **John forced Mary of the necessity of leaving.*
         d. *John forced Mary into leaving.*

We conclude, therefore, that a principle (or a rule of thumb) that leads us to posit one "subcategorization frame" or thematic role pattern for a verb that governs various complement structures is methodologically weak.

Let us consider now the passive constructions corresponding to (82) and (83), given in (87).

(87) $I \begin{Bmatrix} expected \\ persuaded \end{Bmatrix}$ *Mary to be examined by the doctor.*

We might at first suppose that these examples are derived by NP Movement applying to underlying structures of the form given in (88).

(88) $I \begin{Bmatrix} expected \\ persuaded \end{Bmatrix}$ *[e] to be examined Mary by the doctor.*

However, such configurations are ruled out because of the prohibition against predicating of an empty category.[47]

An alternative that we may entertain is that of using Binding to supply the index of the Deep Structure object in these infinitival passives. Suppose that (89) underlies (87).

(89) $I \begin{Bmatrix} expected \\ persuaded \end{Bmatrix}$ *Mary to be examined [e] by the doctor.*

---

[47]This constraint is motivated in Chapter 2, in our discussion of examples such as **The meat was eaten nude* from underlying [e] *ate the meat nude* and **John was promised to leave.*The constraint is discussed further in what follows.

In an analysis of the passive that does not assume NP Movement, an example like (88) will be ruled out by the Binding Condition. As will be discussed, it is not clear how to rule out the examples of the preceding paragraph in such an analysis.

As (90) and (91) show, the role assignments are correct.[48]

(90)   *I expected$_i$ Mary [be examined$_j$ [e] by the doctor]*.
        E$_i$ **A$_i$**   **A$_j$**   **E$_j$**

      Thematic roles: *I*   **goal** of *expect*

                    the doctor   **agent** of *examine*

                    Mary   (i) **theme** of *expect*
                                              (ii) **patient** of *examine*

(91)   *I persuaded$_i$ Mary [be examined$_j$ [e] by the doctor]*.
        E$_i$ **A$_i$**   **A$_j$**   **E$_j$**

      Thematic roles: *I*   (i) **source** of *persuade*
                                            (ii) **agent** of *persuade*

                    the doctor   **agent** of *examine*

                    Mary   (i) **patient** of *persuade*
                                              (ii) **patient** of *examine*
                                              (iii) **theme** of *persuade*

Clearly, it is theoretically undesirable to treat what is obviously a single construction (i.e., the passive) in two different ways (i.e., movement and binding) depending on whether or not it is embedded. Purely on methodological grounds we would be led to abandon NP Movement in passives in favor of Binding in general. We could not reduce all Binding to NP Movement for reasons already discussed in connection with the *tough* construction; see our discussion of Lasnik and Fiengo (1974) at the beginning of Section 2.

However, there are certain facts that militate very clearly against a Binding analysis for passives in general. In our discussion of the simple passive earlier we noted that it is impossible to passivize out of a PP unless the object of that PP is assigned a role by the verb itself. In examples that involve Binding, on the other hand, there is nothing wrong with binding

---

[48]We are assuming at this point that *expect* assigns a thematic role to its direct object in the infinitival construction. We will have reason to question this assumption in Section 3.2, but right now nothing crucial is at stake. Notice that if *expect* does not assign a thematic role to its direct object, the Local Argument Principle of Section 1.3.1 will be violated. However, such a violation does not raise a problem if we adopt a lexical passive, as in the lexical passive analysis it is not necessary to adopt a special principle that requires every surface argument to bear a thematic role with respect to the verb of which it is an argument. This property of passives would follow from the formulation of the lexical passive rule, and no general principle would be required to rule out examples like (89).

[e] in a prepositional phrase; for example, *John was fun to toss the fruit at* [e] is perfectly good. We cannot maintain a Binding approach for the passive, because the corresponding complex passives are not grammatical: **John expected to be tossed the fruit at* [e].

Along similar lines, the passive allows the first object in a double object construction to be omitted, whereas Binding as it was developed in Section 2 does not: *John was given Ø a book; *John would be fun to give* [e] *a book*. In other words, passive and binding are not the same construction.

Other problems with a Binding analysis involve sentences like the following.

(92)   a.   *To be arrested* [e] *would bother John$_i$.*
         b.   *John expected to be arrested* [e].

One problem with (92a) is that *John* does not c-command [e], and therefore cannot bind it. A second problem is that even if *John* can bind [e], this example violates the antecedent internal [e] condition of Delahunty (1981) which disallows a gap inside an antecedent, as will be discussed in Chapter 4.

Furthermore, in our framework, if *John* can bind [e] in these examples then *John* can bind [e] in an example like *To arrest* [e] *would bother John,* with the interpretation "(for us) to arrest John would bother John." If *to arrest* must be predicated of *John* then of course [e] could not be bound by *John,* because of the Distributedness condition. But it seems that the infinitive must have an arbitrary antecedent, because of examples like *To leave the party right now would offend our hosts* (see Section 6 of Chapter 2). Similar examples can be constructed for the passive case: *To be arrested right now would serve no purpose* (the subject of *to be arrested* is not *no purpose*), *To be seen leaving the party so early would offend our hosts.*[49]

3.2. Weighing Alternatives

There are a range of alternative analyses of the passive that should be considered. The central assumptions that are at issue are the following:

1. NP Movement versus no NP Movement in passives
2. Selectional restrictions determined at Deep Structure versus at NP Structure (Chapter 2)

---

[49]One alternative, in a theory assuming Abstract Case, is to have *arrest* but not *be arrested* assign Case to its direct object. A case-marked [e] would have to be interpreted as a "variable" in GB Theory, for example, an interpretation which is ill formed if it is not bound by an operator. It strikes us that this account is somewhat circular, as what we are trying to **explain** is why the only sort of gap that can follow *arrest* is one bound by an operator.

3. PRO versus no PRO

If we assume NP Movement–PRO–Deep Structure selection, then we have essentially the Government–Binding analysis of the passive. Our decision to explore an alternative to this analysis in Chapter 2 was based on two considerations:

1. There is questionable syntactic evidence for PRO.
2. Reducing control to coindexing allows a partial unification of predication and general explanations in terms of the Locality Condition.

A decision to apply selectional restrictions to representations determined at Deep Structure would prevent us from adopting a lexical analysis of the passive construction, where the passive predicate is a lexical entry derived by a lexical rule (such as is found in Bresnan, 1982, and elsewhere). It is at the level of Deep Structure, before the object of a passive is moved into subject position, that it is possible to distinguish all of the examples like the following:

(93)   a. *John ate the meat nude.*
          b. *John ate the meat raw.*
          c. *John promised Mary to leave.*
          d. **The meat was eaten nude.*
          e. *The meat was eaten raw.*
          f. **Mary was promised to leave.*
          g. *Bill struck Fred as intelligent.*
          h. **Fred was struck as intelligent.*
          i. *John$_i$ talked about Mary$_j$ nude$_{i,*j}$.*
          j. **Mary$_j$ was talked about nude$_j$.*

As we noted in Chapter 2, ruling out examples (93f) and (93h) crucially depends on there being an empty subject at Deep Structure; the same device will also rule out (93d) from [*e*] *ate the meat nude.*

It is true, however, that (93d) can be ruled out by doing selection restrictions after NP Movement (or on the passive structure at NP Structure, regardless of whether the passive is transformationally derived or not). It is then simply necessary to require that the predicate *nude* be predicated of *the meat* in order to derive a violation of the selectional restrictions at this level. But at the level of NP Structure, there appears to be no reason why Example (93j) should be ruled out, although there is a good reason (the bijacency requirement of the LC) for ruling it out at Deep Structure.

If selectional restrictions are established at the level of the passive construction, then there must be a level of representation at which the generalization between the active and the passive is captured. Such a level cannot be Deep Structure, by assumption. Presumably it is a level of interpretation, such as R-Structure, at which the selectional restrictions are stated in terms of thematic roles (e.g., "the **patient** must be inanimate"). It is not at all clear how the ungrammatical examples that crucially depend on predication of [e] will be ruled out in such a framework.

The lexical analysis presents problems for us in another way. Certain facts that are explained by the Locality Condition follow directly if NP Movement is viewed as a lexical relation between the arguments governed by a verb; as government is local, any lexical relations involving governed arguments will also be local. However, a transformational NP Movement explains why it is that in English the first NP becomes the passive subject, a fact that is crucially defined in terms of a linear notion of locality, and not in terms of domains of government. Thus we get *John was given the book* and not *The book was given John.*

Notice, furthermore, that to state the passive in terms of a single thematic role, in the case of the dative construction we would have to assume that the indirect object has either the same role as the direct object in a nondative, or the same grammatical relation. That is, if the rule is "assign to the subject of the passive the role of the direct object in the active," then for *John was given the book* to be derived correctly, *John* would have to be the direct object in *Give John the book,* while in *A book was given to John, a book* would have to be the direct object.[50] Or, the rule could be "assign to the subject of the passive the role **R**." On this approach, there would have to be some role **R** that was assigned to the direct object when it immediately follows the verb, and to the indirect object in the double object construction. Neither solution seems to us to be particularly satisfactory.[51] Although there is abundant evidence that a unique role is assigned to the indirect object of the double object construction (see Oehrle 1976), no one has ever shown that this role is also assigned to the direct object of *give* in the corresponding single object construction.[52]

---

[50] As in Bresnan (1982). The formal device used is that of assigning to the indirect object the function OBJ in the double object construction, while the direct object is assigned the function OBJ2. The generalization in the case of the passive is that the SUBJ of the passive is the OBJ of the active. This translates readily into the correct assignment of thematic roles, as Bresnan shows.

[51] In addition, it is in fact not obvious how to rule out NP Movement in a transformational theory that has "move α" as the general schema for rules. But clearly, a unification of the passive construction, elimination of NP Movement in favor of Binding and predication, and further restriction of the class of possible rules would be a desirable result.

[52] In a lexical framework the problem also arises of relating a subject NP of one verb to the object position of another verb, as in well-known examples like *John was expected to be arrested.* In the current framework, *John* is the antecedent of both *expected* and *arrested,* and hence is assigned the "object" role of both. This is the correct result for such sentences. See Bresnan (1982) for essentially this sort of analysis, where the controller of the infinitive is identified by a "lexical control equation."

Departing somewhat from other proposals as to the formulation of a lexical passive (but following a suggestion of Anderson 1977), we suggest the following formulation:

(94)   **Lexical Passive:** Assign to the antecedent of a passive VP a thematic role that is Θ-governed by the active verb.

Notice that this formulation has the virtue of locality discussed earlier; only arguments of a verb can be related by the passive. Thus the Local Argument Principle introduced in Section 1.3.1 follows immediately. Examples like *John was expected to be arrested* are not problematic, as *John* will be the antecedent of both *was expected* and *be arrested*, and hence will be the **theme** of the first and the **patient** of the second.

On the other hand, a lexical passive predicts that both objects in a double object construction can be the subject of the passive, a possibility that has generally been denied in the literature. As noted earlier, *John was given a book* is generally judged to be grammatical, whereas *A book was given John* is not. However, it should be noted that the latter judgment is by no means universal among native speakers, nor do those who judge it to be ungrammatical consider it as bad as **John was given a book to*. We conclude that if the lexical passive is the correct analysis, both passives are grammatical and the unacceptable one requires an explanation of a different sort than has been suggested in the past.

It appears, in summary, that the most stubborn problems for a lexical passive are the ill-formed passives that were noted in (93). We find the lexical approach to be attractive in the context of the general set of assumptions that we have made here. One interesting consequence of a lexical analysis of the passive is that it eliminates the necessity of allowing the rule "move NP" in the grammar (of English, at least). One virtue of this is that we no longer need to stipulate that *Wh* Movement leaves a trace whereas NP Movement does not. Without NP Movement, we may return to the principle that all movements leave a trace.

Consider now the other alternative, an approach that assumes PRO. In such an analysis, (95a) would be derived from (95b), as shown.

(95)   a.   *John expected to be arrested.*
        b.   *John expected [e] to be arrested PRO.* ⇒
             John expected PRO to be arrested.

This analysis is attractive for a variety of reasons that are well known from the literature; it would have the advantage for us of allowing us to unify the passive as NP Movement everywhere. However, for (95b) to be a possible deep structure, we would have to modify our assumption that nothing can be predicated of [e].

Allowing (95b) also allows us a derivation like that in (96).

(96) $John \begin{Bmatrix} expects \\ persuaded \end{Bmatrix}$ [e] *to be arrested Fred.* ⇒

   $John \begin{Bmatrix} expects \\ persuaded \end{Bmatrix}$ *Fred to be arrested.*

But such a derivation requires a significant modification of other assumptions, especially those having to do with the assignment of thematic roles. In (96), the derived direct object of the matrix is the **theme** and, in the case of *persuade*, the **patient** as well. In both cases, *Fred* is the **patient** of *arrested*. In effect, then, while thematic roles are assigned to NPs on the basis of Deep Structure, the determination of which individuals actually get the roles awaits NP Structure. In the approach that we have adopted thus far, a much simpler mechanism for assigning thematic roles is possible.[53]

Let us summarize. There are three alternatives that we have been entertaining: the Deep Structure analysis with Binding, the PRO analysis, and the lexical analysis.

(97)   Deep Structure Analysis:
   1. No PRO
   2. Thematic interpretation on Deep Structure
   3. Generalization of predication to VP complements
   4. Mixed passive analysis (NP Movement and Binding)
   5. Locality applies generally

---

[53]The traditional analysis of infinitival complementation avoids this problem by assigning different underlying structures to *expect* and *persuade*.

(i)   a. *John expects* $\begin{Bmatrix} _s[[e] \text{ to be arrested } \begin{Bmatrix} PRO \\ Bill \end{Bmatrix}] \\ _s[PRO \text{ to arrest Bill}] \end{Bmatrix}$

   b. *John persuaded* $\begin{Bmatrix} Bill \ _s[[e] \text{ to be arrested PRO}] \\ Mary \ _s[PRO \text{ to arrest Bill}] \end{Bmatrix}$

We assume (in view of the abundant evidence) that such an analysis using the GB machinery of Case Theory, Binding Theory and so on can be made to work quite well. Our goal in this book is to pursue the possibility, which we believe is a very plausible one, that much of the intricate linguistic theory that has developed into GB Theory can be reduced to a few simple principles of thematic structure and the Locality Condition.

The PRO analysis given earlier in the text is preferable to the traditional one from the point of view of the syntax, as it allows a simplification in the English base component. (See Section 7.2 of Chapter 2 for discussion.) But because the PRO analysis is problematic for other reasons, we are led to reject both PRO analyses, the traditional one and that of the text.

(98)   PRO Analysis:
1. PRO
2. Thematic interpretation on Deep and NP Structure
3. No generalization of predication to VP complements
4. Unified passive analysis (NP Movement)
5. Locality applies generally

(99)   Lexical Analysis:
1. No PRO
2. Thematic interpretation on NP Structure (= Deep Structure)
3. Generalization of predication to VP complements
4. Unified passive analysis (lexical)
5. Extension of locality to θ-government

Since we have eliminated NP Movement for Raising to Subject in favor of predication, and since there are serious questions about the syntactic reality of PRO, it would clearly be desirable to adopt the lexical analysis and to eliminate NP Movement entirely. The discussion of predication in Chapter 2 remains virtually unchanged if we adopt a lexical analysis, but some major problems then remain, including the analysis of *promise* and *strike*.[54] Regardless of which of the options turns out to be correct, the important point is the central relevance of the LC.

3.3. Dummy *It* and *There*

In this section we discuss the dummy elements *it* and *there*. The way in which dummy elements are integrated into a theory of thematic role assignment depends on whether it is assumed that there is a rule of NP Movement because the base-generated [e] would have to be taken into account. As we have not resolved this question, we will briefly review what implications the dummy elements have for both the NP Movement analysis (which, given our earlier discussion, would probably have to involve PRO) and the lexical passive analysis.

3.3.1. WITH NP MOVEMENT

Suppose, first, that [e] may be an underlying dummy element in English; this is an essential assumption of the NP Movement analysis. On this approach, the passive verb assigns roles to the subject NP in Deep Struc-

---

[54]For an analysis of control in terms of thematic roles see Jackendoff (1972).

ture just as the active form does and it is the rule of UP which deletes the role **E** on the subject NP.

To generate a sentence with the dummy *it* as subject of a verb like *seems* we must assume, in contrast, that *seems* assigns no role to its subject. Some possible deep structures are given in (100).

(100)   a.   *It seems [John likes Mary].*
               0   E   A
         b.   *[e] seems [John likes Mary].*
               0   E   A
         c.   *[e] was hit Mary by John.*
               E   A   E

We might hypothesize that the difference between *it* and *[e]* with respect to Role Assignment is correlated with the well-known fact that (in English), *it* cannot function as the dummy subject of a simple passive.

We may rule out any account of dummy *it* in which *it* is a surface realization of underlying *[e]*. In the passive, as in (100c), substitution of *it* for *[e]* will yield ungrammaticality (as (101) illustrates), and it will not work correctly for the constructions that we discussed in Section 1.4, in which failure of NP Movement yields not dummy *it*, but violations of the Binding Condition. In fact, *it* can only appear in a position where it never gets assigned a role.[55] In contrast, well-formed instances of *[e]* that are assigned roles (e.g., deep structure subject of the passive or object of a *tough* construction) can never be replaced by *it*. It follows, then, that *it* and *[e]* are distinct items and must both be generated in Deep Structure. Thus all of the structures in (100), as well as those in (101), will be generated by the grammar.[56]

(101)   a.   *It seems that John hit Mary.*
         b.   **It was hit Mary (by John).*

It can function as the subject of a passive when there is an extraposed sentential complement, as in *It was believed that the world was flat.* For examples like these we will assume that Role Assignment (optionally) assigns to the extraposed complement the role that a subject may receive, whereas *it* is (optionally) assigned no role. If the options are correctly exercised, the result is a well-formed R-structure. If they are not, the

---

[55]With the exception of the *it* in extraposition constructions, which we will discuss shortly.

[56]Such a view is also consistent with the strong version of the Lexicalist Hypothesis that we assume here.

resulting R-structure is ill-formed, either because *it* has been assigned a role when it should not have been, or the complement has not been assigned a role when it should have been.[57]

Since there is a Deep Structure difference between *it* and [*e*], we will use this difference to account for the ungrammaticality of (101b). Suppose that the lexical item dummy *it* is incapable of being assigned a role at any level of representation, a restriction that we express as (102), subject to further elaboration.

(102)   **it*

$$<t>$$

$$t \in T$$

As (103) shows, precisely the structure underlying (101b) will be ruled out by this restriction.[58]

(103)   a.   *It seems [John likes Mary].*
                 $\emptyset$ E   A
           b.   *[e] seems [John likes Mary].*
                 $\emptyset$ E   A
           c.   *[e] was hit Mary (by John).*
                 E   A   E

---

[57]See Williams (1982) and Chomsky (1981) for discussion of this fact in terms of Case Theory. The case analysis stipulates that the S′ does not receive case, and therefore can remain as the object of the passive verb, which does not assign case to its object. An NP object, which must receive case, must undergo NP Movement into a case-assigning position.

Such an analysis entails that the syntactic structure of the VP containing extraposed S′ and nonextraposed S′ will be the same.

(i)   a.   *John believes that the world is flat.*
          b.   *It is believed (by John) that the world is flat.*

VP Topicalization suggests otherwise:

(ii)   a.   *They said that John believes that the world is flat, and believe that the world is flat he does.*
          b.* *They said that it would be believed that the world was flat, and believed that the world was flat it was.*
          c.   *They said that it would be believed that the world was flat, and believed it was that the world was flat.*

See Delahunty (1982) for more discussion about the proper point of attachment of extraposed S′s.

[58]As noted in Chapter 5, examples like (105b) must be made to yield ungrammaticality if they undergo NP Movement. This can be accomplished by formulating Subject–Verb Agreement in such a way that it filters out any surface structure in which there is no subject or trace of a subject. Of course, for this to work NP Movement must not leave a trace, as we have assumed.

       d. *It was hit Mary (by John).
          E   **A**   **E**

Given our account of predication in Chapter 2, we note that (102) is actually in need of modification. The situation is somewhat more complicated. Specifically, we say that in the case of extraposed infinitives, the infinitive is coindexed with the dummy subject. Example (104) illustrates.

(104)   *It$_i$ is fun [to drink club soda]$_i$.*

On the assumption that coindexing with an NP is tantamount to assigning a thematic role to it, dummy *it* will have a thematic role assigned. Presumably such an assignment would be interpreted as assignment of the thematic role to *arb*.

In order to characterize correctly the difference between (101b) and (104), we propose the modification indicated in (102′):

(102′)   *it

$$\langle t, g, v \rangle \begin{array}{l} t \in T \\ g \in G \end{array}$$

where T = the set of thematic relations, G = the set of grammatical relations, and v = some verbal element.

What (102′) says is that *it* may bear a thematic role or a grammatical relation (or neither) with respect to a given verbal element, but that it may not bear both. This not only accounts for the difference between (101b) and (104), but also for the examples in (105).

(105)   a. *Mary is fun to drink club soda.
           b. *Mary is happy (to drink club soda).*
           c. *It is happy that Mary drinks club soda.
           d. *It is happy (to drink club soda).

Example (105a) is ungrammatical (cf. (104)) because although *Mary* can properly be the antecedent of the VP *to drink club soda*, it cannot occur as the subject of *is fun* because *is fun* in this sense assigns no role to its subject. This results in a violation of the Completeness Condition.[59] Ex-

---

[59]This would also be a violation of the LAP because *Mary* is the subject of *be fun* but bears no thematic role with respect to it in Deep Structure. The LAP is actually in need of slight revision because it must exclude those verbs which simply do not assign a role to a particular position; for example, *seem*, which assigns no role to its subject, or *be fun*, as in (104). Therefore the LAP should read: *If an NP bears a Surface Structure grammatical relation with respect to some element, then it must be assigned a thematic role by that element in Deep Structure, if that element can assign a role to that position.*

amples (105b) and (105c) show that *be happy* is a predicate which does assign a role to its subject, and therefore a lexical NP, but not dummy *it*, can occur in subject position. This explains the ungrammaticality of (105d) as compared with (104). In (105d) *it* can perfectly well be the antecedent of the infinitival VP; it cannot, however, be the subject of a verbal element with respect to which it would also have to bear a thematic role.

Principle (102′) raises an attractive possibility. Suppose that the difference in English between [*e*], *there,* and *it* is as follows: [*e*] must be filled by NP Movement or bound. *There* and *it* cannot have roles and are in complementary distribution with [*e*]. If the predicate has an existential interpretation, we require *there*; otherwise we require *it*. We restate (102′) as (106).

(106)   * $\left\{ \begin{array}{l} it \\ there \end{array} \right\}$

$<t,\ g,\ v>_{t\ \epsilon\ T}$

$g\ \epsilon\ G$

To see how such an analysis works, consider the deep structures in (107).

(107)   a.   *There was hit Mary (by John).*
          b.   *There seems [John likes Mary].*
          c.   *There was a man in the park.*
          d.   *[e] was a man in the park.*

In the case of (107a) we will assume that *was hit Mary (by John)* is not existential and therefore *there* cannot occur. Example (107a) is ungrammatical. Consider next (107b). As *seems* is not an existential predicate, this example also results in ungrammaticality. In (107c) we have no problem generating *there* because *was a man in the park* is an existential predicate. As existential *be* assigns only one role, it would be assigned (by the Role Assignment algorithm) to *a man,* of which *in the park* is predicated. This same role assignment and predication take place in (107d), yielding the appropriate synonymy of the two examples, and if NP Movement applies, we get the grammatical *A man was in the park.*[60]

---

[60]Note that *A man was in the park* could also be base-generated; and since existential *be* assigns only one thematic role, it would give exactly the same result as (107d) with movement. This seems to be a peculiar fact about this one verb because, of course, any other NP Movement in the absence of UP results in a violation of the conditions on well formed R-Structures, as we have already seen.

3.3.2. WITH A LEXICAL ANALYSIS

A potential problem with the preceding approach emerges when we consider infinitival constructions. We have already argued that there are only two viable alternatives for accounting for the passive in infinitives: NP Movement with PRO or a lexical rule. If we adopt the first alternative, we may maintain (106), because the assumption of PRO in [−TENSE] sentences gives the results in (108). But in the lexical alternative, where we would assume coindexing of infinitival VP with an antecedent, it appears that *expect,* as well as *persuade,* will assign **theme** to the dummy NPs. The examples in (109) illustrate.

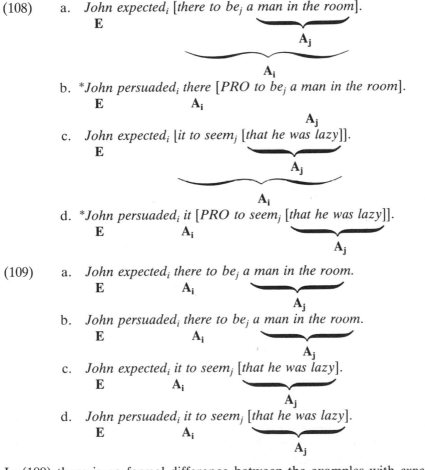

(108)   a.   *John expected$_i$ [there to be$_j$ a man in the room].*
            E

                          A_j

                          A_i

        b.   **John persuaded$_i$ there [PRO to be$_j$ a man in the room].*
            E A_i

                                    A_j

        c.   *John expected$_i$ [it to seem$_j$ [that he was lazy]].*
            E

                          A_j

                          A_i

        d.   **John persuaded$_i$ it [PRO to seem$_j$ [that he was lazy]].*
            E A_i

                                    A_j

(109)   a.   *John expected$_i$ there to be$_j$ a man in the room.*
            E A_i

                                    A_j

        b.   *John persuaded$_i$ there to be$_j$ a man in the room.*
            E A_i

                                    A_j

        c.   *John expected$_i$ it to seem$_j$ [that he was lazy].*
            E A_i

                                    A_j

        d.   *John persuaded$_i$ it to seem$_j$ [that he was lazy].*
            E A_i

                                    A_j

In (109) there is no formal difference between the examples with *expect* and those with *persuade.* If (106) applies to these examples, we would expect all to be ungrammatical, but those with *expect* are not. The solutions, on this approach, are therefore the following: Either *expect* does not assign a thematic role to the NP direct object or (106) must be modified to ignore **theme** assigned to dummies in such cases. The second alternative is not particularly attractive, because it renders vacuous the notion of **theme** as a thematic role with semantic content. In effect it functions as a diacritic for direct objects, much the same as abstract case. We thus conclude that verbs like *expect* do not assign a thematic role to their direct objects in the infinitival construction.

Making this assumption allows us to formulate a rule that expresses in a relatively straightforward way the semantics of *expect*. In the case where the complement is a *that*-clause, the expectation is the proposition expressed by the complement. The S-complement is assigned the **A** of *expect*. Where the complement is infinitival, the content of the expectation is the proposition of which the infinitive is the predicate. Recall that the result of coindexing for predication is the creation of a proposition (see Chapter 2, Section 1). In this case *expect* assigns **A** to the result of the coindexing. Thus *We expect John to leave* and *We expect that John will leave* will have essentially the same interpretation, as will *John expects to leave* and *John expects that he will leave*. In all of these cases the **theme** of *expect* is a proposition. The result of this reformulated role assignment is shown in (110).

(110)   a.   *John expected$_i$ [there] [to be$_j$ a man in the room]*

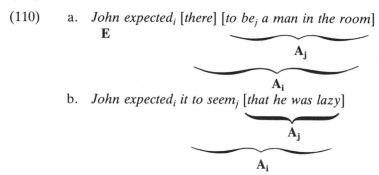

           b.   *John expected$_i$ it to seem$_j$ [that he was lazy]*

The sentences of (110a) and (110b) are well formed because **A** is assigned to the proposition, leaving *it* and *there* with no role, as required by (106).

Given this revised analysis, we can readily capture the lexical difference between *persuade* and *expect* by including in the lexicon the fact that *persuade* requires a **theme**, a **patient**, and a prepositional **goal**, whereas *expect* requires just a propositional **theme**. The advantages of the type of simplification of the base component that results from such lexical information is discussed in detail in Chomsky (1981).

3.3.3. IMPERSONAL CONSTRUCTIONS

Compare next the following examples.

(111)   a.   *It is believed that the world is flat.*
        b.   *⁺It was hit John by Mary.*

Example (111a) may be derived by assigning to the extraposed complement the thematic role that is governed by *believe*, and by assigning no
role to *it*. But then we would expect the same sort of derivation to apply
in the case of Example (111b). We must make the further assumption,
therefore, that the extraposed position in V^2 is propositional, in the sense
of Grimshaw (1979a). Notice that the extraposed position cannot be restricted to S', because of examples like the following, where the "extraposed" constituent is an NP.

(112)   a.   *It's amazing the way Mary wins at the races.*
        b.   *It's obvious* $\left\{ \begin{array}{l} \text{what we should do.} \\ \text{what to do.} \end{array} \right\}$
        c.   *It's disgusting the foods that John eats.*

In languages like French we find a construction precisely like (111b),
the impersonal passive. For example, Kayne (1975, pp. 245–246) cites the
following (the translations are Kayne's):[61]

(113)   a.   *Il a été mangé beaucoup de pommes hier soir.*
             'There were eaten many apples last night.'
        b.   *Il sera détruit une centaine d'habitations.*
             'There will be destroyed about a hundred dwellings.'

We find *il* in French not only in the impersonal passive, but also in the
existential construction and with *semble* 'seems'.

(114)   a.   *Il y a un homme dans le parc.*
             'There is a man in the park.'
        b.   *Il semble que Jean aime bien Marie.*
             'It seems that John likes Mary.'

As in English, the French dummy *il* cannot have a thematic role assigned
to it. What is different between the two languages, apparently, is that in

[61]It appears that the passives in the English translations in (113) cannot have underlying
structures in which *there* is generated in the subject position of a simple passive, because of
the restriction against assigning a thematic role to it. Thus, these examples must be derived
by a "stylistic" rule as we will discuss in what follows, or from an underlying structure in
which *be* is existential, not passive.

French it is possible for *il* to appear with an existential predicate. The analysis of the two languages will be the same, but in English *there* and *it* will be in complementary distribution, depending on whether the predicate has an existential interpretation or not.

It follows from our analysis that the *there* construction in English cannot occur unless the verb is intransitive. An intransitive verb is one that has an interpretation only for one role, essentially, so that if both **E** and **A** are assigned, we get an ill-formed interpretation (as in **John slept the bed*). If Role Assignment assigns only **A** to the direct object and no role to the subject, then in order for there to be a well-formed interpretation for the sentence the subject must be a nonreferring dummy. Otherwise we would get a violation of the Completeness condition. The state of affairs that we are describing occurs just in case the verb is intransitive, the only argument is object, and the subject is a dummy.

The analysis that we propose predicts that French will differ from English in the following way: In intransitive constructions where the subject NP appears in the VP, French will have *il*, and English will have *there* and not *it*. In fact, this prediction appears to be borne out by the following examples.

(115)   a. *Il est arrivé un homme.*
         b. **It arrived a man.*
         c. *There arrived a man.*

English has another *there*, which appears in examples like the following.

(116)   *There walked into the room several elephants wearing pajamas.*

This construction, which Rochemont (1978) calls "stylistic *there* insertion" (see Footnote 61), differs from the cases that we have been discussing here because in (116), the NP *several elephants wearing pajamas* appears in VP-final focus position. We hypothesize, therefore, that sentences like (116) are derived not from deep structures with empty subjects, but by a generalization of Complex NP Shift to subject position. Thus, (116) is derived from underlying (117).

(117)   [*Several elephants wearing pajamas*] *walked into the room*
         FOCUS[*e*].

This generalization of Complex NP Shift allows us to reformulate it as NP − FOCUS[*e*]; that is, we can eliminate the context term V before NP that is found in more traditional treatments (see Culicover and Wexler 1977, for example). Notice that because the subject moves into FOCUS in this construction, extraction is impossible. Contrast the following examples.

(118)   a. *There was a picture of Nixon hanging on the wall.*
         b. *There was hanging on the wall a picture of Nixon.*
         c. *Who was there a picture of hanging on the wall?*
         d. **Who was there hanging on the wall a picture of?*

For further discussion of FOCUS and extraction, see Chapter 5, Section 8.1, and Rochemont (1978, in press).

CHAPTER 4

Wh Movement

All previous accounts of *Wh* Movement in transformational grammar have, to our knowledge, treated it as either an unbounded, long-distance movement (Ross 1967, Bresnan 1977, etc.) or a rule constrained by a condition such as the Binary Principle (Culicover and Wexler 1980) or Subjacency Condition (Chomsky 1973) where the long-distance effect is achieved by iteration of the movement (successive-cyclic *Wh* Movement).[1] We suggest here that neither of these approaches is in fact optimal, and that instead the *Wh* Movement rule is, like all rules, subject to the Locality Condition. In that sense it is a "local" rule, but because of its form and its interaction with possible base configurations of English, it appears to be unbounded.

In this chapter we will discuss in detail *Wh* Movement into COMP. We will see that in order to get the correct results there is no need to consider the rule to be a successive cyclic one and that externally constraining it in such a way misses the significant fact that because of its form this rule can, in principle, operate over an unbounded domain. It will be shown that the interaction between the form of the movement-into-COMP rule and the structure of phrase markers in English results in a rule that seems to be unbounded, although in some examples it affects only adjacent domains. This rule defines its own domain of applicability, as do all rules, based on the interaction of its structural description with the LC.

A basic premise in what follows is that *Wh* Movement must be distinguished from "move NP." It is to be stated in terms of the movement of

---

[1]We are not including here nonmovement accounts, such as that of Koster (1978b) and Gazdar (1981), where the *wh* phrase is generated in COMP position in the base, and binds a gap.

a specific term to a designated position, rather than just in terms of "move category." In other words, this rule makes crucial use of a more complicated structural description. In our discussion of this rule we will distinguish between *Wh* Movement to COMP and movement to FOCUS, which covers the stylistic rules and Topicalization.[2] As was pointed out in Chapter 1, we assume that all movements fall into three basic categories: movement to an argument position, movement to COMP, and movement to FOCUS.[3] We assume that movements are structure preserving and subject to the LC. Movement to a designated position is also subject to the LC and is in the appropriate sense structure preserving (in a sense similar to that of Emonds's [1976] sentence boundary condition).

1. The Rule for Preposing into COMP

Wh Movement in English moves a *wh* phrase (an interrogative or relative phrase) to the left into complementizer position. As COMP is a specifier position, movement of a constituent into COMP position must be, formally, movement of a specifier, if the rule is to conform to the structure-preserving requirement. In a discussion of the rule for preposing into COMP there are essentially two issues that must be addressed: what may move and how the rule gives the effect of long-distance movement. It is known that the constituents affected by *Wh* Movement are NP, AP, and PP. It is important, therefore, that however the rule is written it pick out these terms. Exactly these categories (plus the progressive form of verbs) form the natural class of $[-v]$, according to the feature system suggested for independent reasons in Culicover (1980):

(1)	Gerund	A[4]	N	Passive	V	Progressive	P	?
[N]	+	+	+	−	−	−	−	+
[V]	+	−	−	+	+	−	−	+
[A]	−	+	−	+	−	+	−	+

[2]Topicalization is movement to FOCUS on the left and obviously has different properties from rightward movement to FOCUS. The well-known similarities between *Wh* Movement and topicalization (see Chomsky 1977) we attribute to the fact that both are movements to sentence-boundary, nonargument, designated positions and both are subject to the LC. The rule of Movement to FOCUS is discussed in Chapter 5.

[3]There are also the strictly local rules, which do not concern us here.

[4]We assume that the category A includes adjectives and adverbs. Following Emonds (1976), it seems reasonable to treat the latter as realizations of the former when they are modifiers of verbal rather than nominal heads.

Given the assumption that the rules of core grammar obey the requirement of structure preservation, and given the assumption that *Wh* Movement moves a constituent into COMP which is the specifier of S, then this
rule must be the movement of a specifier. Specifically it must be the movement of the specifier of $[-v]$, that is, the categories NP, AP, and PP. Under
the strictest interpretation of the notion of structure preservation
SPEC$[-v]$ would have to move into exactly another SPEC$[-v]$ position.
However, COMP, by virtue of being the specifier of the M system, is a
$[+v]$ specifier. The SPEC$[-v]$ evidently may move into COMP in weakly
structure-preserving fashion in the sense that it need not match with respect to the feature; only the category type is relevant.

The rule for preposing into COMP we therefore formalize as in (2),
assuming also the condition in (3).

(2)   COMP   –   SPEC$[-v]$ $\Rightarrow$ $2 - \emptyset$
                          $[+\text{WH}]$

(3)   The reordering of a specifier must be construed so as to reorder
        the maximal phrase of which that specifier is the leftmost
        constituent.

It is Condition (3) which assures that the whole $[-v]$ category is fronted.
This condition is basically a positive version of the Left-Branch Condition
(Ross 1967), and would be subject to variation (or perhaps parametrization) if there are languages with left-branch specifiers which allow these
specifiers to be moved away from their heads.

In the structural change of (2) we mean to indicate that the moved
constituent fills an empty COMP. The result is a COMP dominating the
moved constituent. The COMP must be empty because we assume, along
with most researchers, a prohibition against doubly filled nodes. This rule
correctly affects the movement of NP, AP, and PP as the progressive, the
only other $[-v]$ category, does not have a specifier. We analyze AUX, the
logical candidate for specifier of the VP, not as a specifier but rather as
the head of S.

The effects of *Wh* Movement and Condition (3) are as illustrated in (4).
Because of (3) the movement of the specifier affects the movement of the
major category which contains it. (See discussion of the specifier of PP in
Section 5.7 of this chapter.) Consideration of the illustrative examples in
(4) naturally raises many issues, which we will address presently.

To illustrate more precisely the functioning of (2) constrained by (3) we
consider some simple cases as in (5).[5]

---

[5]We eliminate the feature $[-v]$ on nodes for expository convenience. Because of general
conventions, we will refer to the SPEC of N as DET.

(4)   a.

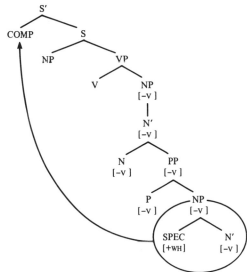

b.

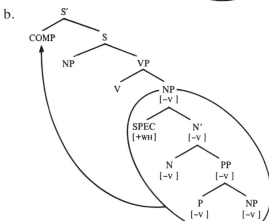

c.

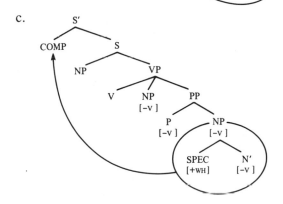

d.

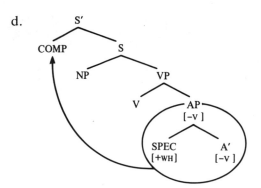

e.

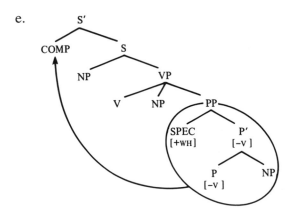

(5)   a.

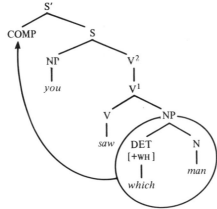

   b.

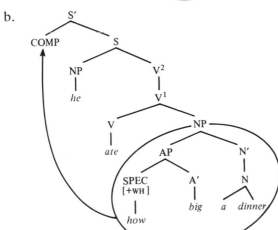

   c.

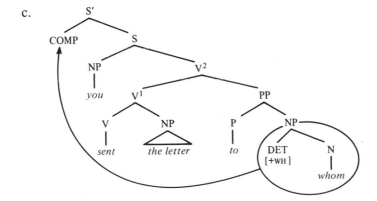

We are assuming that *wh* is generated in the base in specifier position and that unanalyzed *wh* words also have [+wh] determiners. In this way we regularize the syntax of *wh* forms in that they are all identical in at least one property, namely, that of having a [+wh] determiner. In all three cases of (5), where Rule (2) moves the SPEC of [-v], the condition in (3) assures that a whole major category moves to COMP position with the *wh* determiner. The condition is written to assure that in a case like (5b) the movement of the SPEC of the AP affects the larger NP, as the SPEC of the AP is the leftmost constituent of the NP. Next, consider the examples of (6).

(6)   a.

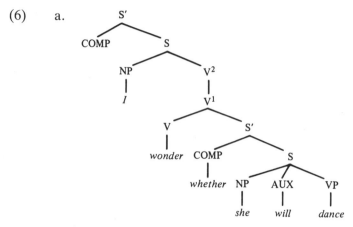

b. *Whether did I wonder she will dance?
c. *Whether she will dance did I wonder?

Whether is a *wh* specifier, but it is not a specifier of [−v].[6] Thus, both Examples (6b) and (6c) are blocked. Neither S′ nor COMP by itself can be reordered by *Wh* Movement. The statement of the *wh* fronting rule as the movement of a [-v] category with *wh* specifier means that exactly the correct constituents are affected by the transformation.

2. Extraction from Embedded *That*-Clauses

In our analysis the base rules for English specify that S′ is realized as COMP S. Given the LC, if an embedded clause has an empty COMP then it will be possible to move a *wh* phrase out of it. If, however, a clause contains a filled COMP, the LC will block movement of a constituent over

---

[6]We assume that S′ is [+v] and [+m]; therefore, *whether* is SPEC[+v, +m].

this COMP and into the COMP of a higher clause. Consider the following examples:

(7)   a. *Who does John $\left\{\begin{array}{l} dispute \\ ridicule \\ repeat \end{array}\right\}$ *(the fact) that Bill saw 0 ?*

      b. *Which discovery did those facts undermine the claim that Harry made 0 ?*

      c. *What did that John bought 0 bother Bill?*

      d. *Which cookie did the fact that Mary ate 0 annoy Tom?*

      e. *Which movie did John eat so much that he could hardly watch 0 ?*

Wh Movement will always produce unacceptable results when a constituent is extracted from a factive *that*-clause [(7a)], a complex NP [(7b), (7d)], a sentential subject [(7c)], or a result clause [(7e)]. In each of these cases there is a COMP (namely, the COMP dominating *that*) which is contained in the variable between the matrix COMP and the moved constituent. A comparison of the examples in (7) with that in (8) illustrates the necessity of a refinement of the notion "contained in the variable" as it is relevant for the LC with respect to the rule of *Wh* Movement.

(8)   a. *Who would the fact that the winner was a woman bother?*

      b.

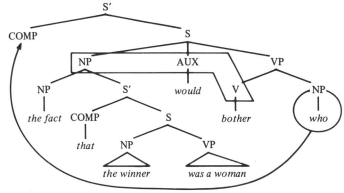

In (8b) the embedded COMP does not block the movement of the object NP because it is in an important respect "too far down" in the phrase marker. It does not c-command the constituent which moves. Evidently the c-command relation is important in the analysis of the variable material for this movement. The nodes of the phrase marker which correspond to the variable in the *Wh* Movement rule and which do c-command the target constituent are indicated by the enclosure in (8b). Compare the examples in (7′), which would be the phrase markers underlying (7a) and (7b), with (8b).

(7′)   a.

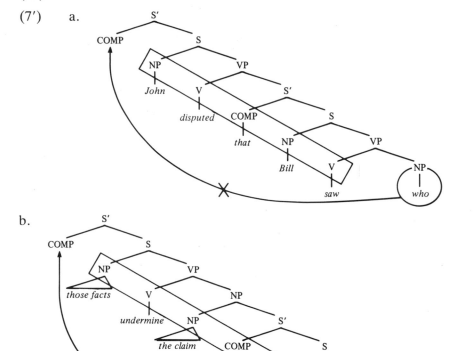

b.

Thus (7′a) and (7′b) illustrate cases where a COMP in the variable material c-commands the constituent to be moved by the rule and the result is ungrammaticality. This brings us to the instantiation of the LC for *Wh* Movement; given in #5:

(9)   ***Locality Condition:*** *All rules are local.*
          ,#1. P Coindex affects an X which is bijacent to NP.
          #2. D Coindex affects the closest preceding NP to X.
          #3. NP Movement affects minimally distant terms.
          #4. Binding affects the closest eligible NP to [e].
          #5. Wh Movement affects relatively adjacent terms.

Referring to the analysis of a phrase marker as indicated by the enclosures in (8b) and (7′) as the "chain of command" (i.e., the set of nodes that c-command the target constituent), we can correctly define "relatively adjacent terms."

(10)   **Definition:** *Two terms, A and B, are* **relatively adjacent** *where*
       (a) A and B are terms of the structural description of an operation which functions on a phrase marker,
       (b) A − B is to be understood as A − X − B with X = the chain of command, and
       (c) X does not contain any instance of an A^i or B^i for $0 \leq i \leq$ max.

Given this definition, #5 of the LC restricts the application of *Wh* Movement to just those cases where the chain of command contains no COMP. (We will see presently that the chain of command is also restricted from containing a *wh*.) We speculate that the fact that it is only the chain of command which is relevant for *Wh* Movement is connected to the fact that a moved *wh* takes scope over the domain which it c-commands. In other words, a COMP in the chain of command would be a "possible" landing site for a moved *wh* whereas a non-c-commanding node would not be.

Consider next the examples in (11)–(13).

(11)   *Who does Mary believe (that) John said (that) Bill hit 0?*

(12)   *Which woman did you* $\left\{ \begin{array}{l} \text{a. } think \ (that) \\ \text{b.*} forget \ why \\ \text{c.*} answer \ that \end{array} \right\}$ *he hit 0 ?*

(13)   a. **What did John quip that Mary wore 0 ?*
       b. **What did John complain that he had to do 0 this evening?*
       (Examples in (13) from Chomsky 1973, citing Dean 1967)

For each of these examples there is a COMP that c-commands the target node. But in (11) and (12a) *Wh* Movement produces acceptable sentences. The important fact illustrated here is that *Wh* Movement is permitted over a **superficially optional** complementizer, that is, over a complementizer that is not obligatory in Surface Structure. As noted in Chomsky (1973), precisely this fact is pointed out by Dean (1967): Verbs that require a following *that* do not allow *Wh* Movement.

In our framework the correlation between the occurrence of an obligatory *that* and the blocking of *Wh* Movement is not accidental. Where a lexically designated complementizer in the variable material c-commands the target *wh*, the rule cannot apply. We assume that certain verbs subcategorize particular complementizers (e.g., *wonder*, [+ ___wh] or *shout*,

[+ ___ *that*] [see Grimshaw 1979a]). *Believe*, on the other hand, subcategorizes simply S′. We chose this representation rather than saying that
believe subcategorizes a bare S because the bare-S analysis seems to be
the equivalent of subcategorizing for [*e*] in COMP. This would be a violation of the Principle of Free Dummies which we discuss in Chapter 5
and which is important in the demonstration of learnability. The relevant
base rules which we assume are therefore as given in (14) (subject to slight
revision in what follows).

(14)   a. VP → V S′
        b. S′ → (COMP) S
            [±WH]

If the S′ complement of a verb is well formed only with a lexically
realized complementizer then it will never be possible to extract anything
from the complement. Thus we predict that verbs that obligatorily take
that, for example, will not allow extraction; this prediction is known to be
correct on the basis of examples involving verbs like *scream*, *whisper*,
shout, etc., which have already been mentioned, and which are further
illustrated in (15) and (16).

(15)   a. *John screamed* $\left\{ \begin{matrix} that \\ *\emptyset \end{matrix} \right\}$ *he had to fix the sink.*

        b. *Mary whispered* $\left\{ \begin{matrix} that \\ *\emptyset \end{matrix} \right\}$ *Fred was very angry.*

        c. *Horace shouted* $\left\{ \begin{matrix} that \\ *\emptyset \end{matrix} \right\}$ *Ivan couldn't do anything.*

(16)   a. **Which sink did John scream that he had to fix?*
        b. **How angry did Mary whisper that Fred was?*
        c. **What did Horace shout that Ivan couldn't do?*

Compare the examples in (16) with those in (17), in which there is no *that*.

(17)   a. *Which sink did John believe he had to fix?*
        b. *How angry did Mary say Fred was?*
        c. *What did Horace think Ivan couldn't do?*

If *that* is added to the examples in (17) they are still grammatical:

(18)   a. *Which sink did John believe that he had to fix?*
        b. *How angry did Mary say that Fred was?*
        c. *What did Horace think that Ivan couldn't do?*

The deep structure for an example like (18a) is as given in (19).

(19)

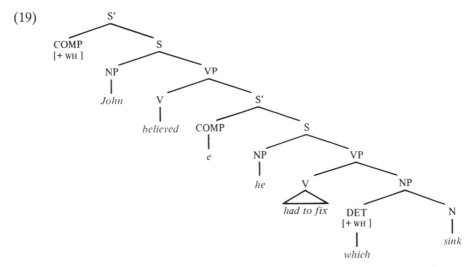

Because the embedded COMP is empty, movement over it may take place. If it were lexically designated, that is, if lexical insertion had taken place in (19) to insert *that*, then *Wh* Movement would be blocked.

In an analysis in which *wh* constituents may (more or less) freely move out of *that* complements, there must be some additional mechanisms to rule out the sorts of derivations illustrated here where extraction is ungrammatical. In the analysis that we are adopting, an additional mechanism is required to insert *that* before the complements of verbs like *believe*, *say*, *expect*, etc. (the superficially optional *that*s). We assume there is a superficial rule, given in (20), which optionally realizes the empty COMPs as *that*.

(20) $_{COMP}[e] \rightarrow that \,/ \underline{\quad}[-v]^{max}$
         [-WH]

The rule in (20) contains a context ($[-v]^{max}$) because, as is well known, *that* cannot be inserted if the subject has been moved (cf. discussions of the *that t* filter; e.g., Chomsky and Lasnik 1977). This is shown in (21a). We state the context in terms of $[-v]$, rather than NP, because of examples like (21b) and (21c).[7]

(21)   a. *Who does John believe that left?*
         b. *I believe that from LA to Boston is a long drive.*

---

[7]As we discussed in Section 6 of Chapter 2, infinitives and gerunds, as in (i), are NPs and therefore $[-v]^{max}$.

(i) *John believed that* $\left\{ \begin{matrix} _{NP}[to\ leave] \\ _{NP}[leaving] \end{matrix} \right\}$ *would be a mistake.*

    c. *I believe that easy to please is the thing to be.*

Before continuing on to other aspects of movement to COMP, we briefly recapitulate our analysis up to this point. We assume that *Wh* Movement is a (weakly) structure-preserving movement to COMP. The rule is formally stated as specifier movement (for reasons of structure preservation in core grammar) and it is universally construed (perhaps subject to parametrization) so as to move the maximal $[-v]$ constituent of which the specifier is the leftmost constituent. The LC predicts that movement to COMP is permitted only where no nonempty COMP or SPEC occurs in the chain of command.[8] We have already illustrated that this prediction is correct with respect to *that*-complementizers. In other words, we have shown that the LC subsumes the Sentential Subject Constraint, the Complex NP Constraint, the generalization about obligatory *that*s pointed out by Dean (1967), plus certain other cases not previously accounted for, at least by these constraints [e.g., the prohibition against extraction from result clauses as in (7e)]. We next illustrate that the LC makes the correct predictions for other complementizers and then that it is also correct about specifiers in the chain of command.[9]

3. *Wh* COMPs in the Chain of Command

Given our statement of the *Wh* Movement rule, the LC says that any c-commanding COMP in the variable material, not only *that*, ought to block the movement. The examples in (22) show cases where an intermediate COMP contains a *wh* term.

(22)   a. **Who does John like the man who saw 0 ?*

---

[8]In a language like Spanish an embedded COMP is always lexically realized, but extraction is permitted:

  (i) *Cuál galleta dijiste   que Benjamín quiere comer?*
      which cookie said-you that Benji   wants to eat

This means that in the relevant sense this *que* is equivalent to the superficially optional *that* in English. It may be possible to capture this similarity in terms of the markedness of the COMP, as *que* + aspect (e.g., clauses that require the subjunctive) and the COMPs *aunque*, *para que*, etc. all block extraction.

[9]Although it is not directly relevant to our discussion of the syntactic properties of *Wh* Movement, we point out that we assume that the semantic scope of *wh* is assigned by a rule of interpretation that applies to Deep Structure, not to Surface Structure. (This rule may possibly be the rule of Quantifier Interpretation of van Reimsdijk and Williams 1982.) The role of Surface Structure in determining the scope of *wh* is to constrain the class of derived structures consistent with a particular scope assignment. The syntactic scope of a moved *wh* constituent at the surface is the S that it c-commands.

   b. ?*What does John forget when to do 0 ?*
   c. ?*What did John remember why he bought 0 ?*
   d. **Who did the man who saw 0 talked to John?*
   e. **What did the man who ate 0 ordered dessert?*
   f. **Which issue is it what they stand for on 0 that we object to?*
   g. **Which mazurka did we question her about who danced 0 ?*

These examples are all correctly predicted to be ungrammatical [see discussion in what follows of cases like the questionable (22b) and (22c)]. The examples of (23) are ungrammatical for essentially the same reason: The COMP *whether* lies in the chain of command.

(23)   a. **What did John forget whether he ate 0 ?*
       b. **Who did John ask whether 0 saw the man?*

A comparison of Examples (22) and (23) with (24) shows why, again, with respect to the variable material, it is important to consider only the nodes in a given phrase marker that c-command the node that corresponds to the rightmost term of the rule.

(24)   a. *When did John forget what Harry would do?*
       b.

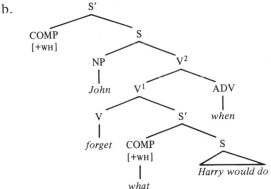

Sentence (24a) represents a case where a *wh* (the *what* in the embedded clause) originates between the COMP and the *wh* to be moved. What is crucial here is that the intervening *wh* does not c-command the target *wh*, as the phrase marker (24b) illustrates. Compare this to a case where the *wh* adverb to be moved is a constituent of the embedded clause.

(25)   a. *John will forget what Harry will do when by next week. (=*
         By next week, John will forget what Harry will do when.)
       b. **When will John forget what Harry will do 0 by next week?*

c.

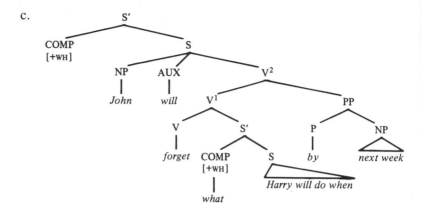

As (25c) illustrates, the embedded COMP c-commands everything in the embedded sentence. Consequently the movement of the embedded *wh* to the matrix COMP results in the ungrammatical (25b). A *wh* cannot be moved across a c-commanding *wh* COMP in the variable material.

Because of the particular branching structure in which COMP appears in English, the LC blocks extraction from embedded questions. Extraction is grammatical, however, from certain embedded questions[10]:

(26)   a.   *Which of the machines do you know how* $\left\{ \begin{array}{l} to\ fix? \\ the\ man\ fixed? \end{array} \right\}$

      b.   *?Who did you wonder when to visit?*

      c.   *?Which car did you ask where to park?*

To the extent that (26b) and (26c) are only marginal, they are certainly better than corresponding examples where the embedded *wh* term is a multiword phrase or where it is not adverbial:

(27)   a.   **Which of these machines do you know in what way the man fixed?*

      b.   **Where did you wonder* $\left\{ \begin{array}{l} what \\ which\ books \end{array} \right\}$ *to put?*

      c.   **Where did you ask* $\left\{ \begin{array}{l} what \\ which\ car \end{array} \right\}$ *to park?*

In order to account for the grammaticality of the examples of (26) we follow up on an observation made by Chomsky (1973) to the effect that the sequence *know how* occurs as a single lexical item, as in the NP *the knowhow*. We suggest that there is a local restructuring rule which forms

---

[10]For some reason, for some speakers, the examples with infinitival complements in (26) are more acceptable.

a single constituent out of a verbal element and a single-word adverbial term.[11] This is illustrated in (28).

(28)   a.

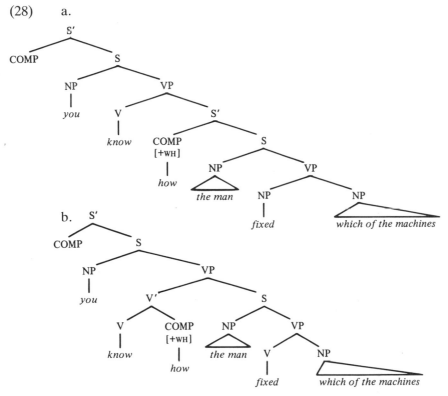

b.

By virtue of the restructuring, as (28b) illustrates, there is no COMP in the chain of command to block the movement of a *wh* term in the embedded clause. Evidence that restructuring provides the correct account of (26) comes from the contrasting acceptability illustrated in the examples of (29) and (30).

(29)   a.   *I figured out how to finance the new house.*
       b.   *What did you figure out how to finance?*
       c.   *I figured it out how to finance the new house.*
       d.   **I figured it out how to finance the new house.*
       d.   **What did you figure it out how to finance?*

---

[11]A similar local reordering rule, restricted to lexical *wh* words (as opposed to multiword phrases), might also be involved in the derivation of examples such as *They gave the book to someone, but I forget who to.* In Ross (1969) this construction is derived by the deletion rule of Sluicing: . . . *but I forget who [they gave the book] to* ⇒ . . . *but I forget who [∅] to;* see van Reimsdijk (1978) for still another analysis.

(30)   a.   *It was obvious when to visit Mary.*
         b.   *Who was it obvious when to visit?*
         c.   *It was obvious to Bill when to visit Mary.*
         d.   **Who was it obvious to Bill when to visit?*

In (29b) and (30b), where restructuring takes place, extraction is allowed. In (29c) there is no contiguous verb for the *how* to restructure with and the result of movement is the ungrammatical (29d). In (30c) the restructuring cannot apply because the *wh* adverb is not adjacent to *be obvious*, and again movement is blocked as illustrated in (30d). Restructuring is a strictly local rule. Where it cannot apply the embedded COMP blocks any extraction out of the embedded clause.

Further evidence for the restructuring rule which we are proposing comes from the rule of Gapping. Gapping deletes verbs, or verbal sequences, but cannot generally delete material in COMP even if it immediately follows the verb. In the examples of (31) and (32) the brackets indicate what is deleted in the second clause.

(31)   a.   *I [expect to try to stay] in the house, and Bill in the office.*
         b.   *I [bet] that the grey horse would win, and Mary that the palomino would (win).*
         c.   *I [asked] who was leaving, and Mary who was staying.*
         d.   **I [bet that] the grey horse would win, and Mary the palomino would (win).*
         e.   **I [asked who was] leaving, and Mary staying.*

If restructuring has applied to make the COMP part of the V constituent, then Gapping can apply:

(32)   a.   **Bill [knows which machines to sell] to women, and John to men.*
         b.   *Bill [knows how to fix] computers, and John calculators.*
         c.   **I [can't figure out in which place to park] my car, or Sam his truck.*
         d.   *I [can't figure out where to park] my car, or Sam his truck.*

Assuming our rule of *Wh* Movement, the LC, and the local restructuring rule (which affects verbal elements followed by *wh* adverbs), we have an accurate account of the extraction possibilities for embedded questions.

4. Extraction from *For–To* Clauses

So far in this chapter we have considered extraction out of clauses introduced by the *wh* complementizers and *that*. We now turn to a consideration of extraction out of embedded clauses introduced by the complementizer *for*. Consider the examples in (33).

(33)   a. *It is annoying to me for children to watch TV.*
        b. *It is annoying for parents for children to watch TV.*

What must be accounted for with respect to examples of this type is that
an NP that follows the preposition *for* may undergo *wh* Movement, but
an NP that follows the complementizer *for* cannot be moved (by any rule).
This is illustrated in (34) and (35).

(34)   a. *Who is it annoying to ∅ for children to watch TV?*
        b. **Who is it annoying to you for ∅ to watch TV?*
        c. *Who is it annoying for ∅ for children to watch TV?*
        d. **Who is it annoying for parents for ∅ to watch TV?*
        e. *What is it annoying (for parents) for children to watch ∅?*

(35)   a.(?)*Who is it easy for ∅ to watch TV?*
        b. *Who is it easy for ∅ for children to watch TV?*
        c. **Who is it easy for parents for ∅ to watch TV?*

Examples (34a), (34c), and (35b) show cases of *Wh* Movement applied
to prepositional objects and the result is grammatical. In contrast, (34b),
(34d), and (35c) show the cases which must be prevented where the *wh*
phrase that has been reordered originated next to the complementizer *for*.
Sentence (34e) again shows an acceptable movement, one where the NP
moved was in the VP of the embedded clause. Sentence (35a) is grammatical but sounds marginal probably because the *for* in this case is easily
misinterpreted as a COMP of the embedded sentence, as in *It would be a
pleasure for children to watch TV.*
    To account for these grammaticality facts we adopt an analysis of *for–
to* clauses based on that of Emonds (1976). This analysis involves a rule
of adjunction to *for* which is similar to Emonds's rule of *for*-phrase formation. Our rule, which we will call P$_*$-formation, functions as in (36).

(36)   a.

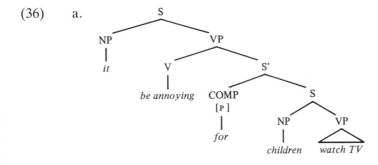

b.

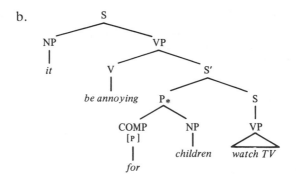

We are assuming here that *for* is a COMP which is a preposition and that the (modified) base rule for S′ is as in (37).

(37)   S′ → COMP S
        $\left\{ \begin{array}{l} [\pm \text{WH}] \\ [\text{P}] \end{array} \right\}$

The COMP can be either *for* or any of the other prepositions that P co-
    [P]
occur with S (e.g., *until, before, if, because, then, although*). With respect to the LC all of these COMPs function identically to block extraction from embedded clauses. *For* presents a special case because of the existence of the rule of P$_*$-formation.[12]

There are several advantages to a rule of P$_*$-formation (or *for*-phrase formation) at the observational level (see Emonds 1976). These include an account of the fact that object (rather than subject) forms of pronouns show up in this position and that no tense morphology shows up on the verb. (See Klima [1969] for discussion of the distribution of object pronouns).

At the theoretical level there is a problem with such a rule in that it results in a structural change without effecting a change in the output string. Rules of this type are ruled out in the learnability proof of Wexler and Culicover (1980) and in Chomsky (1973) and elsewhere. We suggest that such rules not be disallowed but that the result of any structure-

---

[12]We speculate that *for* is a special case because it is, at least in many instances, the realization of the subjunctive in English; see Emonds (1976) and Stockwell, Schachter, and Partee (1973).

changing, string-preserving rule must be frozen.[13] In this case the P_* formed by the adjunction of the NP to the P is frozen. This then explains why the NP sister to the COMP *for* cannot be moved, and hence the ungrammaticality of (34b), (34d), and (35c).

Where *Wh* Movement applies to a prepositional object of the matrix, there is nothing to explain; that is, the results are grammatical, as in (34a), (34c), and (35b). Where *Wh* Movement applies to an NP in the embedded VP the results are grammatical as long as it applies after P_*-formation. If *Wh* Movement, in a given derivation, were applied before P_*-formation the rule would be blocked as there would be a COMP in the chain of command. After P_*-formation the relevant node in the chain of command is a P and nothing stops the application of *Wh* Movement.

As we have argued, the frozen status of the P_* accounts for the ungrammaticality of the movement of an NP that it dominates. What must also be accounted for is the ungrammaticality of the movement of the whole P_*:

(38)   a. *For whom is it annoying to you ∅ to watch TV?*
        b. *For whom is it annoying for parents ∅ to watch TV?*

The ungrammaticality of these examples stems from the fact that there is no rule that moves P alone; the derived frozen P cannot undergo movement rules itself. This follows naturally from the fact that the node created by P_*-formation is not a phrasal node. It is a P and there is no rule in English, including *Wh* Movement, which moves a P.

This discussion of the possibilities for extraction out of *for–to* clauses brings us to a comparison of the LC with Bresnan's Complementizer Constraint on Variables (Bresnan 1976b). This constraint is given in (39).

(39)   **The Complementizer Constraint on Variables:** *For any proper analysis (. . . , X, A, Y, . . .) such that X and Y are variable factors and A is a constant factor to be deleted, if*
        $X = \underline{\quad} COMP$, *the* $\underline{\quad}$ *must be empty (of terminals).*

Since Bresnan here follows Ross (1967) in characterizing Question Movement as a "chopping" rule, and since "chopping" involves both copying and deleting, the constraint in (39) is applicable not only for deletions per se, but also for what we have been considering to be extractions. This

---

[13]A structure of this type (like P_*) must be frozen because if any other rule could apply to the result of a string-preserving rule the evidence of its application would be destroyed. The rule itself in this case would be learnable because of its readily observable consequences (e.g., phonological phrasing and the objective form of pronouns). A reasonable restriction on string-preserving rules, in order for them to be learnable, is that there must be some such observable result of their application.

constraint then means that a rule may apply to *A* either (*a*) where *X* contains COMP and nothing else or (*b*) where COMP is not the rightmost term of *X*. For example, the subject NP of an S may be moved where *X* is the left end variable COMP of S′, but otherwise it may not be moved. From (39), the ungrammaticality of examples like (34b) is properly predicted. This is shown in (40).

(40)

It is annoying to you for ——COMP	*children*	*to watch TV.*	
X	**A**	**Y**	

In this case COMP is the rightmost term of *X* and there are other elements in *X*, so deletion of *A* is blocked.

The constraint in (37) also correctly predicts the grammaticality of (34e). This is illustrated in (41).

(41)

It is annoying (for parents) for children to watch ——COMP	*TV.*	
X	**A**	**Y**

Here, because COMP is not the rightmost constituent of *X*, deletion of the object is permitted. For these two types of cases Bresnan's constraint and our analysis make the same predictions. There is a difference, however, with respect to *that* and *whether* clauses.

As already discussed at length, in Sections 2 and 3 of this chapter, we predict that any extraction whatsoever out of embedded clauses introduced by either *whether* or *that* should be ungrammatical. Bresnan would predict that there is a difference between the result of extracting a subject and that of extracting an object. Consider (42) and (43).

(42) a.

It is annoying to you that ——COMP	*children*	*watch TV.*	
X	**A**	**Y**	

b.

It is annoying to you that ——COMP	*children watch TV.*	
X	**A**	**Y**

(43) a.

You wondered whether ——COMP	*children*	*watch TV.*	
X	**A**	**Y**	

b.

You wondered whether ——COMP	*children watch TV.*	
X	**A**	**Y**

The results of applying *Wh* Movement to the (a) cases of (42) and (43) result in the obviously ungrammatical examples in (44). More interesting are the (b) cases in which an object is moved as shown in (45).

(44) a. *Who is it annoying to you that 0 watch TV?*
      b. *Who did you wonder whether 0 watch TV?*

(45) a.(*)*What is it annoying to you that children watch 0 ?*
      b.(*)*What did you wonder whether children watch 0 ?*

According to Bresnan the examples of (45) ought to be well formed, as the COMP is not the rightmost term of the variable X. By the LC both of the examples of (45) are ungrammatical, as in both cases a *wh* has been moved over a complementizer in the chain of command. According to our judgments and what has generally been claimed in the literature (see references to Dean and Chomsky given earlier) the predictions of the LC are somewhat more accurate than those of the Complementizer Constraint on Variables, and the examples of (45) are correctly prohibited.[14]

Summarizing the analysis of *for–to* clauses, we see that they behave differently from other embedded clauses with respect to *Wh* Movement. The presence of the complementizers *that* and *whether* (or the prepositional complementizers) effectively block *Wh* Movement from affecting any constituent contained in the following clause. Because of the rule of P_*-formation, however, the objects of embedded *for* clauses can be moved by *Wh* Movement. This is because the COMP is not in the chain of command once the restructuring has taken place.

5. Extraction from NP

Let us now consider the question of extraction from gerunds and other nominal constructions. We will see that the LC provides an account of extraction phenomena which has advantages over other current accounts. The LC correctly explains not only the possibilities (or lack of them) for extraction out of embedded clauses, but also the possibilities for movement out of NPs. This is possible because the LC refers crucially to the **form** of the rule, namely, the terms COMP and SPEC.

$$[+\text{WH}]$$

In gerundive nominals, there is a difference in extractability depending on whether there is a possessive NP occurring in the gerund.

---

[14]For some reason Example (45a) sounds better to us than either (45b) or the examples of (44). A related example, *Which TV show does it annoy you the most that your children watch?*, sounds quite acceptable. We have no ready explanation for this fact.

(46)   a. *Which movie did you anticipate seeing?*
         b. **Which movie did you anticipate Harry's seeing?*

The grammaticality difference between (46a) and (46b) might be accounted for by some version of the Specified Subject Condition (Chomsky 1973). For such a constraint the possessive NP would be considered the subject of the larger NP that it occurs in. Extraction by *Wh* Movement would then be prevented because movement cannot take place over a subject except through a COMP node, which an NP does not have.

Our approach will be rather different. For the LC it is not the subject-hood of the possessive NP which is relevant, but rather the fact that it is the specifier (determiner) of the gerundive nominal.[15] This is illustrated by a comparison of (47) and (48), which underlie (46a) and (46b) respectively, assuming an analysis based on Jackendoff (1977) and Akmajian (1977).

(47)

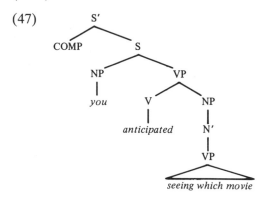

(48)

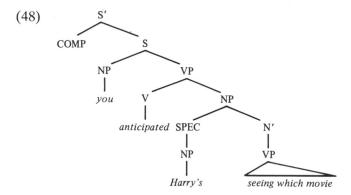

[15]Evidently it is not necessary that the SPEC be [+wh] for the LC. Any c-commanding lexically realized specifier will block *Wh* Movement.

The movement of the *wh* specifier of *which movie* is blocked in (48), but not in (47), because in (48) there is a lexically realized specifier that dominates the possessive NP and c-commands the *wh*. Where there is no specifier of the gerund there is no problem with *Wh* Movement.

The examples in (49) serve to illustrate that it is the specifier of the gerund that is relevant, and not the subjecthood of the possessive NP.

(49)   a. *Which book did you object to John buying?*
        b. **Which book did you object to John's buying?*

We assume that the gerundive nominal in (49a) contains an S (with AUX being the progressive realized as *-ing*) and that the nonpossessive NP in initial position is not a determiner. Whether gerundive nominals of this type are transformationally derived or the gerund is a base configuration (perhaps a small clause in the sense of Williams 1975 and Chomsky 1981), the crucial fact for our analysis is that the NP is not a specifier. Therefore extraction is permitted in the derivation of the grammatical (49a).

There is independent evidence that the structures of (49a) and (49b) are different, and that the subject of the gerund without the possessive marking does not function like a specifier. First of all, the true subject of a gerund can be extracted from the gerund, but the specifier cannot be; this is shown in (50) and (52). Second, the movement of the specifier *wh* effects the movement of the whole NP, by Condition (3), whereas the movement of the [+wh] subject cannot, as illustrated in (51). Example (53) shows that both constructions are NPs and may therefore be topicalized.[16]

(50)   a. *Who would you object to visiting Mary?*
        b. **Whose would you object to visiting Mary?*

(51)   a. **Who visiting Mary would bother you?*
        b. *Whose visiting Mary would bother you?*

(52)   a. *Bill, I would object to visiting Mary.*
        b. **Bill's, I would object to visiting Mary.*

(53)   a. *Bill visiting Mary, I would object to.*
        b. *Bill's visiting Mary, I would object to.*

The distinction in grammaticality illustrated in (49) could also be captured in a framework using (some version of) the Specified Subject Condition providing that it could make use of the sentential nature of the

---

[16]Notice that these facts support our analysis which includes Condition (3) in the sense that what is central to "pied piping" is not simply that a left branch be moved, but rather that a specifier be moved.

gerund in (49a) by saying that it contains a COMP, which would make *Wh* Movement possible. An example that serves to distinguish such an account and ours is given in (54).

(54)   **Which book did you object to the buying of?*

In this case the gerund clearly has a definite specifier but no subject.[17] Extraction by *Wh* Movement is ungrammatical, as the LC predicts. This leads us to a consideration of extraction out of NPs in general.

As the examples of (55) illustrate, extraction out of the complements of NPs without specifiers is permitted, but movement over a lexical specifier is again blocked.

(55)   a.   *Who did you see pictures of?*
         b.   **Who did you see John's pictures of?*
         c.   **Who did you see those pictures of?*
         d.   **Who did you see the picture of?*

It is precisely the class of specifiers that is relevant in the conditioning of *Wh* Movement. Other prehead elements in NP do not block movement:

(56)   a.   *Who did you see some pictures of?*
         b.   *Who did you see seven pictures of?*
         c.   *Who did you see beautiful pictures of?*

Interestingly, the so-called indefinite determiner patterns like the modifiers in (56) rather than like the specifiers in (55):

(57)   *Who did you see a picture of?*

To account for this fact we will assume an analysis of the indefinite "determiner" along the lines of Perlmutter (1969) where it is argued that it is a numeral. *A* is therefore a member of the category Quantifier and predictably does not block *Wh* Movement. The grammar then must require deletion of *a* after definite determiners, so that examples like **the a man* are blocked (compare: *the several men*).

In this discussion of extraction out of NPs, the NP Constraint of Horn (1974) and Bach and Horn (1977) is relevant. It says that there is no extraction whatsoever out of noun phrases. Our analysis predicts that there is extraction out of NPs with no specifiers. To compare the two analyses it is important to carefully choose the illustrative examples. Consider the following examples, based on Horn (1974).

---

[17]One could assume that *the* is a subject in this case, but then it would not be clear whether a coherent notion of subject exists that is any different from the notion SPEC.

(58)   a. *Which cavern did Jack search for a road into?
        b. *Which forest did Jack build a cabin in?   (≠ where)
        c. *Who did you deplore the brutal attack on?
        d. Who do you deplore brutal attacks on?
        e. *What did they witness the destruction of?
        f. What is it terrible to witness mindless destruction of?

        g. What did John $\left\{ \begin{array}{l} drink \\ (?)see \\ *break \end{array} \right\}$ a glass of?

The (c) and (e) examples are predictably bad because there is movement
out of an overtly specified NP. Horn would have to predict that the examples in (d) and (f) are also ungrammatical. We suggest, however, that
they are in fact grammatical. Their possible strangeness is attributable to
the fact that NPs with no overt specifiers in the relevant positions are a
bit strange even when no *Wh* Movement is involved, for example:

(59)   a.(?)You deplore brutal attacks on children.
        b.(?)It is terrible to witness mindless destruction of cities.

To the extent that an NP with no lexical specifier can be used in some
position, it is grammatical to extract from it, at least as far as the LC is
concerned.

   For the (a) and (b) examples of (58) the LC would predict well-formedness. For Horn, (a) is ungrammatical and (b) is ungrammatical in the
intended meaning (i.e., the NP rather than NP PP reading). We suggest,
however, that (58a) is in fact grammatical and (58b) is in fact ambiguous,
just as the corresponding examples in (60).

(60)   a. Which cavern did Jack discover a road into?
        b. Which city did Jack buy a house in?

   Example (60a) seems to be perfectly grammatical, and (60b) is certainly
ambiguous: The question could be either about the location of the house
or about where Jack did the buying. Although for some unexplained reason (58a) and (58b) seem less acceptable than the sentences of (60), we
claim that all are grammatical and that extraction can take place out of
NP.

   As these disputed grammaticality judgments do not constitute clear-cut
evidence one way or the other, we continue on to the examples of (58g).
Here again the LC cannot explain a case of ungrammaticality. However,
here the ill-formedness of *What did John break a glass of?* has nothing to
do with *Wh* Movement. The corresponding example where no movement
has taken place is also ill formed:

(61)   *John broke a glass of milk.[18]

The cases of (58g) with *drink* and *see* present no such puzzle.

Next we come to some very interesting examples, also discussed by Horn. In illustrating the prohibition of movement out of NPs which could certainly not be derived by relative clause reduction, he mentions NPs such as *the belief in god*, which are often considered immune to extraction. The LC explains this apparent immunity in terms of the fact that such NPs are usually definite. Notice that to the extent that an indefinite environment can be constructed, *Wh* Movement is acceptable:

(62)   a. *Who would it be impossible to question John's belief in?
        b. Who is it important to have a strong belief in?
        c. Who is it a waste of time to even hope for a belief in?

The relative grammaticality of (62b) and (62c) illustrates the fact that it is the specifier rather than a particular type of noun that determines the movement possibilities.

There is one particular type of example from Horn which might at first glance seem to contradict the theory of *Wh* Movement we are proposing. The examples involve copular structures where the predicate noun phrase appears to be specified by the definite determiner.

(63)   a. What city is John the mayor of?
        b. *What city did you see the mayor of?

We say "appears to be specified" because in point of fact *the* in just these copular structures is a lexicalized part of the noun. (For detailed discussion of this see Culicover 1980.) This fact is illustrated in (64a) and (64c), where the noun can appear with no determiner in exactly the same sense. The case of (64b) illustrates that it is only in the copular structure that this analysis is relevant, which is completely consistent with the extraction facts. Finally, (64d), which contrasts with (64c), shows that extraction is impossible when *the* is in fact a syntactic specifier.

(64)   a. John is (the) mayor of Los Angeles.
        b. We saw *(the) mayor of Los Angeles.

---

[18]Tom Smith-Stark suggests (p.c.) that the ungrammaticality of these examples has to do with the fact that *a glass of* in these cases is a measure phrase (i.e., that *glass* is not the head of the NP) and that things that come in glasses are not usually "breakable." These examples are ungrammatical for the same reason that (i) and (ii) are.

(i) *John broke the milk.
(ii) a.*John broke a liter of milk.
     b.*What did John break a liter of?

    c.   *Which city is John (the) mayor of?*
    d. **Which city did you insult (the) mayor of?*

The preceding analysis is also relevant to the well-known examples from Ross (1967):

(65)   a.   *The government prescribes the height of the lettering on the covers of the reports.*
        b.   *These are the reports which the government prescribes the height of the lettering on the covers of 0.*
        c.   *These are the reports the covers of which the government prescribes the height of the lettering on 0.*
        d.   *These are the reports the lettering on the covers of which the government prescribes the height of 0.*

The puzzle presented here is that any of the constituents contained within the NP object of *prescribe* may be moved by *Wh* Movement, as shown in (65) with movements of the various NPs (the PPs may also move but we return to this issue in Section 7). For a constituent to be moved by this rule it must have a specifier, in particular a *wh* specifier. However, for a term contained in a larger domain to be extracted from that larger domain there must be no c-commanding specifier. The extraction of *the reports* from the larger NP would seem to violate the LC. But notice that in the example underlying the relative clauses, (65a), the determiner is optional, just as in (64a). (*The* might not be optional with *height*, but this would be irrelevant as *the height* is undoubtedly a measure phrase inside QP.)

(66)   *The government prescribes ?(the) height of lettering on covers of reports.*

In these examples the specifier *the* has a generic reading. We suggest that the generic is a surface realization of the underlying specifier [*e*] in English. As this specifier is lexically null, it does not block extraction. This point can be readily illustrated, as in (67):

(67)   a.   *I enjoy (the) theater in New York.*
        b.   *What city do you enjoy (the) theater in?*

Sentence (67a) with *the* is ambiguous with respect to the interpretation of the NP; it could be either definite or generic. Sentence (67b) illustrates that *Wh* Movement can apply over the generic specifier, but not over the definite *the*: It has only the one, generic, reading. The only specifier that can occur in the chain of command without causing ungrammaticality is the generic specifier, a realization of [*e*]. The LC correctly accounts for the facts here because it ignores empty nodes in the chain of command.[19]

Finally, returning to our discussion of the NP Constraint, we come to the issue of the impossibility of extraction from subjects. As Horn correctly points out, his constraint, which prohibits movement out of any NP whatsoever, is more general than Chomsky's Subject Condition, which specifically prohibits extraction from just those NPs in subject position. Nothing thus far in the LC theory will account for the ungrammaticality of *Wh* Movement out of a subject with no overt specifier, as in (68).

(68)   *Who did a book about annoy Tom?*

In order to account for this fact about subjects, we adapt an analysis based on the "antecedent-internal *e* condition" of Delahunty (1981). Although our use of the term "antecedent" is different from Delahunty's, the basic insight is his. Informally, the generalization is that an antecedent (either grammatical subject or antecedent determined by coindexing) cannot contain a gap.[20] Since all grammatical subjects are antecedents this obviously accounts for the often-noticed island nature of subjects. This particular account has some other interesting advantages as well, as illustrated in (69)–(72).

(69)   *Who did they expect a book about to be on the table?*

(70)   a.   *John kept a picture of Mary.*
         b.   *John kept a picture of Mary near him.*
         c.   *Who did John keep a picture of?*
         d.   *Who did John keep a picture of near him?*

(71)   a.   *Mary gave Alex a book about horses.*
         b.   *Mary gave Alex a book about horses open (to p. 21).*
         c.   *What did Mary give Alex a book about?*
         d.   *What did Mary give Alex a book about open (to p. 21)?*

---

[19]We are suggesting that generics that lack surface specifiers also lack deep specifiers, whereas generics with surface *the* are derived from an underlying [*e*] specifier. The difference between these two sorts of generics is one of definiteness; a specified NP is "definite" in the relevant sense, whereas an unspecified NP is "indefinite." This difference shows up clearly with examples like the following.

   (i)   a. *I like to eat rabbit.*
         b. *I am studying the rabbit.*
   (ii) a. *Rabbit upsets my stomach.*
         b. *The rabbit interests me.*

The indefinite interpretation is that of generic mass, whereas the definite interpretation is that of generic species.

[20]We do not state this condition in terms of extraction because Delahunty has shown that clefts are base generated. The condition can be seen as a way to formalize an insight, due originally to Bach, that there is no extraction out of presupposed information.

(72)   a. *John loaded paintings of Mary into the truck.*
          b. *John loaded paintings of Mary into the truck still wet.*
          c. *Who did John load paintings of into the truck?*
          d. **Who did John load paintings of into the truck still wet?*

For sentences like (69) we assume an analysis (as discussed in Chapter 2) where *expect* takes as its complements an NP followed by an infinitival VP rather than an untensed S. In other words, the object of *expect* is at no time in the derivation the structural subject of an embedded clause. It is, however, the antecedent of the infinitival predicate. By accounting for the ungrammaticality of (69) by the "antecedent" constraint, we need not consider the object NP to be the syntactic subject of the infinitive in order to be able to invoke a condition relevant to subjects.

The examples in (70)–(72) illustrate an advantage of the antecedent constraint over either the NP Constraint or the Subject Condition. In these cases extraction is permitted from object NPs [the (c) examples] except when they are antecedents [the (d) examples], by virtue of being coindexed with some predicate.

As is well known, there can be no movement out of any constituent moved into COMP (or FOCUS) position. Assuming that movement into nonargument position leaves a trace (that this is a necessary assumption is discussed in Chapter 5), then *Wh* Movement into COMP (and movement into FOCUS; i.e., Topicalization or the stylistic rules) leaves a trace. We generalize the relevant notion of "antecedent" to include the relationship between a moved constituent and its trace. The proposed condition therefore predicts that there can be no movement out of a constituent in COMP or FOCUS (see Delahunty, 1981, for more discussion).

The examples of (73) show that the antecedent constraint must be stated in terms of a "gap."

(73)   a. *Every boy thinks that some picture of Bill is ugly.*
          b. **Who does every boy think that some picture of is ugly?*
          c. *Every boy thinks that some picture of him is ugly.*

In (73a) *some picture of Bill* is the antecedent of *is ugly*, and (73b) shows that it may not contain a gap. In (73c) *some picture of him* is the antecedent of *is ugly* and at the same time contains a constituent, *him*, which itself has an antecedent, *every boy*. An antecedent may contain a term that is bound by some other antecedent as long as that term is not empty, that is, a gap. The antecedent constraint therefore is formalized as in (74), where the coindexing indicates the binding relationships and *e* indicates the gap.

(74)   * $\ldots A_i \ldots {}_{A_j}[\ldots e_i \ldots] \ldots C_j \ldots$

In summary, with respect to NPs, we have shown that the LC prevents extraction from overtly specified NPs but allows extraction from NPs with lexically null specifiers. Additionally, we have shown that the Subject Condition is actually a subcase of a constraint against extraction out of any antecedent. We now continue on to a discussion of cases of multiple whs.

6. Multiple *Wh*

The following sentences illustrate multiple occurrences of *wh*.

(75)   a. *What crimes does the FBI know how to solve?*
           b. **What crimes does the FBI know whether to solve?*
           c. **What books does John know to whom to give?*
           d. **To whom does John know what books to give?*
           e. *John knows what books to give to whom.*
           f. *John knows to whom to give what books.*
           g. **John knows what who saw.*
           h. *John knows who saw what.*
           i. **Who does John know saw what?*
           j. **What does John know who saw?*
           k. *Who saw what?*
           l. **What did who see?*

[Examples (a)–(h) are from Chomsky 1973, pp. 244–245]

Most current accounts of the syntactic distribution of multiple *wh*s use some version of what Chomsky (1973) has called the Superiority Condition (see, e.g., Wilkins 1977, 1980a). This condition and related ones seek to explain the apparent fact that where there is more than one *wh* in a string, if one of them is a subject then it is more "prominent" with respect to the rule of *Wh* Movement than is any object. This apparent prominence is illustrated in examples like (75g) versus (75h) and (75k) versus (75l). The movement of a *wh* object rather than the subject (i.e., movement of the object over the subject) results in ungrammaticality.

Before discussing our account of this issue, where we will show that in fact subjects are not necessarily more prominent than objects for *Wh* Movement, we will look at the more straightforward examples. Consider first (75a)–(75d), repeated here.

(75)   a. *What crimes does the FBI know how to solve?*
           b. **What crimes does the FBI know whether to solve?*
           c. **What books does John know to whom to give?*
           d. **To whom does John know what books to give?*

Examples like (75a) we already discussed in Section 3 of this chapter.

There has been a restructuring of *know* and *how* to form a complex verbal form *know how*. Therefore (75a) does not represent a violation of the LC.[21] The ungrammatical examples (75b)–(75d) are all explained as violations of the LC. This is illustrated in (76).

(76)

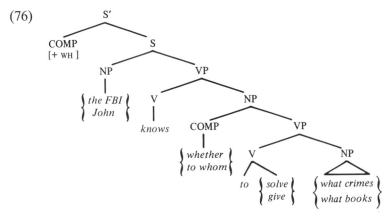

Each of these cases is the result of extracting a *wh* across a lexically designated [+WH] COMP. This is a violation of the LC and predictably results in ungrammaticality.[22] In (75e)–(75f), the movement of either *wh* into embedded COMP position is fine, and this is illustrated in (77).

(75) e. *John knows what books to give to whom.*
      f. *John knows to whom to give what books.*

(77)

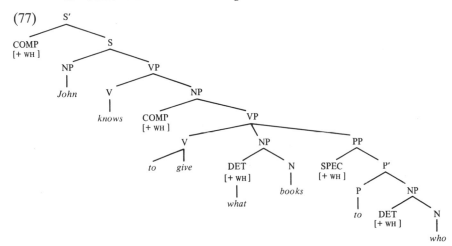

---

[21]For some speakers (75b) is well formed. This would mean that *whether* was considered an adverb and undergoes the restructuring rule. We will assume throughout that (75b) is ungrammatical.

[22]The phrase marker in (76) indicates our analysis, discussed in Chapter 2, where the infinitival complement to a verb like *know* is an NP (not an S′).

As can be seen in (77) either *wh* term can be moved without violating the LC. In neither case would there be a SPEC or COMP in the chain of command.[23]

This brings us to (75g) versus (75h) and (75k) versus (75l), which appear to illustrate the prominence of the *wh* subject. Any account of multiple *wh*s which maintains simply that objects may not be reordered over subjects cannot explain examples like (78b) or (79b).

(78)   a. *John knows which women chose which books.*
       b. *John knows which books which women chose.*

(79)   a. *Which women chose which books?*
       b. *Which books did which women choose?*

We suggest that the apparent prominence of *wh* subjects in the examples generally discussed in the literature is due to the choice of the lexicalized *wh* form *who* (or *what*) in subject position. Compare (80a) with (80b).

(80)   a.

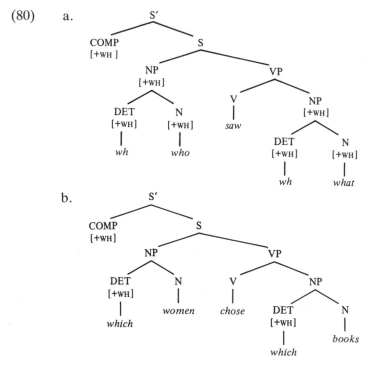

Example (80a) illustrates our assumption that *who* is a lexicalized *wh* form which inherently contains the feature [+WH]. Assuming additionally that an NP inherits the features of its head, we have an account of the gram-

---

[23]We will discuss the specifier of PP in Section 7 of this chapter.

maticality distinction between (78b) and (75g) or between (78b) and (75l). Movement of the object NP in (80a) means a reordering over a c-commanding [+WH] constituent, in this case the NP, which is a violation of the LC. The reordering of the object in (80b) involves no such violation as the subject NP is not [+WH]. By the LC *Wh* Movement is prohibited when there occurs any lexically realized COMP, SPEC, or [+WH] in the chain of command.

Returning to (75), the only examples left to discuss are (75i) and (75j), which are repeated here.

(75)   i. *Who does John know saw what?*
         j. *What does John know who saw?*

These could be the result of a movement into the embedded COMP and then a second application of the movement into the matrix COMP. They could also be the result of a single movement from the embedded clause into the matrix, but this would be out because of the requirements on the syntactic scope of *wh*. The intermediate structures, assuming the first movement into the embedded COMP, are as given in (81).

(81)   a.

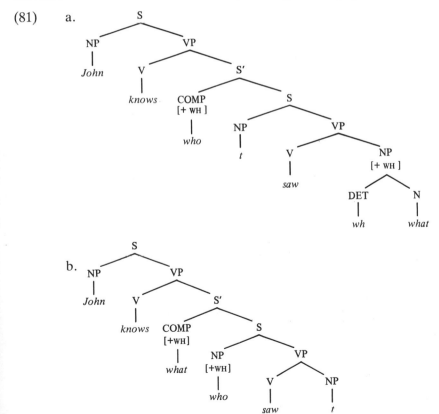

Example (81b) would be ungrammatical in itself because it represents a violation of the LC: *what* has moved across the [+WH] NP. However, (81a) is well formed and what must be explained is why *who* cannot move again into the matrix COMP. As far as the movement rule itself is concerned, there is nothing to prevent a second application. The result of such a second application, however, would mean that the verb *know,* which governs a [+WH] complement, would not co-occur with a [+WH] complement. Assuming, as we mentioned briefly in Footnote 9 of this chapter, that the semantic scope of *wh* is determined in Deep Structure, then *know* would take a complement containing a *wh* whose scope were exactly that complement. The syntactic scope of *wh* at S-Structure must then be consistent with its semantic scope. As the syntactic scope of *wh* is the whole domain it c-commands, there would be violation of this consistency requirement if in (81a) the *who* were to move again into the matrix COMP position. The result here is that once a constituent has moved into the embedded COMP position of a verb that requires a *wh* complement, it can move no further.[24]

With this understanding of the scope of *wh,* the LC provides an account of all the examples of (75) and has done so without recourse to other conditions on rule application and without the overgeneration inherent in the successive-cyclic account of *Wh* Movement.[25]

7. SPEC in Prepositional Phrases

We next consider the constellation of facts that has come to be known as P-stranding.[26] So far our analysis of *wh* obviously accounts for (82a), but (82b) needs further discussion [see Examples (4c) and (4e) given in Section 1].

(82)   a.   *Who did she dance with?*
         b.   *With whom did she dance?*

In order for the whole PP to move as in (82b) it is necessary that the PP have a specifier. This is exactly what we propose: PP, like the other

---

[24]Notice that where a verb does not subcategorize a [+WH] COMP (e.g., a verb like *believe*), the issue of the iteration of *Wh* Movement is irrelevant as there could be no movement into the embedded [−WH] COMP by *Wh* Movement in the first place (i.e., **John believed who saw the boy*).

[25]It is not clear how an example like (75i) or that in Footnote 24 would be ruled out in a theory generally requiring successive-cyclic *Wh* Movement.

[26]See Ross (1967), Chomsky (1981), van Reimsdijk (1978), Hornstein and Weinberg (1981), and Kayne (1981a).

three phrasal categories, has a specifier and this specifier may be either
[+wh] or [−wh]. (For discussion of the specifier of PP see Jackendoff
1973, 1977; see also van Reimsdijk 1978, where it is argued, for different
reasons, that PP has a COMP.) Only where the PP is generated with a
[+wh] specifier may *Wh* Movement affect it. The phrase markers in (83a)
and (83b) underlie the examples (82a) and (82b), respectively.

(83)   a.

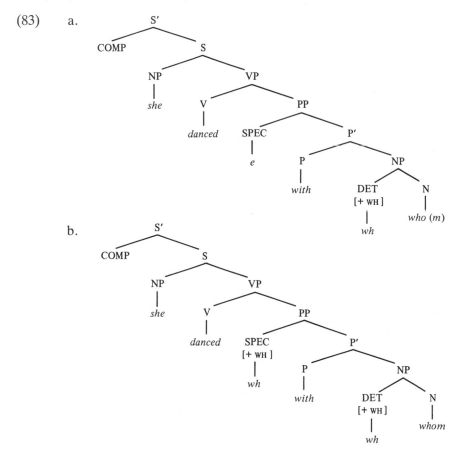

b.

To (83b) the only movement which can apply affects the whole PP. Where
the PP has a designated specifier the LC will prevent extraction from it.

This assumption that PP can have a [+wh] specifier regularizes the
analysis of *where* along the lines of the analysis of *who* and *what*. *Where*
is the realization of $_{P''}[_{SPEC}[wh]\ _P[where]]$. Other cases where the [+wh]
specifier is realized overtly on the PP would be, for example, in *whereby*,
when, *whence*, *wherefrom*, and *wherefor(e)*.

Our analysis of PP naturally requires that the specifier often have no overt realization. This is generally the case with the [−wh] specifier. The [−wh] specifier can, however, be realized as *right* or *just* or by various types of measure phrases (depending on the analysis of the PPs). That these constituents are indeed specifiers is illustrated in (84) and (85).

(84)   a.   *The man put the money right into the drawer.*
       b.   **Which drawer did the man put the money right into?*
       c.   *The woman parked the car just behind the barn.*
       d.   **Which barn did the woman park the car just behind?*

(85)   a.   *We drove seven more miles into the forest.*
       b.   **Which forest did you drive seven more miles into?*

Where the PP is overtly specified there can be no extraction from it.

Our analysis thus far provides for an account of both "pied piping" [by Condition (3) of Section 1] and P-stranding in English. However, as various researchers have recently commented, P-stranding is a very infrequent phenomenon in the languages of the world. In other words, an extraction from PP that leaves behind just the P is ungrammatical in the great majority of languages. This ungrammaticality is illustrated in (86) from Spanish.

(86)   a.   *A quién mandó la   carta 0 ?*
             to whom sent-he the letter
       b.   **Quién mandó la   carta a 0 ?*
             who   sent-he the letter to

In order to account for the facts of (86) and the general prohibition against P-stranding it would be possible to reformulate Condition (3) from Section 1, repeated here.

(3)   *The reordering of a specifier must be construed so as to reorder the maximal phrase of which that specifier is the leftmost constituent.*

Condition (3) could be reformulated so that extractions always affected the movement of a P along with any specified constituent within a PP. Any deviation from the reformulated (3) would then represent a marked case, perhaps requiring a complication of the SD of the rule of *Wh* Fronting.

Alternatively, the difference between languages that allow P-stranding and those that do not might be accounted for in terms of optional versus obligatory specifiers. Where the specifier of some category is obligatorily nonempty, as might be the case for PP, there can be no extraction from that category by *Wh* Movement.[27]

Another alternative account for the possibility of P-stranding in English could incorporate (some version of) the analysis of Hornstein and Weinberg (1981). This would make use of a restructuring rule which functions within VP (Ps outside of VP not being strandable in English).

For the present we adopt none of these alternatives. We suggest instead that the issue of whether or not Ps can be stranded by *Wh* Movement is not really of particular syntactic interest; that is, it does not represent a deep syntactic difference between languages. English permits stranded Ps because it happens both to lack a system of surface case and to permit certain prosodic structures which are not possible in many other languages. We predict that Ps can be left behind by a movement rule only if three separate conditions (none of which is syntactic) happen to be met: (*a*) Ps arc not obligatorily surface case assigners;[28] (*b*) Ps (prepositions or postpositions) are not encliticized onto their NPs; and (*c*) Ps are not obligatorily atonal. English (and a few other languages) happens to exhibit these three characteristics which, when taken together, allow Ps to occur alone in their PPs. We speculate that in languages where Ps are surface case assigners they must assign morphological case to their NPs in strictly local fashion (and not via a trace). Where Ps are clitics they must cliticize onto nonempty NPs, and not [*e*]. Finally, if Ps are obligatorily atonal (as in Spanish) they may not occur in a position that receives any emphasis in sentential stress contours, for example, in VP-final position. English is a language which essentially lacks a system of morphological case and whose

---

[27]There is some evidence that specifiers in Spanish are never really optional. Any constituent in subject position, for instance, must have an overtly realized specifier:

  (i) **Caballos comen pasto.*
       horses   eat   grass
  (ii) *Los caballos comen pasto.*
       the horses eat   grass
  (iii) *Los niños   comieron tacos.*
        the children ate   tacos
  (iv) **Tacos fueron comidos por los niños.*
        tacos were eaten   by the childen
  (v) *Los tacos fueron comidos por los niños.*
        the tacos were eaten   by the children

Under such an analysis, in Spanish, for there to be extraction out of the complement of an NP, there would first have to be extraposition of the constituent out of the NP. If there were no such rightward movement out of PP then there could be no P-stranding by Wh Movement.

[28]Kayne (1981b) attributes the difference in the grammaticality of P-stranding to a distinction between languages that assign "inherent case," the unmarked case, and languages such as English, which have lost this system.

prosodic structure indicates that Ps are not necessarily clitics and that they can in fact bear heavy stress.

In summary then, *Wh* Movement operates freely on all $[-v]$ constituents with $[+wh]$ specifiers. Syntactically, both examples like (82a) and (82b) are well formed. In many languages, however, a string corresponding to (82a) would be "unpronounceable" because of other (morphological and prosodic) factors.

Our analysis of *Wh* Movement has shown that this rule is subject to the LC. While illustrating the LC effects, we have assumed that *Wh* Movement moves a term into a nonargument position (COMP) and that, unlike NP Movement, it leaves a trace (which, as other investigators have shown, has effects on the phonological realization of sentences). In the chapter which follows we will show the necessity of these assumptions for learnability.

CHAPTER 5

Learnability and Locality

In the preceding chapters we explored the consequences of adopting a particular set of hypotheses about the nature of linguistic theory and the organization of grammar. In many respects these hypotheses are identical to or are versions of proposals in current linguistic theory, but we have made many simplifications so that the question of learnability could be addressed more easily.[1] In this chapter we propose to provide a theoretical foundation for this set of hypotheses in terms of learnability theory.

In the first section we will provide a review of learnability theory, pointing out the crucial assumptions and methodology. In the second section we will discuss the relevance of the restricted theory of structural descriptions, showing that the impoverished theory we are assuming can do a good deal of the work of other constraints. In the third section, we will suggest a revision of the learnability framework, which crucially involves a generalization of the Locality Condition. In the fourth section we will consider the problem of learning grammatical relations given thematic and Surface Structure input. Sections 5 and 6 investigate the types of errors

---

[1]Consider the Empty Category Principle (ECP) of current work (e.g., Chomsky 1981, Kayne 1981b), which stipulates that [*e*] must be "governed" in some particular sense. Assuming that some version of ECP is correct, we would like to understand why it is, and why it takes the particular form that it does. But we are unable to pursue this issue here.

In the course of this chapter we will assume that knowledge of phrase structure is used by the learner to make inferences about the possible presence of empty categories in Surface Structure. An alternative approach involving the ECP, following a point of view suggested in work by Stowell (1981) and Kayne (1983), would be to replace knowledge of phrase structure with a version of ECP and an abstract notion of "government," from which empty categories could be hypothesized. We will not speculate here about how we would have to revise the learning framework to address the learnability question for the government and binding theory.

contributed by transformations in this theory; Section 7 outlines preliminaries for a degree-0 learnability proof. Section 8 provides a brief discussion of some empirical consequences of the degree-0 theory.

1. A Brief Review of Learnability Theory

Because of the availability of Wexler and Culicover (1980) (henceforth *FPLA*), in which learnability theory is reviewed in detail and then considerably elaborated, the survey that we give here will disregard many technical details. Our intention is to address those particular aspects of earlier work which require revision so that they will conform to more recent linguistic theory. The reader is encouraged to consult *FPLA* for a more comprehensive introduction.

1.1. First Results

The earliest results in mathematical learnability theory were reported by Gold (1967). Gold investigated the "identifiability" of classes of languages in the Chomsky hierarchy (finite state, context free, etc.). Given data from one language in a given class, he asked, does there exist a learning procedure that can, before a particular finite time, determine which language in the class the data is taken from? Because the class of grammars for natural languages does not appear to fit into the Chomsky hierarchy, Gold's methodology has in general proven to be more relevant to the investigation of natural language learnability than have his particular results, but there is one negative result that is worth mentioning here: **There is no learning procedure that can identify a context-free grammar taken from the class of all context-free grammars given only a(n infinite) set of grammatical sentences from the language generated by the grammar.** The importance of this result follows from the fact that the class of transformational grammars includes the class of context-free grammars, and the data presented to the learner seems to consist essentially of grammatical sentences, which does not allow the learning of even the context-free grammars in Gold's framework.

This dilemma is resolved in the language learnability theory of Wexler and Hamburger (Wexler and Hamburger 1973; Hamburger and Wexler 1973, 1975; Wexler and Culicover 1980). From the point of view of linguistics, this approach makes three advances beyond Gold's work. First, it directly addresses the question of the learnability of transformational grammar, which Gold's work does not. Second, it introduces a significant enrichment of the data available to the learner. Third, it demonstrates that the adoption of constraints on rules of grammar can narrow the class of transformational grammars in such a way that a previously unlearnable class becomes learnable. We will elaborate these points in the next section.

1.2. The Degree-2 Theory

The early research on the learnability of transformational grammar was concerned, as was Gold's work, with the identifiability of the class of grammars given plausible input to the learning procedure. To prove identifiability it is necessary to show that there exists a finite time such that any grammar of the class can be identified before that time on the basis of data from the language that it generates. Crucially, there is no demand in this work that the time be reasonably short, in spite of what we know about the relatively short amount of time that it takes human children to learn their language(s). The goal of the degree-2 theory is to provide a learnability framework that is **feasible,** in the sense of Chomsky (1965): "Can the [learning mechanisms] succeed in producing grammars within the given constraints of time and access, and with the range of observed uniformity of output? [pp. 53–54]." In other words, the learning procedure must not only learn, but it must learn "easily," given the sort of primary data that is available to human children, and in the time span that we believe to hold for language learning. (See *FPLA*, pp. 21ff.)

The core of the degree-2 theory is the requirement that all of the evidence about the grammar of the language to be learned be present in relatively simple sentences. The theory thus rules out the possibility that there are rules of language that can be observed to operate only on very complex sentences, such as sentences with many levels of embedding.[2] Whether or not such rules exist is of course an empirical question, but it is worth observing that none have yet emerged in the course of empirical work on natural languages.

To summarize a bit more fully, the degree-2 theory is built on the following:

---

[2]We must distinguish between rules allowed by the theory of grammar that are not in the grammars of any language because of considerations of feasibility and rules of a particular grammar that cannot be acquired by the learner under certain conditions. If we stipulate that rule R is part of grammar G, then it would be incorrect to say that a learner had **acquired** grammar G unless the learner had constructed a grammar with rule R in it, or at least a grammar G' that satisfies a reasonable condition of equivalence with G.

On the other hand, there may well be rules allowed by the theory that will never be part of the grammar of any natural language. For discussion, see Lasnik (1981).

1.2.1. THE SETTING

The language learner L is presented with an infinite sequence of items of data from some language in the class of possible languages. The task that L has is to guess a grammar that will generate the language before some constant time t, where t does not depend on the language to be learned. It is assumed, therefore, that there is a principled bound on the time that it takes for any possible human language to be learned, although of course there may be individual differences among human language learners, and some languages may turn out to be learned more quickly than others.

1.2.2. ASSUMPTIONS ABOUT THE LEARNER

1. The learner does not have a memory for sentences it encountered in the past; it is only aware of the currently presented datum and its current hypothesis as to what the grammar of the language is.

There is no empirical evidence, so far as we know, that language learners are capable of remembering substantial quantities of linguistic data relevant to the language-learning task. So far as we know, any memory for past data is at best sporadic. However, assuming that the learner has no memory for past data introduces the possibility that a crucial datum occurred in the learner's environment too soon for the learner to take it into account in formulating the correct grammar.

The theory must ensure that important data are not irretrievably lost before they can be used; at the same time the learner is assumed to have no memory for past data. This problem is resolved by the assumption that all data have a greater than zero probability of occurrence; thus every datum will reoccur any number of times in the infinite stream of input data (see 1.2.4).

The prohibition against memory for linguistic data also raises a problem if it turns out that the learner has to **compare** pieces of data in order to arrive at the correct grammar. Whether there are rules of grammar that require comparison of data is an empirical question, and the degree-2 theory assumes that there are not. (See the discussion of "instantaneous" learning in Chomsky 1975, pp. 121–122 and *FPLA*, pp. 94–97.)[3]

---

[3]The learnability theory makes the minimal assumptions regarding memory in the learner, assumptions that appear to accord with empirical observations. The proof demonstrates that even with these very minimal assumptions, learning can occur. If more memory is attributed to the learner, then it may have the effect of facilitating learning (i.e., reducing the time). But without error-free memory for past data, the burden of limiting the range of hypotheses available to the learner must be placed on the formal constraints. See *FPLA*, Chapter 3, for discussion.

2. If the learner wants to change its hypothesis as to what the grammar of the language is, it may add a new rule to its grammar, or it may eliminate a rule from its grammar, depending on the evidence. Changing a rule is not allowed. It is an empirical question whether human learners change their grammars by adding and deleting rules one by one as assumed in the degree-2 theory. It is possible that they may approach the final grammar by modifying rules that they have already hypothesized. Or they may never abandon any rules at all, but simply add rules to the previous grammar as time goes on. In order for the last state of affairs to hold, the learners must be extraordinarily accurate in their initial hypotheses. We will return to this point in what follows.

3. At each point in time, then, the learner has a current hypothesis as to what the target grammar might be, and is presented with a datum from the actual target language. The learner determines the validity of its current hypothesis by ascertaining whether the new datum is consistent with that hypothesis. The formal representation of this testing procedure will be given in 1.2.7.

1.2.3. WHAT CONSTITUTES LEARNING

The degree-2 theory adopts the learning criterion of Gold (1967) that learning occurs when there is a time t such that the learner's hypothesized grammar is consistent with all new data about the language. Prior to this time, the learner occasionally has encountered data that its grammar could not "handle," in a sense to be made more precise in what follows. Such data resulted in a reformulation of the grammar. But after t, no such mismatch occurs. It is possible to imagine alternative criteria (see *FPLA*, Chapter 2), but currently there is no overwhelming empirical motivation for changing the criterion of the degree-2 theory.

1.2.4. THE CLASS OF GRAMMARS

The degree-2 theory assumes that the class of grammars that the learner must select from is the class of transformational grammars as specified in the *Aspects* theory of Chomsky (1965). To simplify the learning problem, it is assumed that the base component is universal, so that all that the learner really has to learn is the transformational component. In other words, the learner does not have to learn both the context-free phrase structure grammar that constitutes the base component **and** the transformational component that maps between base phrase markers and surface structures.

1.2.5. DATA

1. In the degree-2 theory, as in all prior work on language identifiability, there is a requirement that all relevant data have a greater than zero probability of occurring. Thus, in an infinite stream of data, say, sentences from the language, every sentence will occur not only once, but an infinite number of times. Crucially, no data relevant to the selection of the correct grammar will be withheld, and if it occurs too soon in the learning process, it will occur again. This assumption obviates in part the need for the learner to remember past data.

2. The data consist of (b, s) pairs, where b is a base phrase marker and s a surface string. Inasmuch as the learner could not actually be presented directly with base phrase markers, it is presumed that the learner possesses a procedure for determining the base phrase marker corresponding to a surface string from the string itself and the context in which it is uttered. Presumably, the most crucial aspect of the context is a plausible interpretation of the string, in some sense its "meaning."

1.2.6. THE LEARNER'S TASK

In the idealization of the degree-2 theory, the learner in essence has already available to it all lexical items that will appear in sentences of the language. The data consists, then, of examples of how these lexical items can be grammatically arranged, and what the examples mean. The task for the learner is to hypothesize the mapping T of transformational rules relating base phrase markers to the surface strings. The learner does not have to learn the base component, or the lexicon, which is a severe simplification of the task facing any human language learner, of course. Despite this radical simplification of the learner's task, the proof of learnability in the degree-2 framework is of considerable complexity and has considerable empirical consequences. (See *FPLA*, Chapter 4 for the proof, and Chapter 5, as well as Culicover and Wexler, 1977, for extensive discussion of some empirical consequences of the theory.)

1.2.7. THE LINGUISTIC EVIDENCE

The learner determines the grammar based on the linguistic evidence. The data, recall, consists of (b, s) pairs. What is to be learned is the mapping $T: b \rightarrow s$ (for all b generated by the base component). The evidence for the learner, then, consists of whether or not its currently hypothesized grammar actually maps b into s.

Let T_L be the currently hypothesized transformational component of the learner L, and let T_A be the target (or "adult") transformational component. Given a base phrase marker b, let $|R'| = T_L(b)$ be the surface **structure** that results from application of T_L to the underlying phrase marker b. Similarly, $|R| = T_A(b)$ is the surface structure that results from application of T_A to b.

The terminal string corresponding to a phrase marker is indicated by putting an asterisk before the expression defining the phrase marker. In the case of the surface structures discussed in the preceding paragraph, $s' = {}^*T_L(b)$ refers to the string generated by the learner's transformational component from b. The surface string s presented to L as part of the (b, s) pair is thus expressed as $s = {}^*T_A(b)$.

We say that there is an **error** in the learner's transformational component if the surface structure that it generates for b is different from the surface structure that the adult transformational component generates. However, even if the two structures are different, the terminal strings might be the same. Because the learner is presented with the strings and not the structures, in order for there to be evidence about an error, the strings must be different. There is a **detectable error** in the learner's transformational component if the string $s' = {}^*T_L(b)$ is not the same as the string $s = {}^*T_A(b)$ that the adult's transformational component generates.

The evidence that the learner has for the correctness of its hypotheses consists, then, of matches or discrepancies between s, the surface string that actually corresponds to b in the language to be learned, and s', the surface string that the learner's transformational component associates with b.

1.2.8. DEGREE-2 LEARNABILITY

The goal of the proof of degree-2 learnability is to demonstrate that the learner L can learn the correct transformational component given relatively simple data only. The measure of complexity of data is expressed in terms of the degree of embedding of the recursive node S in a phrase marker. A simple S that dominates no other S nodes is of degree 0; a phrase marker in which the top S node dominates another S node is of degree 1, and so on. A degree-2 phrase marker is therefore of the form given in (1).

(1)

In the degree-2 theory, S is the only recursive node that contributes to the complexity of the phrase marker, as measured by degree.

The method of the degree-2 proof is to demonstrate that if there is a detectable error in the learner's grammar, the error is detectable on a phrase marker of degree 2 or less.[4] Let us call this property of a class of grammars the **degree-2 property.** The demonstration that a class of grammars in fact has the degree-2 property allows a model of language learning with the essential property outlined in the introductory remarks to this section: The learner requires only relatively simple primary data as evidence for the rules of the grammar. Crucially, there is no rule of grammar, in the degree-2 theory, that is exemplified **only** by data of greater than degree 2.[5] As in this theory the only evidence for the learner consists of detectable errors, there cannot be any detectable error on a datum of greater than degree 2 that does not also appear on a datum of less than or equal to degree 2.

1.2.9. COUNTEREXAMPLES TO THE DEGREE-2 PROPERTY

As shown in *FPLA,* Chapter 4, there are possible grammars that can be constructed within the broad framework of transformational grammar that lack the degree-2 property. It is possible to construct counterexamples to the degree-2 property, where there is a detectable error (i.e., a detectable difference between the learner's transformational component and the adult's), but this error is not detectable on a phrase marker of degree 2 or less. We give one such example here in detail, because understanding of the methodology of the degree-2 proof will be important in our discussion of proposed revisions of the degree-2 theory in Sections 3 and 4 of this chapter. The example is taken from *FPLA,* Chapter 4, modified along the lines of Culicover (1980) and Wilkins (1980b).

In the degree-2 theory it is assumed that the sorts of errors that a learner can make in the acquisition of a transformational component are errors of attachment. The learner is aware from the input data that there is transformation in the target grammar that moves a constituent to a certain position in the phrase marker. In hypothesizing the transformation, the learner correctly guesses the position to which this constituent is moved, but incorrectly guesses the constituent to which the moved constituent is

---

[4]The proof, due to Wexler (1980), is given in detail in Chapter 4 of *FPLA.*

[5]Of course, there may also be particular rules that are exemplified by primary data more complex than degree 2.

to be attached. Consider the transformation in the adult component illustrated in (2).

(2)

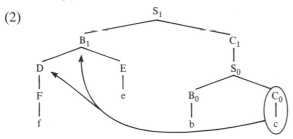

Lower case letters indicate lexical items. The terminal string in the base is *febc*. The transformation in question attaches C_0 to the right of D, as a daughter of B_1. Given (2) as a base phrase marker, the surface string in the input (b, s) pair will then be *fceb*.

The error that the learner makes is to hypothesize that C is attached as a right sister of D rather than as a right sister of F. The surface string is consistent with this error. Only more complex examples, in which D is moved, would reveal whether C was a daughter of D or of B. A counterexample to the degree-2 property would be one in which the error is in fact revealed by a sequence of transformations that occurs only on a phrase marker of degree 3 or greater.

To construct the counterexample, we embed S_1 in a degree-3 structure, given in (3).

(3)

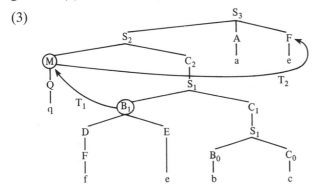

Except for the difference in where C_0 is attached when it is raised into S_1, the two transformational components (the learner's and the adult's) are identical. In both there is a transformation that raises B_1 into S_2 and makes it a sister of Q, as shown by the arrow labeled T_1. In both there is a transformation that raises M into S_3 and makes it a sister of E, as shown by the arrow labeled T_2. Notice that the raising of B_1 and then of M have the crucial property of not making the error in the learner's component detectable. Even though C_0 has been incorrectly attached, neither of these two transformations applies to D, and so neither yields a terminal string that reveals the error. Only a transformation that moves the constituent that the moved C_0 was incorrectly attached to will reveal the error.

Such a transformation finally applies at the level of S_3. After the two raising transformations, the intermediate phrase marker has the form of (4).

(4)   a.   Child:

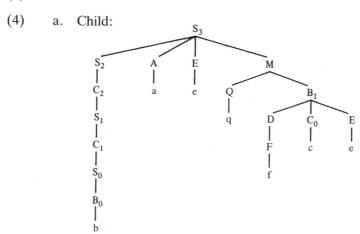

       b.   Adult:

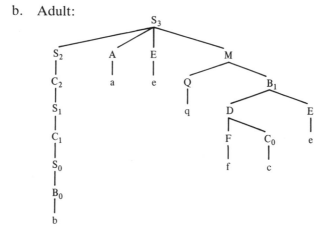

Suppose that there is a transformation that moves D to the right of A (T_3). This transformation reveals the error: The terminal string produced by the learner's grammar is *bafeqce,* whereas that produced by the adult's grammar is *bafceqe.* Because of the incorrect attachment of C_0 by the child, *c* does not move along with D as it does in the adult's grammar. Thus we have a detectable error on a phrase marker of degree 3.

The counterexample is constructed in such a way that there is no phrase marker of less than degree 3 in which the error of the learner's grammar will be revealed, that is, is detectable. The crucial transformation, that which moves D to the left, requires an A to the left of D: $A - D \Rightarrow A + D - \emptyset$. This configuration arises only after M (and therefore D) has been raised to the right of A. Furthermore, M will dominate D only if B_1 has been raised into M. The transformation on which the error is made is also a raising rule. Thus we need a sequence of three raising rules to create the detectable error; a degree-3 phrase marker is required in order for such a sequence to be possible. The example that we have constructed thus constitutes a counterexample to degree-2 learnability because it violates the degree-2 property.

The proof of degree-2 learnability of transformational grammar is accomplished by constraining the class of grammars in such a way that no counterexamples of the sort that has been illustrated here can be constructed. In the illustration, the concealed error was revealed only after a succession of raising transformations had applied. One way of ruling out this particular type of counterexample is to not permit a transformation to apply to a constituent contained in a raised constituent. This principle, the Raising Principle of *FPLA,* will block the movement of D to the right of A in (4).

The full learnability proof of *FPLA,* Chapter 4, invokes a number of principles, constraints and assumptions, the purpose of which is to rule out the construction of a variety of counterexamples to the degree-2 property of the general sort illustrated in the preceding discussion. No doubt there are alternative constraints that will serve the same purpose as these constraints.

The constraints of *FPLA* are of some interest because they appear to have valid empirical consequences. For example, it was shown in Culicover and Wexler (1977) that one principle, the Binary Principle, accounts for the impossibility of extracting out of a subject, a relative clause or other complex NP, or an embedded question. The Binary Principle also blocks passivization of a subject of a tensed S, allowing passivization of the subject of an infinitive, and it bounds rules of extraposition. Another principle, the Freezing Principle, explains a variety of phenomena having to do with Dative and Complex NP Shift in English, and requires an analysis of conjoined structures and Right Node Raising that involves no change in phrase structure, but only lexical reduction. The Raising Principle correctly predicts that constituents that are extraposed cannot be analyzed by extraction transformations.

Whether or not these particular constraints are correct ones, the fact that constraints motivated by considerations of learnability from degree-2 data turn out to have plausible empirical consequences is intriguing and important. If we replace these constraints with others, or if we make substantive changes in the degree-2 theory, we would nevertheless want still to be able to explain at least the same range of grammaticality patterns.

In the next section, we will show how a theory of movement rules with less expressive power than the *Aspects* framework, such as the one we are assuming here, rules out the set of counterexamples that are ruled out in the degree-2 framework by the set of constraints that have been mentioned. As the restrictive theory is the one in which the Locality Condition is relevant, this discussion will lend plausibility to the claim that the Locality Condition and its related principles may be crucially tied to learnability. Following that, in Section 3, we will show how a more restrictive learnability theory will not allow us to maintain the constraints of the degree-2 theory, but is consistent with a natural generalization of the Locality Condition.

2. Constraints on Rule Form and Degree-2 Learnability

In this section we consider the implications for degree-2 learnability of severely limiting the form of structural descriptions of transformational operations. The restrictions on rule form are exactly those which we have assumed throughout our discussion of locality, namely, both context terms and the specification of internal variables are disallowed. In other words, the form of rules is limited to the specification of the category that moves and the category of the landing site. (These two terms might be given in the structural description itself or might be determined by universal constraints such as the structure preservation requirement or a theory of possible landing sites.) We will see that with this reduced expressive power with respect to structural descriptions, the examples used in *FPLA* to motivate the Binary Principle (BP) and the Freezing Principle (FP) can be accounted for without any constraints on rule functioning.[6] We will also see, however, that even this strong constraint on rule form (no contexts

---

[6]**Binary Principle:** *A transformation may apply no deeper in a phrase marker than the immediate constituents of the next B-cyclic node below the one at which the transformation is applying.* (See Chapter 3 of the text.)

Freezing Principle: *If a node A of a phrase marker is frozen, no node dominated by A may be analyzed by a transformation. If the immediate structure of a node in a phrase marker is nonbase, that node is frozen.* (FPLA, p. 119)

and no specified variables) does not reduce the learnability problem to triviality. There are still errors that can be made and in order to assure that any detectable error will show up on a small (degree-2) phrase marker (p-m) it is still necessary to constrain rule functioning by specifying that all raising must be structure preserving (see also Williams, 1981, for discussion of structure-preserving raising).

Following *FPLA* and the earlier work in learnability, we continue, in this section, to assume that each datum consists of a base structure–surface string pair (b, s) and that the learner must learn the transformation that relates the pair.[7] We assume that rules which move constituents result in sister-adjunctions.[8] A further assumption, and the one that we will be examining here, is the strict constraint on rule form, that rules may not contain strictly contextual terms and that they may not specify internal variables. The second part of the constraint entails that the rules themselves cannot specify the adjacency of terms. Between any two terms of a structural description there is an inherent variable.

With these two stipulations on rule form, we know exactly what all rules must look like. For sister-adjunctions there are exactly four possibilities: $A - B \Rightarrow 1 + 2 - \emptyset$, $A - B \Rightarrow 2 + 1 - \emptyset$, $A - B \Rightarrow \emptyset - 1 + 2$, $A - B \Rightarrow \emptyset - 2 + 1$. Here, of course, the term that the moved category adjoins to is considered the target, and therefore is not considered a context term. The example in (5) shows a datum [a (b, s) pair] which could be presented to the learner and two of the guesses that the learner could make.

(5) $b =$

$s = $ a d g e f h

Possible rules: $D - G \Rightarrow 1 + 2 - \emptyset$

$E - G \Rightarrow 2 + 1 - \emptyset$

To examine our proposed constraint on rule form, we first consider the examples from Chapter 4 of *FPLA* which demonstrate the relative neces-

---

[7]Later in this chapter, in Section 3, we suggest a different characterization of the data presented to the learner.

[8]We consider only sister-adjunction here as it is the only type of rule considered in *FPLA*.

sity of the BP. Given the base rules in (6), we can construct the p-m in (7) [(48) in *FPLA*].

(6)

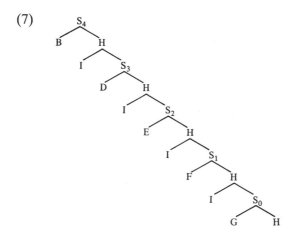

$$S \rightarrow \left\{ \begin{array}{c} B \\ D \\ E \\ F \\ G \end{array} \right\} H$$

$$H \rightarrow \quad I \quad (S)$$

(7)

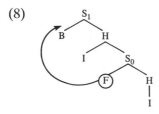

A transformation with the structural description B – X – D – Y – E – Z – F – U – G – V (X, Y, Z, U, V = variables) will apply to this degree-4 p-m. This transformation cannot apply to any smaller degree p-m, and therefore it causes no detectable error on a small (degree-2) p-m.

This example is readily handled (i.e., the BP is shown to be not necessary for this example) in *FPLA* by a revision of the Principle of No Bottom Context (NBC). This revision says that only the context of the matrix (top) S can be used in a transformation. For instance, we might have the rule B – X – F – Y $\Rightarrow$ 3 + 1 – 2 – $\emptyset$ – 4 which does not violate NBC and which not only can apply to (7) but can also apply where S_3 and S_2 are dropped and the p-m is of small degree as in (8) [(49b) in *FPLA*].

(8)

As NBC is, of course, a subcase of "no context," our new assumptions give the same result here. (Recall that for adjunctions as we are considering them, B in the rule here is considered the target; it is not a context.)

Our next example [(50) in *FPLA*] is one where NBC is not a sufficient constraint.[9]

(9)   a.

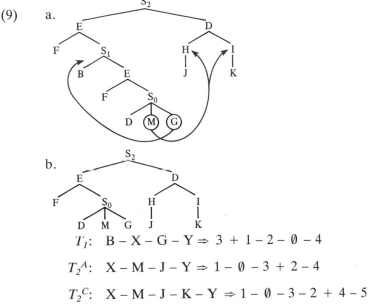

b.

$$T_1: \quad B - X - G - Y \Rightarrow 3 + 1 - 2 - \emptyset - 4$$

$$T_2^A: \quad X - M - J - Y \Rightarrow 1 - \emptyset - 3 + 2 - 4$$

$$T_2^C: \quad X - M - J - K - Y \Rightarrow 1 - \emptyset - 3 - 2 + 4 - 5$$

The raising of M in (9) is the error-producing rule, T_2^A versus T_2^C. The error is exposed on the S_3 cycle where H (or I) is raised. The raising of M, as can be seen in the SDs of rules T_2 requires that M be adjacent to J; no variable is written into the rule. This means that M can be raised only where no G occurs between M and J, or in other words where T_1 has applied. This in turn means that none of these rules will apply in (9b), the p-m made by dropping S_1 of (9a). As there is therefore no error in (9b) there is no detectable error. Without the BP an error is caused where the smallest p-m is as in (9a) and a degree-3 p-m will be the smallest one where the error is detected. Therefore in the *FPLA* theory the BP is necessary.

In the theory we are assuming adjacency cannot be specified.[10] For rules like T_2 there will always be an unstated but inherent variable between any two terms, and thus here between M and J. Therefore the error-producing rule can apply whether or not T_1 has applied. Rule T_2 can apply, for

---

[9]The subscript on the rule indicates the S-domain in which the rule applies. The superscripts A and C indicate the rule for the adult and the child, respectively.

[10]Adjacency cannot be specified in the Lasnik and Kupin (1977) formalization of a theory of transformations.

instance, in (9b) causing the error which will then be detected on the degree-2 p-m.

Next we consider (10) [(52) in *FPLA*; we skip *FPLA's* (51) because (52) is the interesting case related to it].

(10)   a.

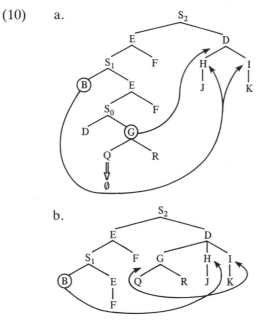

         b.

T_0: $D - Q - X \Rightarrow 1 - \emptyset - 3$

$T_{2,0}$: $X - G - Y - H - Z \Rightarrow 1 - \emptyset - 3 - 2 + 4 - 5$

$T_{2,1}{}^{A}$: $X - B - Y - G - Z - J - W \Rightarrow 1 - \emptyset - 3 - 4 - 5 - 6 + 2 - 7$

$T_{2,1}{}^{C}$: $X - B - Y - G - Z - K - W \Rightarrow 1 - \emptyset - 3 - 4 - 5 - 2 + 6 - 7$

T_2: $X - Q - Y - B - Z \Rightarrow 1 - 4 + 2 - 3 - \emptyset - 5$

In (10a) the first transformation deletes Q. At S_1 no transformation applies. At S_2, first G is raised from S_0 ($T_{2,0}$), then B is raised from S_1 to S_2 ($T_{2,1}$), causing the error. This example is constructed so that the raising of B is dependent on a G in S_2. In (10a) the G is in S_2 because it has been moved there by $T_{2,0}$.

In the smaller p-m in (10b) the error-causing movement of B also applies. In this case it can apply because the G in S_2 upon which it is dependent is there in the base. Note that (10b) is constructed from (10a) by dropping S_0 and by assuming that the base includes the rules D → G H I and G → Q R.

Next T_2 can apply. What T_2 does is move B to the left of Q. The effect that this rule has is that it "undoes" the error caused by the raising of B.

This rule applies in (10b) because there is a Q. It cannot apply in (10a) because the Q has been deleted by T_0 in S_0. (It is important to remember that G → R is not a base rule; the only way to get a G dominating an R but not a Q is by deleting Q, here in the environment of D.) As no error exists in (10b) after T_2 applies, there is certainly no detectable error.

In (10a), where T_2 cannot apply to "undo" the error, it is exposed on S_3 where H (or I) is raised. Without the BP (which would prevent the raising of G) there is no degree-2 p-m where the error can be detected. So for *FPLA* the BP seems to be necessary.

In the framework that we are assuming rules may not indicate contexts. In particular, the error-causing raising of B cannot be written so as to depend on the context G. Therefore, the movement of B applies whether or not G has been raised; in other words, it can apply in (10a) where S_0 is dropped off. This means that there is a detectable degree-2 error without assuming the BP.

Unless other examples can be constructed to show the (relative) necessity of the BP, it seems that disallowing contexts and assuming that there is an inherent variable between any two terms of an SD, gives equally good results for degree-2 learnability.

Assuming that the constraints on rule form can handle the examples used to illustrate the necessity of the BP for the learnability proof, we examine next the examples illustrating the (relative) necessity of the FP to see if they can be similarly accounted for.

In *FPLA* two examples are given to show the relative necessity of the FP. The first example [(54)] is shown here in (11).

(11)   a.

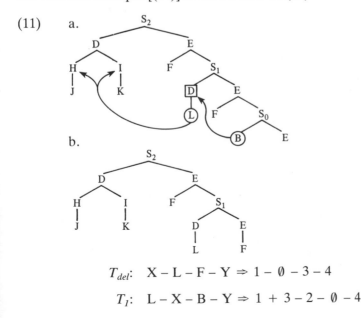

b.

$$T_{del}: \quad X - L - F - Y \Rightarrow 1 - \emptyset - 3 - 4$$

$$T_I: \quad L - X - B - Y \Rightarrow 1 + 3 - 2 - \emptyset - 4$$

In this example the first assumption is that D → L B is not a base rule. Then the first rule is one that raises B to the right of L under D. Because D cannot dominate L B in the base the only way for this configuration to arise is by transformation. If the FP held, the node D would be frozen, as shown by the box around it in (11a). The discussion in *FPLA* assumes, however, that the FP does not hold (in order to show its necessity). Next, at cycle S_2, L is raised causing an error. This error is not detected until S_3 where H (or I) is raised.

Phrase marker (11b) is constructed by dropping S_0 to try to show that there is a small p-m on which this error is detectable. As things stand, L can be raised to cause the error in (11b) which is then detected (by the raising of H or I) in a degree-2 p-m. In *FPLA* it is suggested then that there is a transformation that deletes L in (11b) so that no error is created, but which does not apply in (11a) so that the error remains undetected in (11a) until S_3. This transformation is the T_{del} X – L – F – Y ⇒ 1 – ∅ – 3 – 4. By this rule L is deleted when it occurs immediately to the left of an F. Hence L is deleted in (11b) but not in (11a). Therefore, without the FP, there is an error that remains undetected until degree-3. In *FPLA* this demonstrates the relative necessity of the FP.

By the constraints we are considering here the deletion rule would be disallowed for two reasons. First, there must be an inherent variable between L and F in the SD. This means that the rule could equally well apply in (11a) so that no error would be created. Second, the term F in the rule is strictly contextual so it could not be mentioned anyway. The deletion transformation is not a possible rule.[11] In this case, then, the error-producing T_1 could apply in (11b) as well as in (11a) so there is a degree-2 p-m where the error is detected. For this example the FP (which by freezing D in [11a] would prevent the error-causing raising of L) is not necessary.

The second example used in *FPLA* to show the necessity of the FP does not involve deletion; (56) of *FPLA* is given here in (12).

---

[11]Given that deletion rules invariably mention context terms the question arises as to whether they are possible rules. Perhaps a better question is whether categories can be deleted, or if it is only morphological material which is ever deleted. Maybe the things (categories) that are subject to movement operations are not the things (terminal symbols) that are subject to deletion. If this dichotomy in fact exists, then it looks like there are (at least) two separate things to be learned and we might expect that the constraints on deletion rules would be different from those on movements. Or it might be the case that the learning of deletions is completely trivial if the base is given. See also Williams's (1981) discussion of S-essential deletion.

(12)

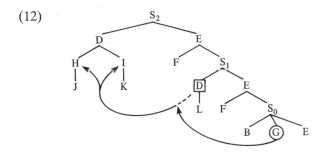

First G is raised to the left of L under D and D → G L is not a base rule. With the FP, D would be frozen after this raising. Again, to show its necessity, *FPLA* does not assume the FP. Therefore the next rule, which raises G, can apply to cause an error. This raising of G applies only when it has been moved into that position (as it cannot be there in the base). Say that in the adult component the rule specifying this second raising of G is $J - X - F - G - Y \Rightarrow 1 + 4 - 2 - 3 - \emptyset - 5$. In the child component the rule would specify a left-adjunction to K. By this rule, G is raised in S_2 and the error-exposing rule applies on S_3. Again the FP, to freeze D and disallow the error-causing rule, seems to be necessary.

From our viewpoint, the error-producing rule in (12) violates both parts of the constraint on rule form. It includes the context term F, and it also requires that no variable material occur between F and G, or in other words that F and G be adjacent. In *FPLA* the example was constructed so as not to violate any of the other constraints in order to show the importance of the FP. In particular, in order not to violate the BP it must be the case that G does not move directly from S_0 to S_2. For this reason the error-producing rule uses F as an adjacent context. The term G must move first to the left of L, creating the p-m in which the FP must be invoked. In our model here the movement of G to J in S_2 must be written without F and this means that it can apply to move G from S_0 in a single movement (we do not assume the BP). The small p-m in which it applies is similar to (12) but with S_1 dropped. Therefore the error is exposed on a degree-2 p-m, when H is subsequently raised. As far as these examples are concerned the FP, like the BP, is unnecessary if we have strict constraints on rule form.

Thus far we have not seen any counterexamples to degree-2 learnability. It is important now to show that even though constraining rule form is very powerful and seems to make the BP and FP unnecessary, it is not powerful enough to prevent errors from occurring. In other words, it does not make learning the grammar a trivial problem. In fact, a constraint on rule functioning remains necessary. To show this we need look no farther than the examples in *FPLA* used to show the relative necessity of the Raising Principle (RP).[12]

(13)

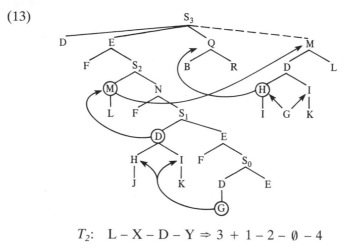

$$T_2: \quad L - X - D - Y \Rightarrow 3 + 1 - 2 - \emptyset - 4$$

$$T_3: \quad X - M - Y - Q \Rightarrow 1 - \emptyset - 3 - 4 + 2$$

$$T_3': \quad X - B - Y - H - Z \Rightarrow 1 - 4 + 2 - 3 - \emptyset - 5$$

The first transformation that applies in (13) raises G at level S_1 which causes the error. At level S_2 D, which dominates the error, is raised by T_2. At level S_3 M, which dominates D which still dominates the error, is raised by T_3. So far the error is not exposed. Next H is moved, say to the left of B, by T_3', which does expose the error, on a degree-3 p-m. The error cannot be exposed on any smaller p-m because the error-producing rule cannot apply (its SD is not met) until the H is to the right of the B. This can only occur when H is moved along with M (because there is no rule moving H itself). And H can only be under M by moving there with D. Assuming that there is no RP the state of affairs in (13)—the degree-3 detectable error—is not prevented by any of *FPLA*'s constraints. Nor is it prevented by our constraints on rule form. None of the rules uses a strictly contextual term and none of the rules needs to specify adjacency. The RP would prevent the movement of H by T_3' because once a node is raised (e.g., M or D) it cannot be analyzed by any subsequent transformation. The RP is therefore necessary to prevent the error from showing up.

An alternative to the RP is to require that all raising be structure preserving (see also Williams, 1981, for discussion of this issue). If this were

[12]*Raising Principle: If a node A is raised, then no node that A dominates may be used to fit a transformation (FPLA, p. 143).*

the case, then in (13) M in S_3 would have had to be possible as a base structure (as would D under M). We would therefore have examples like (14).

(14)   a.

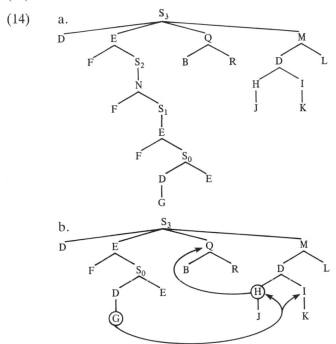

b.

Phrase marker (14a) shows M (and D) in base position in S_3. The error-causing movement is the raising of G. (This must also be structure preserving, so G must be generated in the base both as a right sister of J and as a left sister of K.) As levels S_1 and S_2 are unaffected we drop them and we are left with (14b), where the movement of G causes the error and where T_3' applies to show the error in a small (degree-1) p-m.

A comparison of (13) and (14) leads to an interesting issue. In (13), where the RP is used, there is an error which can never be detected. In (14), with structure-preserving raising, the error is detected on a small p-m. It might therefore be possible, using the new constraints, to assure that the child grammar is the same as the adult grammar, instead of just an equivalent grammar. We will not pursue this alternative here and, in fact, it is not even clear if this would be a desirable result from the point of view of explanatory adequacy.

In any case, with structure-preserving raising or with the RP the results seem to be fine for degree-2 learnability. Interestingly, assuming our general framework (i.e., the rule form constraints), there is an example which is correctly handled by the structure-preservation requirement, but not by the RP.[13]

(15)

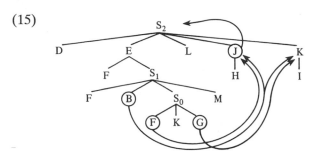

$$T: \quad G - I \Rightarrow \emptyset \;\; - 1 \; + 2$$
$$T': \quad F - H \Rightarrow \emptyset \;\; - 2 \; + 1$$
$$T^A: \quad B - F \Rightarrow \emptyset \;\; - 2 \; + 1$$
$$T^C: \quad B - G \Rightarrow \emptyset \;\; - 1 \; + 2$$

With respect to (15) we assume, for now, no constraints other than those on rule form. We then apply the given transformations which do not violate those constraints. First, G is raised to become a left sister to I and F is raised to become a right sister to H.[14] The next thing that happens is that B raises, causing the error. In the adult component B is attached to the right of F; in the child component B is attached to the left of G. The error is exposed on S_3 when J is raised.

With no constraints on rule functioning, in particular with no BP, the detectable error in (15) is degree 3. The important thing here is that the RP will not help as it is not violated. No raised constituent is being analyzed. Stipulating that all raising must be structure preserving is the constraint that does help. In that case the p-m can be constructed where F and G are in S_2 in the base and where S_0 is dropped. The error, the movement of B, is then created and detected in a degree-2 p-m. The

---

[13]We thank Ken Wexler for this example.

[14]Notice that these two rules together violate the Principle of Uniqueness of S-Essential Transformations (USET). For discussion of the fact that USET is obviously wrong on linguistic grounds, see Williams (1981). Notice also that the Adjacency Constraint of *FPLA*, which rules out other violations of USET and which is at least somewhat more plausible linguistically, does not rule out this violation. We thank Ken Wexler for this discussion of USET and adjacency.

constraints on rule form therefore require structure-preserving raising rather than the RP.[15]

Besides the fact that structure-preserving raising gives the correct result in (15), it is interesting for another reason. There has been speculation, for instance by Baker (1977), that restrictions on rule form might replace conditions on rule functioning such as the BP and the FP. We see here that constrained rule form is not sufficient. To assure degree-2 error detectability we must assume (at least) one additional constraint which turns out to be a constraint on rule functioning. We must require that raising function in structure-preserving fashion.

Having now discussed our proposed alternatives to the BP, FP, and RP in the degree-2 theory, it is important to stress that this new approach is only interesting insofar as it also provides for an adequate theory of grammar. Our underlying assumption is that learnability requirements explain principles of grammar. In Chomskyan terms, learnability provides a way for achieving explanatory adequacy. As such, we assume that a given set of constraints will be supported on linguistic grounds as well as be important to demonstrate learnability. We have already illustrated the importance of the LC as a principle of grammar. The LC presupposes the conditions on rule form that we have discussed here and provides for a syntactic framework that needs neither the FP nor the BP (nor the Subjacency Condition).

In what follows, rather than pursue any further the implications of our assumptions for degree-2 learnability, we will suggest a revision of the learnability framework in which the LC plays a crucial role.

3. Reconsideration of the Degree-2 Theory

For ease of reference, we summarize here the central assumptions of the degree-2 theory that were introduced in Section 1 of this chapter.

I.   The setting
     1. Infinite sequence of data
     2. Each datum has a probability of occurrence of >0

II. The learner
     1. No memory for past data
     2. Rejects or adds rules according to the evidence

---

[15]Williams (1981) has observed that structure-preserving raising in itself makes the FP unnecessary.

III.   Criterion for learning
       There exists a time t such that the learner never changes its
       hypothesis after t.

IV.   Class of grammars
       1. Universal base
       2. Class of transformational components in the *Aspects*
          framework

V.   Data
       (b, s) pairs, where b is a base phrase marker and s is a
       corresponding surface string

VI.   Learner's task
       Hypothesize a correct transformational component

VII.   The linguistic evidence
       Detectable errors, in which the surface string corresponding to
       b in the learner's component is not the same as the surface
       string presented to the learner. That is, $^*T_L(b) \neq {}^*T_A(b)$.

VIII. Degree-2 learnability
       If a detectable error exists on a phrase marker, then it exists on
       a phrase marker of degree ≤ 2.

The assumptions may be grouped into two categories. In one category
we have I–III, assumptions having to do with the general prerequisites for
learning. In the other category are assumptions IV–VIII, which specify
the particular details of the acquisition of grammars. Although changes in
I–III could have empirical consequences, we will focus our attention on
those assumptions that bear more directly on the problem of language
acquisition per se.

3.1. Defining the Class of Grammars

3.1.1. THE UNIVERSAL BASE

As noted in *FPLA*, Chapter 7, the assumption that there is a universal
base component is empirically untenable. There the possibility was pur-
sued that there is a small class of possible base components, which can be
distinguished one from the other on the basis of very simple primary data.
The particular hypothesis that was examined was the following: (a) that
there is a fixed set of universal syntactic categories; and (b) that the rules
for expanding any phrasal category X^n differ from language to language
only in the relative order of the immediate constituents of the node X^n.
Thus, for binary branching, if B and C are the immediate constituents of

A, and if D and E are the immediate constituents of C, then only the following are possible base grammars.

(16)   A → B C
        C → D E

(17)   A → B C
        C → E D

(18)   A → C B
        C → D E

(19)   A → C B
        C → E D

Such a hypothesis, which was called the Invariance Principle, makes rather specific predictions about universals of word order. In particular, assuming that there are no reordering transformations involving the categories in (16)–(19), the only possible orderings of B, D, and E are those in which B does not appear between D and E: BDE, EDB, DEB, BED, *DBE, *EBD.

In general it does not appear that the Invariance Principle accounts for the full range of word order typology. Given a set of plausible phrase structure rules for English, there are certain permutations that yield word orders that do not appear to occur in other languages, and there are certain word orders that are not accounted for by permutation of the English constituent structures. The latter situation is exemplified by the VSO languages, which cannot be generated if V and O are immediate constituents of VP, and by the so-called "free word-order" languages, which do not seem to display any particular underlying canonical structures in the extreme cases (see Hale 1973 on Walbiri, and Lapointe 1980).[16]

---

[16]There is always the possibility, of course, that there are no "deep VSO" languages, except perhaps those in which the verb governs the "subject," that is, "deep ergative" languages. This was discussed in Wexler and Culicover (1974) and Culicover and Wexler (1974). At that time, the two obstacles to the apparent correctness of this hypothesis were (i) that not all superficial VSO languages could be analyzed as ergative, and (ii) given the Freezing Principle, deriving superficial VSO from deep SVO or SOV would predict the absolute impossibility of extraction from VSO sentences. This prediction is empirically false, as shown by languages like Arabic, in which extraction is relatively free.

Without the Freezing Principle, (ii) is no longer a problem, of course, and it might be possible to resurrect the Invariance Principle, perhaps in a different form. A natural avenue to pursue, for example, would be one involving government, as suggested by Kayne (personal communication, 1982). We may say that α governs β if α and β are sisters; languages would then differ on the linear relationship of governor and governed. All languages would observe universal constraints on government. Notice that underlying nonergative VSO languages are still a problem, since the common factor in this view of government and in the earlier Invariance Principle is that a verb and its direct object were sisters, universally.

3.1.2. THE CLASS OF TRANSFORMATIONAL COMPONENTS

The degree-2 theory assumes that the learner is to formulate a hypothesis the form of which is a set of transformational rules in the *Aspects* framework of Chomsky (1965). Subsequent work in linguistic theory has proceeded toward the goal of modifying the *Aspects* framework so as to render it both far less permissive in the class of grammars that it will allow and more descriptively adequate.

A review of the methodology of the degree-2 theory shows that a change in the class of grammars itself could have the consequence of ruling out certain counterexamples to the degree-2 property. The degree-2 theory is based on detectable errors that result from the misattachment of a moved constituent. A modification of the typical counterexample to the degree-2 property is given in Section 1 in connection with our discussion of the Raising Principle.[17]

The empirical evidence from the study of the course of language acquisition suggests that attachment errors, if they occur at all, are extremely rare. There is no basis from empirical observation of children learning language to believe that attachment errors form a primary part of the evidence for the child as to the form of its grammar.[18] The empirical evidence suggests, in fact, that the transformations are learned relatively directly; once the child is ready to hypothesize the transformation, the correct formal statement of the transformation in the child's grammar appears to follow directly.

3.2. The Data

The assumption that the learner is presented with (b, s) pairs is clearly counterfactual. On the other hand, it is reasonable to assume that the linguistic data consists in part of grammatical strings, and that there is little if any correction for grammatical errors, or any other kind of explicit linguistic instruction (see *FPLA*, Chapter 3, for extensive discussion). Given that surface strings alone are insufficient as data for learning any reasonably complex class of grammars,[19] we are faced with the same di-

---

[17]It might be thought that the consequence of ruling out the counterexamples by changing the class of grammars is a desirable one. However, such a move would not be desirable if it failed to explain the empirical phenomena that the learnability constraints account for. Ruling out the counterexamples to the degree-2 property is of limited linguistic interest unless the way in which the counterexamples are ruled out has consequences for linguistic theory.

[18]This claim is based on our analysis of the language development literature, especially Klima and Bellugi (1966) and Brown (1973), and from discussion with Ed Matthei. It is entirely possible, of course, that the evidence for attachment errors is in the literature, and that it has yet to be noticed.

[19]Demonstrated in Gold (1967) and Wexler and Hamburger (1973).

lemma as before if we propose to abandon the notion that b is part of the input data.

In *FPLA* and elsewhere it was assumed without further discussion that the learner is provided with sufficient semantic information about the sentence being presented to be able to construct b. If we do not assume that the base is universal, this assumption becomes considerably more problematic.

One possible objection to the assumption that the learner is presented with sufficient semantic information to hypothesize b is that the learner, having this amount of information about the sentence, would not have to learn the grammar. This view of the matter is misleading, however. The assumption is simply that the learner has **sufficient** information to construct b. It may not be necessary to know the full meaning of the s in order to be able to construct b (or a satisfactory partial representation of b). Suppose, for example, that the learner hears the sentence *The alligator with the purple gills is eating Horace,* where *Horace* refers to a pet fish. Suppose that the learner does not know the meaning of the first noun phrase, but knows (*a*) that it is an NP, because of the definite article *the,* (*b*) that *is eating Horace* means "is V-ing Horace," because of the morphology of the progressive aspect. The learner will then have enough information to construct a partial base phrase marker in which *is eating Horace* is the VP, *Horace* is the direct object, and *the alligator with the purple gills* is dominated by NP. While this partial base phrase marker will not provide the learner with all of the syntactic information that there is to know about the sentence, it could conceivably provide crucial evidence for some rule of the language. Although the degree-2 theory is not formulated in terms of partial base phrase markers, a workable modification of the degree-2 theory along these lines should be possible. It would appear more productive, however, to question directly the notion that the learner constructs any base phrase marker whatever from the input string and the context.

3.3. Thematic Roles

In a more realistic model of language acquisition, the learner not only is ignorant of the grammar, it is ignorant of the lexicon as well. Pursuing an approach suggested by work of Bresnan (1978, 1982), Pinker (1982), and others, let us consider in the current context the extent to which what is to be learned is implicit in the lexicon itself or explicitly represented in the entries for particular lexical items.

To know the meaning of a verb is to know at least the thematic roles of the participants in the action or state expressed by the verb. What the possible thematic roles are depends not only on a linguistic theory but also on a theory of perception and a theory of action. We must assume, first of all, that the human being is innately endowed with the ability to perceive objects in space, to distinguish one from the other, to determine their physical properties, and to perceive the properties of their motion in space. A theory of perception must account for our ability to perceive and distinguish these things.[20]

A theory of action, on the other hand, must account for our ability to recognize a group of objects (usually animate) in motion over time as engaged in an instance of an identifiable action, which may be a special instance of a more general class of actions. It may be the case that to some extent language instructs us in recognizing certain sets of actions as constituting a single more general act, but it is the theory of action itself that determines the class of possible actions that language can express.

Along these lines we may distinguish two classes of thematic roles, the extensional (perception) and the intensional (action). The extensional thematic roles categorize objects as physical entities in terms of their perceived properties. The thematic relations of Gruber (1965) are in general of this sort: **source**, **goal**, and **theme**. For example, an object that changes position or state is a **theme** in Gruber's sense.[21] The intensional thematic roles are those that categorize objects according to their status as actors in an action. The notions **agent**, **patient**, **instrument**, **benefactee**, and so on, are not applicable in general to objects in terms of their extensionally perceivable physical and spatial properties, but are assigned to objects based on our natural theories of human action.[22]

On this view of thematic roles, it is possible for an argument of a verb to possess more than one thematic role, as there is in general no logical disjunction between the extensional and intensional roles. Thus we differ on specifics with the Θ-Criterion of Chomsky (1981): "Each argument bears one and only one Θ-role, and each Θ-role is assigned to one and

---

[20]We must also have a general theory of cognition to account for our ability to categorize the objects and properties that we perceive and to identify them as instances of more general categories. A theory of cognition will presumably constrain the expressive range of a human language. See Jackendoff (in press) for explorations into the nature of this relationship.

[21]The notion of **theme** may be generalized to include changes of state and possession, as in Jackendoff (1972). This extended notion comprises intensional as well as extensional roles. In distinguishing between these two sorts of thematic role, we are assuming a suitably fine-grained analysis of the thematic roles.

[22]It is possible that the theories of action, perception, and cognition do not suffice to explain precisely what the linguistically relevant thematic roles are, but only provide a superset.

only one argument [p. 36]." Our view admits, with Jackendoff (1972), the option of assigning more than one thematic role to an argument, but we restrict the possibilities along the lines suggested by Chomsky: There cannot be dual assignment by a verb of intensional roles, or of extensional roles, to a single argument. A more precise formulation of the restrictions on assignment of thematic roles appears in Chapter 3 in terms of Completeness and Distributedness.

Let us consider a simple example from English. The sentence *John ate the radish* describes some act of John's perpetrated on some radish. *John* is the **agent** and *the radish* is the **patient**. That the eater is the **agent** and the thing eaten the **patient** has nothing directly to do with the verb *eat*, but with our understanding of the act of eating, of what it involves. In contrast, the rules of English determine that we are going to understand this sentence as meaning "John ate the radish," and not the other way around. Presumably this has nothing to do with the meaning of the verb *eat*, but depends on the grammar of English.

Thematic roles have a dual status. On the one hand, they are integral parts of the definition of particular acts or states as such, quite independent of the linguistic expressions used to refer to these acts or states. Let us call this the "defining function" of the thematic roles. In this sense, the thematic roles are assigned to mental representations of objects, concepts, etc. On the other hand, the thematic roles are assigned by verbs to entities that are the referents of arguments of the verbs in the linguistic expressions themselves. Let us call the assignment of thematic roles by verbs (and adjectives) the "linguistic function" of the thematic roles.[23]

It seems to us most natural to view the defining function of thematic roles as the primary one. The defining function constrains the linguistic function, in the sense that a verb cannot assign to an argument a thematic role that is not implicated in the definition of the act or state that the verb expresses. A verb assigns certain roles to certain arguments because (*a*) the verb refers to a particular act or state in which those roles have a

---

[23]Implicit in this characterization of thematic roles is the claim that only verbs, prepositions, and adjectives assign thematic roles, and that nouns do not. We believe that this is correct, and that nouns only implicate thematic roles by virtue of the verbs (or adjectives) that they implicate. To refer to an example discussed in Chapter 1, the noun *message* implicates that a message is sent, and the verb *send* governs **source** and **goal**. Precisely how this relationship of implication is to be expressed is an open question. Moreover, it raises the question of precisely how to interpret Completeness and Distributedness, which require that all referring NPs map into (representations of) sets of individuals in R-Structure to which thematic roles are assigned. Given our assumptions, the relationship of implication must play a role in the mapping from syntactic structure into R-Structure.

defining function, and (b) the arguments refer to the entities that play these roles in the particular act or state.[24]

The lexicon has, in this way of thinking, two distinct parts. One part has to do with the defining function of the thematic roles, the other part with the linguistic function. The defining function is language independent: An act or a state is in part **defined by** the thematic roles played by various entities. The linguistic function is in part language specific: Given a particular verb, the thematic roles constrain the function of the rules of the language that specify assignment of thematic roles to the objects that the arguments refer to.

The task of the language learner with respect to thematic roles is thus threefold. First, it must learn the defining function of the thematic roles (not a strictly linguistic task). Second, it must learn the rules of the language that determine which thematic roles are assigned to which arguments. Third, it must learn that certain thematic roles must be expressed for certain verbs.

In Chapter 1 we advanced the hypothesis that thematic role assignment in the unmarked case is determined directly by the grammatical roles assigned to NPs. In order for a verb to deviate from the unmarked mapping, it must so specify in its lexical entry. The learner must therefore solve the following problems, for any language: (a) how are the grammatical relations indicated? (b) how are the grammatical relations mapped into thematic roles? and (c) what are the idiosyncratic properties of the verbs, if any?

4. Detectable Errors in a Degree-0 Theory

Suppose that we abandon the assumption that the learner is presented with (b, s) pairs. We assume that the learner is presented with surface strings, but instead of base phrase markers, the learner is presented with information concerning the thematic roles of individuals in the context. That is, the information includes (R, s) pairs, where R designates a set of

---

[24]By using "refer" we invoke the correct philosophical and psychological interpretation of the word, whatever it might turn out to be. A plausible view is that in using certain expressions in sentences, speakers "refer" if they have a mental representation that they associate (a) with the expression and (b) with some object, set of objects, concept, etc. In this sense speakers can be said to refer to objects, and derivatively, expressions can be said to refer to objects if they are used by speakers to refer, and so on. We will use "refer" in these senses in this chapter.

thematic roles.[25] The task for the learner is no longer that of acquiring a transformational component. Rather, it is in essence that of determining how the grammatical relations are expressed in the target language. We will suppose that universally there are three grammatical relations, subject, object, indirect object; for our purposes there is no need to distinguish between the object of a verb and the object of a preposition.[26]

As in the degree-2 theory, the crucial part of the learning process must involve the formulation of hypotheses by the learner, and the modification of these hypotheses in case there is evidence that an error had been made. Generalizing from the degree-2 theory, we investigate the set of mappings between levels that the learner must hypothesize, and the kinds of errors that would produce detectable errors for each of these mappings.

A plausible procedure for determining the correctness of a hypothesized grammar is the following:

(20)   *Learning Schema (LS):*

    i. Given the input string s, construct the surface structure.

    ii. Given the surface structure and the base component,[27] construct the S-structure $|S(s)|$ (or more simply, $|S|$).

    iii. Given $|S|$ and the transformations, reconstruct the deep structure, assigning the Deep Grammatical Relations.

    iv. Given the Deep Grammatical Relations, construct the R-structure.

    v. Compare the R-structure with the target R-structure.

    vi. If there is a mismatch, then there is a detectable error.[28]

[25]Actually, what we must assume is that the learner is presented with the defining roles of a particular verb. That is, what the learner is exposed to is a context in which various salient entities possess certain salient thematic roles. From the fact that these entities are the referents of the NPs in the sentence, the learner must construct an R-structure, which serves as the first member of the pair (R, s) that the learner uses as input data. We are assuming that this is more plausible than the task of constructing a base phrase marker from the real-world context.

[26]See Chapter 1 for an outline of the theory of grammatical relations that we are assuming.

[27]We are of course assuming here that the learner has already constructed a base component, or enough of the base component to account for the input s. In fact, the way LS works, the learner cannot even assign the wrong interpretation to a sentence if it is unable to assign a structure to the input string.

[28]Stages (i)–(v) are precisely the steps that could be attributed to a language comprehension device. After assigning an interpretation to a sentence based on its grammar, the learner compares aspects of this interpretation (the R-structure) with the evidence available from the environment. There is no reason to believe, a priori, that the language learner makes use of a qualitatively different procedure for comprehension than does the adult speaker-hearer. We will return to this point in Section 8.4.

As formulated here the procedure outlined in LS has a number of stages where there could be errors in the learner's grammar. Following the methodology of the degree-2 theory, we will not attempt to account first for the earliest stages of language acquisition, that is, those stages during which the rules of the base component are hypothesized.[29] As an idealization, we will also assume that the procedure of Stage (iv) does not have to be acquired, but is already given. Thus the task of the learner is to determine what the deep structure of a sentence is given the surface string.[30]

We will assume that the set of rules given by Universal Grammar for the assignment of grammatical relations to syntactic mechanisms are of the form $<\gamma, \mu>$, where γ is taken from the set G of DGRs, and μ from the set M of syntactic mechanisms.[31] Let us call the set of such rules for a particular language L $\{<\gamma, \mu>\}_L$.

A further consideration concerns Stage (i). For simplicity we will assume that the learner can go directly from the surface string to the surface structure, where the surface structure crucially contains traces of constit-

---

[29]We discuss the problem of learning the basic rules for assigning grammatical relations in Section 7.

[30]We thus deliberately ignore the possibility that overgeneralization errors may occur when the learner fails to recognize that a particular verb does not fit into the normal paradigm given by the schema of Chapter 1:

Role Assignment:
  (i) Assign lexically idiosyncratic roles.
  (ii) Assign **theme** to the object if there is one. Otherwise assign **theme** to the subject.
  *(iii) (a) Assign **goal** to subject or (b) assign **patient** to object and **agent** to subject or (c) **instrument** to subject or . . . .*

For empirical evidence concerning such errors, see C. Chomsky (1969). A typical example is that the child assigns to *easy* the thematic structure governed by *eager*. Presumably the latter is unmarked, the former marked, as discussed in Section 2 of Chapter 3.

The child must have some way of revising the lexical entries of marked items like *easy*. The mismatch between the real world and the child's grammar would certainly provide the evidence on the basis of which to revise the lexicon.

We must guarantee that the child does not constantly revise the lexicon when in fact it is the grammar itself that must be changed. Suppose, for instance, that the child learning English believes that the subject follows the verb, in general. The child could maintain this hypothesis and treat every verb in the language as idiosyncratic. Every new verb would then lead to a new detectable error. But given that there is a greater than 0 probability of the child revising the grammar, at some point the grammar would be restructured, and from that point on the child's hypothesis would be consistent with all new data. Of course, the formerly idiosyncratic lexical entries would all have to be revised to take into account this restructuring.

[31]A syntactic mechanism μ is a particular case mark, a particular agreement rule, or a particular configuration. For example, one such mechanism, which we call syntactic subject, is the configuration [S, NP] (the NP immediately dominated by S) in the *Aspects* framework.

uents moved into nonargument positions and other empty categories.[32] The data available to the learner consists of $(R, |S|)$ pairs, where R is an R-structure and $|S|$ is an S-structure. Effectively, the R-structure is available to the learner directly from the context in which the sentence is uttered.[33] We can now define the conditions under which there will be a detectable error involving the matching of grammatical relations and syntactic mechanisms. Let $R(|S|)$ be the R-structure (the set of thematic roles) assigned to the NPs in $|S|$, while $DS(|S|)$ is the deep structure of $|S|$.

(21) *Definition: Given an adult's grammar A and a learner's grammar C*
    (i) *C makes a GR-error on some datum $(R, |S|)$ iff $DS_A(|S|) \neq DS_C(|S|)$*
    (ii) *C makes a detectable GR-error on some datum $(R, |S|)$ iff $R_C(|S|) \neq R_A(|S|)$*

Part (i) of the definition says that there is a GR-error if the grammatical relations assigned by the learner to the NPs in a sentence are not the grammatical relations that the adult's grammar assigns. Such an error will occur if $\{<\gamma, \mu>\}_A \neq \{<\gamma, \mu>\}_C$, given the idealization that we have made. Part (ii) says that this error is detectable if at least one of these NPs thereby is assigned a thematic role that is in conflict with the thematic roles that appear in the input data to the learner.[34] If there is a detectable error, then for some NP_i in $|S|$, the R-structure of the learner and the R-structure of the adult differ on the assignment of a thematic relation to this NP.

---

[32]There seems to be considerable empirical evidence to support the view that traces of movements into nonargument positions are phonologically real (see Bresnan 1971, Chomsky and Lasnik 1977, Culicover and Rochemont 1983, Jaeggli 1980, and van Riemsdijk and Williams 1982). On the other hand, there is little, if any, theory-independent evidence to support the view that rules like NP Movement leave traces. In Section 8.2 we will suggest a learnability basis for the distinction between these two sorts of movements.

[33]This does not mean that the entire meaning of the sentence is available to the learner, only that the thematic roles are associated with the individuals referred to in the sentence. We might assume that at an early stage of cognitive development the set of roles that can be perceived by the learner is relatively restricted, perhaps to **theme** only. Recognition of a more highly differentiated set of thematic roles by the learner might correlate with the growth of the learner's linguistic competence, measured in part by the relative complexity of utterances and in part by the abstractness of the subject matter.

[34]We will speak informally of the thematic role as assigned to the NP. Actually the thematic role is assigned to the representation of the referent of the NP in R-Structure.

In order for two R-structures to differ, some NP must be assigned one thematic role in one and a different thematic role in the other. That is, for NP_i, thematic roles $t \neq t'$ and domains $k \neq k'$,

(i) $<i, t, k> \in R_A$ & $<i, t, k> \notin R_C$ & $<i, t', k> \in R_C$, or
(ii) $<i, t, k> \in R_A$ & $<i, t, k> \notin R_C$ & $<i, t, k'> \in R_C$, or
(iii) both (i) and (ii).[35]

We will consider the nonassignment of a thematic relation to an NP in one of the two R-structures to constitute a difference between them, for reasons that will be obvious. Errors of type (i) are those in which an NP has been assigned the wrong thematic role; this can occur if it is assigned the wrong grammatical relation, for example.[36] Errors of Type (ii) are those in which the NP is misconstrued with the wrong clause in the sentence, which can occur because of incorrect coindexing with an empty category, or because of an incorrect parsing of the sentence.

Consider the example of *John ate the radish.* Suppose the learner hypothesizes that the first NP is the object, and that the second NP is the subject. By Role Assignment, *John* is assigned **A** and *radish* is assigned **E**. By the lexical specification of *eat*, *John* has the **patient** role and *the radish* has the **agent** role. So, if *John* is clearly the **agent** of the act of eating and if *the radish* is clearly the **patient** of the act of eating (in the observable context), this misassignment would constitute a detectable GR-error.

Once the learner has settled on a scheme for assigning DGRs to simple structures, the central problem of learning transformations is to figure out

---

[35]Notice that our definition of detectable GR-error probably cannot be simplified to the requirement that the thematic role of the entity referred to by the NP in question not appear in the set of thematic roles that appear in the input data to the learner, that is: $<i, t, k> \in R_A$ & $<i, t, k> \notin R_C$. If this were the case, then the learner could simply fail to notice the thematic role of a particular object in a context, and this would constitute a detectable GR-error. Given that such errors are the basis for changing the grammar, there would be reason for the learner to change its grammar every time it was not paying attention or otherwise not aware of the thematic role of some object in the context that was mentioned in a sentence. As lack of awareness may occur at any time, and as there must be a time at which detectable errors no longer occur [by our criterion for learning (III)], it does not appear reasonable to allow lack of awareness of a thematic role to constitute the basis for a detectable error. Rather, the correct basis must be different assignments of thematic roles to the same individual.

[36]Another way such errors can occur is if the learner fails to recognize that a given verb does not possess the unmarked pattern of thematic roles. An example is the common **I learnt him how to swim,* where the learner incorrectly takes the subject NP of *learn* to be the **agent** instead of the **recipient**.

what the DGRs of moved NPs are.[37] In general, the learner can make two sorts of errors: (*a*) assign no DGR to the NP, because it is not clear from the surface structure what its underlying DGR is, and (*b*) assign the wrong DGR to an NP, not realizing that it had been moved to a new argument position. We will deal with both cases in Section 5.

5. Detectable GR-Errors Produced by Transformations

We consider now the interaction between the rules assigning DGRs to NPs and the transformational rules that may potentially provide another source of errors for the learner. There are three types of movement transformations that must be taken into account: structure-preserving movements into nonargument position (e.g., *Wh* Movement), structure-preserving movements into argument positions (e.g., NP Movement), and non-structure-preserving movements. We will consider the first two types in this section, and the third in Section 6.

While it is possible for a learner to hypothesize a transformation correctly, we must be concerned with the range of detectable errors that the learner can make. We motivate the Locality Condition by showing how it constrains an otherwise overly expressive linguistic theory. In the linguistic theory that we are assuming here, transformations are not in general bounded, and may in principle apply to phrase markers of any degree of complexity. Thus, without constraints, we can imagine the possibility of interactions between transformations applying on complex phrase markers that yield detectable errors only on complex phrase markers; *FPLA* provides numerous examples of such interactions.

5.1. Movement to COMP

There are several ways for an NP to end up in initial position in Surface Structure. It can be moved into an initial COMP position, it can be generated in an initial position that has a unique grammatical relation associated with it, or it can be placed in that position by linearization in a nonconfigurational language. The problem for the learner is to figure out which of these possibilities is exemplified in the input data.

---

[37]There may be additional problems connected with nonmovement transformations, but we will restrict our attention to movement transformations here. Our remarks concerning movement of NP to an empty argument position hold mutatis mutandis for a theory in which "move NP" is supplanted by a lexical relation.

If the language indicates grammatical relations through inflectional morphology on the NPs, then reordering of constituents will not interfere with the assignment of DGRs, and thus GR-errors will not occur after the stage at which the learner discovers that the language in fact crucially utilizes morphology. Thus the learner does not need to assume movement if it recognizes that the language is a nonconfigurational language that marks DGRs morphologically.[38]

Let us consider an example involving strict word order. Suppose that the language has a topicalization transformation. The learner has already formulated the following hypothesis:

H1:   The subject is the NP preceding the V; the object is the NP immediately following the V.

The learner now encounters the sentence *Beans I was eating* paired with the assignment of thematic roles given in *R*.

R: (i)   *<beans*, **patient**, *eat>*
       (ii) *<I*, **agent**, *eat>*

The learner's hypothesis supports *R*(ii), but not *R*(i). The learner now has two alternatives. First, it can hypothesize that there is an alternative set of syntactic mechanisms in which object is sentence initial and subject immediately precedes the verb. Call this the Base Hypothesis. Second, it can hypothesize that the language has relatively free constituent order. Call this the Nonconfigurational Hypothesis. Third, it can hypothesize a transformation, by inducing the existence of a trace in Surface Structure corresponding to underlying object position in this sentence. Call this the Transformational Hypothesis.

Given that the Base Hypothesis and the Nonconfigurational Hypothesis are available to the learner, we must explain how they are abandoned in favor of the Transformational Hypothesis. We must also explain the basis on which the Transformational Hypothesis is arrived at given the input data.

Let us assume that the Nonconfigurational Hypothesis will be maintained just until the learner discovers that there is no true inflectional

---

[38]If the syntactic mechanism makes crucial use of morphological marking, then the main problem facing the learner is to identify the precise phonological patterns that indicate that an NP is in a particular case. We might speculate that the relative difficulty of determining the morphological structure of words and in particular the indicators of case and agreement marking would lead the learner to adopt a word-order strategy before entertaining others. Such appears to be the case in languages with case marking and relatively free word order. See Slobin (1966).

correlation with the grammatical relation that was assigned to the fronted constituent.[39]

To rule out the Base Hypothesis, we could adopt a principle to the effect that for every DGR there is only one syntactic mechanism that expresses it. But such a principle is empirically false, if by "syntactic mechanism" we mean a particular configuration or morphological marking. Languages that mark surface grammatical relations by case typically use different markers for different cases, and others mix morphology and configuration. Thus there must be direct evidence against the Base Hypothesis.

Presumably, the presence in topicalized position of a constituent that is not the object of the verb could provide sufficient evidence against the Base Hypothesis. If the learner shares the prejudices of the linguist as to what constitutes a significant generalization, sentences like the following will indicate that not all fronted constituents are objects, or at least objects of the expected verb.

(22)   a.   *John, everyone thinks Mary likes.*
       b.   *On Tuesday we're going to Grandma's house.*
       c.   *To John, I gave the beans, and to Mary, the sausages.*
       d.   *John, I gave the beans to.*

If the learner identifies initial position with object, then there will be a detectable GR-error on examples like those in (22).

Suppose that the S-structure of a topicalized sentence is of the form $_{S'}[NP_i \,_S[NP_j \ldots [e] \ldots]]$.[40] If the learner has adopted the Base Hypothesis, the DGR object is assigned to NP_i and some DGR is assigned to $[e]$, depending on its syntactic position. If $[e]$ is an object, then there will be two NPs with the same DGR. Thus these two NPs will be assigned the same role, say **A**. The mapping into R-structure will not yield a GR-error on this particular example, as the NPs in the learner's R-structure will have the same thematic roles assigned to them as do the NPs in the input R-structure.[41]

If $[e]$ is not an object, then there will be examples in which some other

---

[39]We are assuming that a nonconfigurational language must mark grammatical relations by inflection, either on the verb or on the NPs. It is difficult to see how else grammatical relations could be effectively marked in such a language. Significantly, there is no basis for hypothesizing a movement transformation in a language that does not use constituent order and hierarchical structure to mark grammatical relations, for two reasons: (*a*) by assumption, inflectional marking is sufficient to signify the grammatical function of any NP in such a language; and (*b*) there is no basis for hypothesizing gaps without constituent-order generalizations.

[40]We assume for now that the learner has a procedure for recognizing empty categories in Surface Structure. See Section 8.4 for discussion.

[41]While the Distributedness condition rules out assignment of the same roles to different sets of individuals, it does not produce a detectable GR-error in the case where one NP is empty and bound by the other.

NP_k is an object. Then there will be a violation of the Distributedness requirement (two sets of individuals with the same role) and a detectable error.

The detectable GR-error causes rejection of a rule assigning object to the first constituent in the S. If object is no longer assigned to the fronted NP, then this NP will not be assigned a role. To force the hypothesization of a movement transformation, we invoke the Completeness condition, that is, the requirement that every lexical NP must have a role assigned to it. Given this requirement, $_{S'}[NP_i \ _S[NP_j \ \ldots \ [e] \ \ldots \ ]]$ cannot be the deep structure, as NP_i would not have a role assigned to it by any configurational syntactic mechanism. On this basis the learner hypothesizes that the grammar includes a transformational rule of movement to COMP (COMP being the constituent that precedes the subject).[42]

We are assuming as part of our discussion of the learning schema LS a learning procedure (LP) that is related to the learning procedure of the degree-2 theory. As in the degree-2 theory, we must incorporate the hypothesization of transformations into LP for the degree-0 theory, a preliminary version of which is the following:

(23)   *LP: If there is a detectable GR-error in the child's grammar, then*
          (a) if the NP c-commands[43] an [e] and cannot have a role assigned to it, assume a movement transformation;

---

[42]An equivalent approach would be to assume, along the lines of Koster (1978b), that the fronted constituent is generated in Deep Structure in COMP position and inherits a thematic role by binding [e]. Because it is not in an argument position governed by the verb it cannot be assigned a thematic role directly, so it must be assigned a role by Coindexing with [e]. The rule of Coindexing for such cases must be the mirror image of *Wh* Fronting, and thematic interpretation must be ordered after Coindexing.

We prefer the transformational formulation because it allows us to capture certain facts by applying the Locality Condition to the transformation "move *Wh* to COMP." (See Chapter 4 for discussion.) It is conceivable that the same generalizations could be captured as well in the alternative sketched out in the preceding paragraph, but we will not pursue this question here. For some discussion, see the reviews of Koster (1978b) by Culicover (1980) and Wilkins (1981a).

[43]More generally, a fronted constituent that has been moved to COMP will c-command its trace, because COMP c-commands S. This relationship is not equivalent to the "binding" of a variable by an NP, since if the fronted constituent is not an NP but contains an NP, the trace of the fronted constituent does not correspond to a variable in the representation of the logical form of the sentence. Thus, *to whom did you give the book* [e] does not have a logical form in which there is a variable ranging over expressions of the semantic type corresponding to "*to* NP," but one in which there is a variable ranging over persons. See van Riemsdijk and Williams (1982) for discussion of this point.

Moreover, it is not apparent that the relationship between a fronted constituent and the gap in a relative clause is the semantic one of variable binding, but nevertheless the c-command relationship holds. What is crucial to the hypothesization of movement, in the current framework, is the identification of a gap in the syntactic structure.

(*b*) *otherwise find the syntactic mechanism exemplified on NP. Add a rule* $<\gamma, \mu>$ *for some* γ.[44]

5.2. Movement to COMP: The Complex Case

It will be useful to define a particular type of GR-error.

(24)   A **Misassignment Error** is a detectable GR-error where, for some NPs with indices $\mathbf{I} = \{i, i', \ldots\}$, thematic roles $\mathbf{T} = \{t, t', \ldots\}$ and domains $\mathbf{K} = \{k, k', \ldots\}$, the child's R-structure R_C and the adult's R-structure R_A are distinct subsets of $\mathbf{I} \times \mathbf{T} \times \mathbf{K}$ (the set of all triples $<i, t, k>$, $i \in \mathbf{I}$, $t \in \mathbf{T}$, $k \in \mathbf{K}$) and moreover R_A and R_C are well formed.

In other words, all of the right thematic roles are assigned, but to the wrong entities. This type of error can occur in the simple sentence when the learner is first determining the mapping between grammatical relations and syntactic mechanisms, for example. Presumably, in such a case the real-world context, which defines the R-structure presented to the learner, causes the error to be detectable.

Given that the basic rules of the grammar are established, the other way that a Misassignment Error can occur is if an NP is assumed by the learner to "bind" the wrong [*e*]. Such a state of affairs can arise when there are two [*e*]s in a sentence that the NP c-commands. We will consider the kinds of problems that arise for the learner if the class of grammars allows languages in which there is a systematic ambiguity in the identification of the underlying grammatical functions of moved constituents. Suppose that the following example is grammatical in such a language.

(25)   *What did you tell John who* [*e*] *hit* [*e*]*?*

While data presented to the learner contain the empty categories, it is implausible to assume that the data also indicate the indices on these [*e*]s. Therefore the learner must carry out some coindexing procedure to determine the deep structure and then compare the consequences of this procedure with the input R-structure. If there is no principle for assigning indices and if indices are assigned randomly, there will always be a datum

---

[44]LP is assumed to apply at a stage after the base component has been formulated. If we broaden LP to take into account learning of both the base component and transformations, then we will have to prevent it from constantly using transformed sentences to reject correct prior hypotheses about the base component. We will not deal with this more complex situation here in detail, but we do touch on it in what follows.

for which the learner's hypothesis is incorrect, and therefore there will always be detectable GR-errors on these complex sentences. In other words, if both $[what_i \ldots who_j \ldots [e_i] \ldots [e_j] \ldots]$ and $[what_i \ldots who_j \ldots [e_j] \ldots [e_i] \ldots]$ are well formed, there will always be an error on a datum where there is one assignment of indices but the child hypothesizes the other. As COMP cannot be doubly filled (and there is, of course, only a single COMP in any S'), complex sentences are the only sentences on which such errors will occur, thus giving us a counterexample to degree-0 learnability.[45] This is another type of Misassignment Error, which we must rule out.

The Locality Condition provides a principled basis for assigning indices to $[e]$: Coindex $[e]$ with the closest c-commanding NP that lacks a grammatical relation. In Example (25), either both $[e]$s will be coindexed with *who,* or one $[e]$ will not be coindexed at all, depending on other assumptions about coindexing. Thus the sentence will be ill formed, either because *who* is assigned two DGRs or because one of the two $[e]$s is not bound.

The Locality Condition constitutes the unmarked case. We can see how a language can in fact allow sentences like (25) while conforming to LC. If the learner encounters such sentences, it will have to develop an auxiliary rule of coindexing, as the simple rule "coindex" is blocked by LC. The auxiliary rule, in order to avoid the LC, must specifically mention the intervening context that otherwise would cause LC to be invoked.

Consider the structure in (26).

(26) $wh_i \ldots [wh_j \ldots [e] \ldots]$

A simple rule that will permit a violation of LC is one that mentions the intervening *wh*:

---

[45]We show in Section 6 that all movement transformations must be structure preserving if degree-0 learnability is to hold. This requirement extends to movements into COMP and in fact all nonargument positions. A prediction that follows is that if a language appears to have doubly filled COMP, either one of the elements in COMP is a morphological marker and not a moved constituent, or at least one of the fronted constituents is not in COMP. In order for something to be fronted but not in COMP (or in a designated TOPIC position), the language would have to be nonconfigurational, and hence mark grammatical relations either with case or with verbal agreement.

Thus, in English we have contrasts like the following, pointed out by Delahunty (1981):

(i)   *To John, what did you give [e] [e]?*
(ii) **To whom, the book did you give [e] [e]?*

These examples suggest that there are distinct TOPIC and COMP positions. Otherwise, we would expect (ii) to be grammatical, if PP and NP could both appear in COMP.

(27)   *Extended Coindexing:*[46] wh_i wh $[e]$
$$1 \quad 2 \quad 3 \Rightarrow 1\ 2\ 3_i$$

The LC will not allow the leftmost *wh* to bind $[e]$ without further specification of the structural condition. A structural description such as (26) occurs just in case the lower *wh* is not fronted, but is in initial deep structure position. For example, a subject NP in a language like English would satisfy this criterion. Whether a subject NP undergoes *Wh* Movement to adjacent COMP is an open question.[47]

Consider next the structure in (28).

(28) $wh_i \ldots [wh_j \ldots [e] \ldots [e] \ldots]$

Extended Coindexing will allow wh_i to bind either $[e]$, as the first $[e]$ will not block the binding of the second $[e]$. An empty node is not a factor in the application of the LC. As such a structure would in principle yield ambiguity, we would predict that application of Extended Coindexing will be further constrained for such cases. Those languages that allow structures like (26) will require additional machinery if structures like (28) must also be allowed.

---

[46]Extended Coindexing is a procedure in the learner's (or hearer's) parser that is the inverse of Extended *Wh* Movement for languages that allow extraction from *wh* islands. We presume that in general *Wh* Movement and Coindexing are two facets of the same rule; if a language has (Extended) *Wh* Movement then the learner-hearer must have a procedure for coindexing fronted constituents and their traces in surface structures.

[47]To pursue the matter briefly, let us assume that a function of *Wh* Movement is to signal the scope of the interrogative. It is a straightforward matter to define "scope" so that an interrogative attached to S will have scope over the entire S if there is no interrogative in COMP that takes precedence. [Such disjunctive definitions are not uncommon in linguistic theory; see Kayne's (1981b) definition of "proper government" for a case in point.]

This formulation of "scope" would be supported by consideration of negative sentences. It is shown in Culicover (1981) that positive tags are grammatical when negation has sentential scope. For example,

(i) *John didn't see a single man, did he?*
(ii) *Not a single man did John see, did he?*

In (i), sentential scope occurs when negation is attached to S. In (ii), it occurs when a negative constituent is moved into COMP. Example (iii) shows that a negative subject can also have sentential scope.

(iii) *Not many people were at the movies, were they?*

It is thus reasonable to conclude that the same definition of "scope" can be used for interrogatives. Thus there is no semantic motivation for applying *Wh* Movement to subjects within a single clause.

For theoretical motivation against movement of subjects, we recall the constraint in *FPLA* against string-preserving, structure-changing movement. (See Chapter 4, Section 4 for discussion.)

We cannot explore here the full range of possible weakenings of LC. The sort of language that we have been describing may in fact exist; see the discussion of Danish by Erteschik (1973) and of Swedish by Engdahl (1980). To enrich the theory satisfactorily, we would have to develop a principled account of the sorts of violations of LC that are possible, a task that would take us far afield.[48]

Notice also that ambiguity in the case of structures like (28) arises just in case the two fronted *wh*s are both NP arguments of verbs. Suppose that one *wh* (at least) is adverbial. Then the two *wh*s are functionally distinguished by their surface syntactic form. Thus a language could further avoid systematic ambiguity by specifying in the Extended *Wh* Movement transformation that the *wh* phrase to be moved over a *wh* in COMP not be NP. This presumes, of course, that the traces of the two *wh*s are also distinguishable in the surface structure.

Danish is a language that allows this type of Extended *Wh* Movement. There is some reason to believe that the way that Danish avoids the problem raised by structures like (28) is by replacing an [*e*] in subject position by the dummy element *det* ('it'). Thus in the structure wh_i . . . [wh_j *det* . . . [*e*]] *det* indicates that the *wh* adjacent to it binds it, leaving only one possible coindexing of the structure. (See Erteschik 1973.)

If marked violations of LC are permitted in the theory, they cannot be permitted to produce errors in a degree-0 theory. Either the degree-0 requirement must be relaxed for such phenomena, or the theory of grammar constrains them so narrowly that errors are impossible.

In summary, then, there are two ways to rule out Misassignment Errors. The first type of error is detectable from context. For the second type, a language must disallow *wh* . . . *wh* . . . [*e*] . . . [*e*], have a disambiguating mechanism, or allow it only where there is no chance of ambiguity (e.g., where one moved constituent is an NP and the other is an ADV).

5.3. Movements to Argument Positions

We consider next the problem of learning that an NP that bears a surface grammatical relation with respect to a particular verb is in fact to be assigned the thematic role assigned by that verb to some other grammatical

---

[48]One possibility worth pursuing is that "marked" rules may mention one context predicate. Interestingly, Lasnik and Kupin's (1977, p. 180) restrictive formalism for transformations allows exactly one context predicate.

In order for a rule to have the effect of extracting a constituent from a lower clause, the particular context predicate would have to be (a particular form of) COMP, for example, COMP X *wh* Y *wh* Z $\Rightarrow$ 5 2 3 4 0 6. Such a rule would violate NBC of the degree-2 theory of *FPLA*.

argument position. At the point at which the learner recognizes that the surface structure alone is not sufficient to assign the correct thematic roles, the theory must make available to the learner the appropriate class of hypotheses.

For expository convenience we will characterize what is to be acquired as an NP Movement transformation. As we noted in Chapter 3, it is entirely possible that the class of phenomena captured by NP Movement are in fact to be expressed as a lexical rule. If so, then the range of hypotheses will not involve NP Movement, but the corresponding lexical rules.[49]

A transformation moving an NP from one argument position to another presents a special problem for the learner. Other things being equal, the learner proceeds on the basis that the Surface Structure position of an NP is an indication of its grammatical relation. Structure-preserving movements to argument positions are thus potentially misleading.

Consider a simple example of NP Movement in English.

(29)   *John was tripped (by the dog).*

Suppose that the learner has never encountered a passive before. It may recognize the presence of *was*, but not knowing its significance, may ignore it or speculate that it is some kind of subtle aspectual marker, not an indicator of voice.

Suppose that there is no *by*-phrase (or that the learner ignores the *by*-phrase). Because there is then no object in this sentence, the role **A** is assigned to the only argument governed by the verb, in this case *John*. **A** is realized as **theme**. The input data has *John* as {**theme, patient**}. If the learner knows the verb *tripped*, then the information is already available that *trip* governs **theme**, **patient**, and **agent** in the transitive use, and **theme** in the intransitive use.[50]

---

[49]See Bresnan (1982) and Bresnan and Kaplan (1982) for one formalism in which lexical rules may be expressed. They assume that a lexical rule assigns to one grammatical argument of the verb the thematic role associated with another grammatical argument. In Chapter 3 we suggest a modification, in which one of the thematic roles governed by a morphologically marked verb is directly assigned to the subject regardless of the grammatical relation with which it would be associated. In either case, what would have to be learned is the relevant morphology, and the relevant thematic roles or arguments.

[50]The learner applies the following schema, repeated from Chapter 1.

Role Assignment:
  (i) *Assign lexically idiosyncratic roles.*
  (ii) *Assign **theme** to the object if there is one. Otherwise assign **theme** to the subject.*
  (iii) *(a) Assign **goal** to subject or (b) assign **patient** to object and **agent** to subject or (c) **instrument** to subject or . . . .*

(30)   Input data: *John*   **theme**

_____
                                             patient
_____

         Learner's interpretation:

                           John   **theme**

_____

Suppose that the learner attempts to take the *by*-phrase into account. There is no basis for hypothesizing NP Movement in the English passive as long as the main verb is hypothesized to be *tripped*. If the learner does not identify the passive morphology, a Misassignment Error for this sentence may arise through the strategy of assigning object to the object of the *by*-phrase.[51]

Alternatively, the learner may revise the lexical entry for *trip* to conform to the input data shown in (30): Intransitive *trip* is then exceptional for the learner in that its subject, marked **A**, is not only a **theme** but a **patient**.[52] This strategy will be contradicted by any subsequent input in which *trip* is used actively, as *John tripped*.

If the learner hypothesizes that *by* assigns **E** to its object, then there will still be an error, because the surface subject will not be assigned **patient** (as presumably it was never the object) although the object of the *by*-phrase will be assigned **agent**.

In summary, then, the plausible strategies available to the learner for constructing a nontransformational analysis of the passive result in GR-errors. The learner cannot be allowed to reject the rules for assigning grammatical relations that work correctly for all active sentences.

The input data has *John* as **patient** and *the dog* as **agent**. In order for *John* to be **patient** of *tripped* it must possess some other grammatical relation than what it appears to possess. By a process of reconstruction, we

---

[51]The language acquisition literature suggests that this is in fact what children do. See Bever (1970).

[52]It is not clear that such an option should be allowed. We know of no verbs where the subject of an intransitive active gets the thematic role **patient**. The difference between middle verbs and passive with respect to the thematic roles of the surface subject is in fact good reason to treat the surface subject of the middle verbs as a deep subject and the surface subject of the passive as an deep object.

can deduce that *John* would be **patient** if it were the object of *tripped.*[53] This must be the basis for hypothesizing a transformation of NP Movement in the case of the passive. In the case of Misassignment Errors then, the learning procedure must allow for the possibility that the learner's grammar assigns DGRs correctly, and that the NPs in a passive sentence have been moved to new positions in Surface Structure.[54]

The problem before the learner, then, is to distinguish between those cases in which its rules for assigning grammatical relations are simply wrong and those cases in which movement has applied. In order to guarantee convergence of the learning procedure, we must assume that the existence of a complete set of rules for assigning grammatical relations places a high priority on the hypothesization of a movement transformation.

We saw earlier that the Locality Condition rules out Misassignment Errors that result from indexing errors. If a Misassignment Error does occur, the learner must test whether an NP Movement derivation would yield an interpretation consistent with the input data. If the learner hypothesizes that *John* is the deep object in (29), and if all movements are structure preserving, the subject must be empty in Deep Structure. As Distributedness does not allow the assignment of two roles to one NP, the function of the passive participle must therefore be that of deleting the role assigned to the empty subject. We will presume that this function is in fact the rule of Universal Passive, mentioned in Chapter 3, which is triggered by some mechanism such as the passive participle. The task for the learner is to recognize that its language contains such a mechanism (see also Footnote 54).

To summarize this discussion, we add to LP a subprocedure for hypothesizing NP Movement. It is given as (*b*) in the following revision:

[53]The corresponding hypothesis in a lexical analysis would be that the passive morphology requires the assignment to the subject of (*a*) the thematic role of the direct object, (*b*) the **patient** role, or (*c*) any role governed by the verb. Which of these alternatives is in fact to be allowed by the theory depends in part on empirical considerations. See Bresnan (1982).

[54]A natural strategy to pursue in the case of the passive would be to say that English has the following rules for assignment of DGRs:

(*a*) <object, [NP, VP]>;
(*b*) <object, [NP, S]> in the context *be* V + *en*;
(*c*) <subject, [NP, S]> otherwise.

However, allowing (*b*) greatly increases the expressive power of the theory, and considerably relaxes the constraints on what constitutes a possible "syntactic mechanism." Contextual information that appears in structural descriptions in the Standard Theory would be recapitulated in the rules for assigning grammatical relations to syntactic mechanisms.

(23′)   **LP:**   *If there is a detectable GR-error in the child's grammar,*
          then
          (a) if the NP c-commands an [e] and cannot have a role
               assigned to it, assume a movement transformation;
          (b) if there is a Misassignment Error, then hypothesize a
               movement transformation;
          (c) otherwise find the syntactic mechanism exemplified on
               NP. Add a rule $<\gamma, \mu>$ for some γ.

Naturally, whether or not the hypothesis specified by LP is viable depends on additional considerations, including the grammatical constraints on derivations and on the state of the grammar.[55] As we noted earlier, (*b*) works only when the learner can determine the morphological indicator of Universal Passive (or of some related transformation that deletes roles). If there is no way that the learner at some particular stage can accommodate a detectable GR-error, then we might presume that the error is simply ignored.

5.4. Movement to Argument Positions in Complex Sentences

Suppose (31) were a possible input datum.

(31)   S-structure: *[John was told [that Mary would see]]*

         R-structure:

NP	Verb	Role
John	*told*	**theme**
		goal
arb		**source**
Mary	*see*	**goal**[56]

As NP Movement does not leave a trace, the S-structure does not indicate whether *John* is the object of *told* or of *see*. If the learner assumes the latter, there will be a detectable GR-error. The learner's R-structure will be that of (32).

---

[55]This also assumes that a transformational operation can move at most one constituent. There can be no interchange of NPs for instance.
[56]It would be more accurate to classify the subject of *see* as an **experiencer**.

(32)   R-structure:

NP	Verb	Role
arb	*told*	**source**
Mary	*see*	**goal**
John		**theme**
		source

As we saw in the case of movement to COMP in complex sentences, the potential for systematic ambiguity must be ruled out in principle. In the earlier case, systematic ambiguity occurred only in complex sentences where there were two movements, because such movements leave traces. But where there are no traces, even a single movement produces the potentiality for such ambiguity, as the preceding example shows.

We could rule out examples like (32) by requiring NP Movement to be clause bound. However, it would be preferable to extend an already motivated constraint rather than adopting a new one.

The Locality Condition in fact rules out the case that we have considered, and all movements of NP over an intervening NP. The empirical consequences of adopting LC for NP Movement are discussed in Chapter 3.

An interesting consequence of the alternative view of the passive, which is that it is a lexical rule, is that the locality of the rule, in effect the clause-boundedness condition, follows directly from the fact that the definition of grammatical relations is local. Specifically, the theory of grammar allows the formulation of primitive grammatical relations in terms of very simple syntactic configurations; no grammatical relation can be defined on a structure involving more than one VP, for example.[57] So, if a lexical rule is defined as a mapping between thematic roles and grammatical relations governed by a verb, the rule will apply locally as a consequence of the local definition of grammatical relations. Similarly, if the thematic roles are assigned in terms of the grammatical relations, and if a lexical rule is defined as a relation between thematic roles assigned to designated grammatical relations, the lexical rules will be local.

To summarize to this point, what we have demonstrated is that if all movements are structure preserving and if the base component is severely constrained, the LC will rule out detectable GR-errors that appear only

---

[57]See *FPLA*, Chapter 7.

in complex sentences.[58] We will recapitulate these observations more systematically in Section 7. We turn first to the problem of non-structure-preserving movements.

6. Non-Structure-Preserving Movement Transformations

In Sections 6.1–6.3 we will look again at the interactions between non-structure-preserving transformations and raising transformations, which apply in complex sentences.

6.1. The Role of Raising Transformations

In Section 2 we discussed the fact that even in an extremely restrictive theory, raising transformations must be specifically constrained in order for degree-2 learnability to hold. Here we consider raising transformations again, this time in the context of a degree-0 theory. First let us review the status of these rules in the degree-2 theory.

Perhaps the most consequential assumption of the degree-2 theory is the degree-2 property itself. As suggested in *FPLA*, Chapter 1, the descriptive consequences of a theory of language learnability vary radically depending on the bound on the complexity of the primary data utilized by the learner. Within the general framework of language learnability of which the degree-2 theory is a special case, this bound determines the extent to which transformations can relate parts of a phrase marker that are not underlying clausemates.

To utilize an example from Chapter 1 of *FPLA*, suppose that raising transformations are permitted by the theory of grammar. Consider the tree in (33).

---

[58]Notice, however, that it is not sufficient to rule out all such errors. Consider Example (i).

　(i) *John was told [would see Mary].

Nothing so far would rule out the hypothesis that *John* was the subject of *see* in Deep Structure. It must be the case that NP Movement leaves no trace so that the example is ruled out by conditions on the well-formedness of the agreement morphology. Alternatively, it could be the case that agreement takes place at NP Structure.

(33)

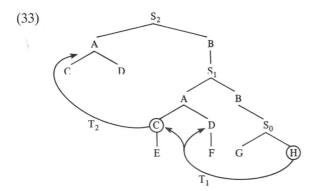

Suppose that the transformation T_1 raises H to a position between C and D on S_1, creating an error through misattachment. Transformation T_2 raises C to the left of A in S_2.

An error-producing raising transformation T_1 will produce an error only on a degree-1 phrase marker, **if it is exclusively a raising transformation**. Given that there are raising transformations, the transformation T_2 that produces a detectable error following the application of T_1 may also be exclusively a raising transformation. Thus the theory permits a grammar in which two raising transformations produce a detectable error only on a degree-2 phrase marker; neither transformation will produce a detectable error by itself on a degree-1 phrase marker. If the theory of grammar permits raising transformations in the context of this general theory of language learnability, we cannot impose a degree-1 restriction on the class of grammars. The example just outlined shows that there are detectable errors that occur only on a degree-2 phrase marker, and not on any smaller phrase marker.

Restricting raising transformations in the degree-2 theory is accomplished by blocking the analysis of a raised constituent. In general, if a constituent that contains an error cannot be analyzed by a transformation, then there is no detectable error. The Raising Principle, discussed earlier, is an explicit statement that raised constituents cannot be analyzed. It is possible to imagine other, less direct devices for accomplishing the same end. In Chapter 7 of *FPLA* it is suggested that if all raising is into COMP, and if all attachment to COMP is non-structure-preserving, the Freezing Principle will block analysis of any raised constituent. However, it is also noted there that there seem to be instances of raising that are not attachment to COMP, for example, extraposition. Either such transformations do not allow the construction of counterexamples to the degree-2 property or the Raising Principle cannot be dispensed with in favor of the Freezing Principle in the degree-2 theory. In fact, as we showed in Section 2, even severe restrictions on the form of rules do not allow elimination of the Raising Principle or a constraint that gives at least the same results.

6.2. Transformational Errors in a Degree-0 Theory

In general, a transformation can produce two sorts of errors. First, it can attach a constituent in the wrong way, yielding a **structural error**. Second, it can yield a surface structure that is not correctly interpreted by the learner's grammar, which we will call an **indexing error**. Both sorts of errors show up as GR-errors, as we have seen.

The degree-2 theory is concerned with structural errors. In the degree-0 theory, it is possible to construct a comparable situation in which a transformation is learned incorrectly on a simple (or even complex) datum: The learner assigns the wrong surface structure to a sentence exemplifying this transformation. On the basis of this wrong surface structure, the learner hypothesizes an incorrect rule of the form $<\gamma, \mu>$ to assign a grammatical relation to the incorrectly attached constituent. On some complex datum the GR-error is revealed, but it is never revealed on simpler data. Such a situation is illustrated by the following.

(34)

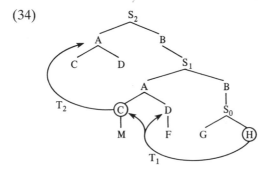

Suppose that in this language the grammatical relation γ is associated with the configuration [H, C]. In the adult grammar T_1 must attach H under C, whereas in the child's grammar H is attached to D.

In the case of simple sentences of the form *mhfg* the learner has a GR-error but no detectable GR-error, because the learner will adduce that there is an empty category into which H is moved, and this empty category bears the DGR that in the adult's grammar is represented as [H, C]; thus the learner adopts [H, D] for this grammatical relation.

In a more complex sentence to which T_2 applies, the input to the learner will be a surface string of the form *mhcdfg*, where *mh* has been moved to the left of C in the higher S. The learner cannot assign a grammatical relation to h, because it does not appear in a configuration with which a grammatical relation is associated in the learner's grammar. Significantly, h must be assigned a grammatical relation with respect to the lower S, but there is no syntactic mechanism of the lower S that the learner can use. The configuration [H, C] is ruled out because the learner has already used [H, D] to express this grammatical relation. Therefore there is a detectable GR-error on this structure in the form of a violation of the Distributedness condition.[59]

6.3. Restricting Raising in a Degree-0 Theory

In order to be degree-0 learnable the class of grammars provided by the linguistic theory must have the following property.

(35) **Degree-0 property:** *If the learner's grammar makes a detectable error, it makes a detectable error on a datum of degree 0.*

In the preceding section we saw a counterexample to degree-0 learnability involving a raising transformation. We can construct other examples in which the error is not revealed by a raising transformation, but caused by a raising transformation. As a raising transformation is a degree-1 transformation (an S-essential transformation in the sense of *FPLA*), if it produces an error at all it will be on a degree 1 or greater phrase marker. Any subsequent transformation that reveals the error will produce a counterexample to the degree-0 property.

We have to consider two essential cases, then. In Case I, the error is revealed by a raising transformation. In Case II, the error is caused by a raising transformation. It appears that the following constraints would rule out both of these cases:

1. There are no raising transformations.

---

[59]It is immaterial whether or not the movement of H leaves a trace. The presence of a trace simply indicates that the position to which H is moved does not assign a grammatical relation. But in the simple sentence, the particular configuration of the position to which H is moved is not known to the learner. The error is then an error in the base component, rather than a GR-error.

If the theory specifies a priori what the configuration is to which H is moved, then there can be no error regardless of whether the movement of H leaves a trace. As the problem is to eliminate errors on degree-1 phrase markers which are not detectable on degree-0 phrase markers, tightening the theory in this way constitutes a solution to the problem. See the next section for fuller discussion.

2. Transformations do not produce errors.[60]
3. There are no transformations.

Clearly (1) cannot be true in a transformational theory as there is empirical evidence for raising (i.e., unbounded movement) in many languages. Notice that the example that we gave did not require that the transformation always raise; it was sufficient to have a transformation that applies unboundedly, and to construct the example so that the error would appear just in case the unbounded movement occurred.

If the theory of grammar allows transformations, (3) cannot be true either; hence (2) must be true. That is, all movement transformations must be structure preserving.[61]

Thus we arrive at the following alternatives: Either there are no transformations or transformations do not produce errors. A "configurational" theory of the sort proposed by Koster (1978a, 1980) bears serious consideration not only because of its restrictiveness but also because of its implications for degree-0 learnability. In order for us to pursue Koster's approach here we would have to assume not only that so-called unbounded transformations like *Wh* Fronting are in fact to be reformulated as binding of a variable by a quantifier, but that **all** "stylistic" movement transformations such as Extraposition, Complex NP Shift, Inversion, and Stylistic Inversion are actually base configurations. The implications of such an approach for a theory of the base are potentially serious, and the danger in taking such an approach is that problems in the learnability of transformations are simply replaced by problems in the learnability of the base component; it is still necessary to figure out which are the canonical structures and which are the stylistic alternatives.

Rather than risk uncharted waters, let us adopt for now the less radical alternative—that there are transformations, but that for reasons having to do with the theory of grammar they do not cause attachment errors. As discussed earlier, the requirement that all movement transformations be structure preserving, along with a principle such as the Locality Condition, will allow us to maintain the degree-0 property.

---

[60]The constraint could not simply be that raising transformations do not produce errors, because of Case I. The demonstration in Section 2 that raising transformations are structure preserving must be coupled with the requirement that transformations that feed raising transformations produce no errors in order for there to be no degree-1 errors at all.

[61]If they are not structure preserving in the strong sense, that is, substitutions for empty categories, then the "landing site" of every movement transformation must be unambiguously specified by the theory (see Baltin 1981). The structure-preserving hypothesis, being the more restrictive, is the one that we prefer to adopt here.

It is not obvious that the structure-preserving property can be maintained for all movement transformations, for precisely the same reason that we cannot assume that all transformations are actually alternative base configurations in a "configurational" approach: Other movement transformations such as Extraposition, Complex NP Shift, Inversion, and Stylistic Inversion do not in general appear to have this property. We argue in Section 8 that contrary to appearances, such "stylistic" rules are structure preserving.[62]

7. Preliminaries for a Proof of Degree-0 Learnability

In order for a formal proof of degree-0 learnability to be possible, the class of grammars must be formalized. No formalization exists for the class of grammars that we have been considering in this book, and so an attempt at a formal learnability proof would be premature. However, it is still possible to demonstrate certain requirements that such a proof would impose on the class of grammars, and to suggest formal constraints that would satisfy these requirements.

7.1. Transparency

The most fundamental requirement on a class of grammars with respect to learnability is that the learning procedure **converge** on a correct hypothesis in bounded time, where convergence means staying with the correct hypothesis. This means that mismatches between the learner's grammar and the adult's grammar must fall off as time progresses.

Transparency is a property that ensures that mismatches are not likely to occur as the grammar continues to develop. Suppose that the class of grammars allows the assignment of more than one deep structure, and hence more than one R-structure, to a sentence with any S-structure $|S|$.

---

[62]We are led to this position by the fact that we have already shown, in this section, that all movement transformations must be structure preserving in order for the degree-0 property to hold.

The structure-preserving requirement must be expressed in such a way that movements into COMP are structure preserving. There thus must be another position, similar to COMP, which renders "stylistic" movement transformations like Extraposition and Complex NP Shift structure preserving in the same way that COMP renders *Wh* Movement structure preserving. If Topicalization is not movement to COMP, there must be a designated TOPIC position as well. The only other transformations to consider are local permutations, which are not problematic as they involve terminal categories and not arguments (Emonds 1976).

Thus we would have languages that are systematically ambiguous. Such languages would not be learnable by our criteria, because at any time there is a chance that a detectable GR-error will occur in the form of a mismatch between the R-structure assigned to the sentence by the learner and the R-structure associated with the sentence by the adult. Without the transparency property, then, we will always have detectable GR-errors.

In the degree-2 theory the only kinds of detectable errors that can occur are attachment errors, where the mismatches occur because the surface strings produced by the two grammars differ. In the current theory there are in principle two kinds of detectable errors: attachment errors and GR-errors. We eliminate the possibility of the first kind of error by imposing the requirement that all movement transformations be structure preserving.[63] Then to prove learnability we will have to show that the class of grammars is transparent.

7.2. Proving Transparency: Fundamental Transparency

As noted, to prove transparency we must show that no systematic ambiguity exists in the language. There are two sorts of systematic ambiguity that we have to be concerned with: (*a*) **fundamental** systematic ambiguity, where the ambiguity arises from an overabundance of rules for assigning grammatical relations to particular syntactic mechanisms, and (*b*) **complex** systematic ambiguity, where the ambiguity arises in complex structures but not in simpler structures. Typically, the second type will be a consequence of either insufficient constraints on binding possibilities or illegal movements without traces.

We will say that a class of grammars that lacks the first type of ambiguity has the property of **fundamental transparency**, while a class that lacks the second type of ambiguity has the property of **complex transparency**. Fundamental transparency leads to a proof of degree-0 learnability only if complex transparency also holds.

In previous sections we avoided the issue of fundamental transparency by assuming that the learner had mastered the syntactic mechanisms marking the basic grammatical relations. An example that violates fundamental transparency would be one in which the grammar to be learned had the following form:

---

[63]See Section 6 for discussion of how the structure-preserving requirement eliminates attachment errors. The rest of the job is done by the categorial component, which does not allow movements to the same linear position in the string with different attachment possibilities. See Section 5, *FPLA*, chapter 7, and Culicover (to appear) for discussion.

(36)   {<subject, [NP, S]>
        <subject, [NP, VP]>
        <object, [NP, S]>
        <object, [NP, VP]>}

In other words, either grammatical relation can be expressed by one of the same two syntactic devices. The mapping {<γ, μ>} is thus many–many. A strong restriction that would guarantee fundamental transparency would be the following:

(37)   **Strict Biuniqueness**: The mapping $\gamma \to \mu$ is one–one, and the mapping $\mu \to \gamma$ is one–one.

Most likely Strict Biuniqueness is too strong, as the learnability problems arise only when there are two grammatical relations marked by the same syntactic mechanism. A weaker restriction which would have different empirical consequences is:

(38)   **Syntactic Uniqueness**: The mapping $\mu \to \gamma$ is one–one.

Suppose that Syntactic Uniqueness is not only a principle of grammar, but a principle of the learning procedure as well. If a learner has hypothesized <γ, μ> for some μ, then the learner cannot hypothesize another rule involving μ without rejecting the first. As this mapping involves very small sets of elements, eventually a correct hypothesis will be arrived at, by rejecting old hypotheses in favor of new ones at least some of the time.

The learning procedure must function in such a way that correct hypotheses are not systematically rejected. As we are concerned about grammatical relations, we must look at NPs that have been moved transformationally. If they are moved to an argument position, there is always the possibility that a moved NP is taken as an indication that the syntactic mechanism associated with that NP signals the underlying grammatical relation of that NP. The learner will eventually hypothesize that NP Movement is involved. If it does not hypothesize NP Movement, it will continue to produce the same error on subsequent examples of the same type.[64]

---

[64]The learner must be able to hypothesize that if a sentence can in principle be derived by using NP Movement (or a lexical rule, in the alternative theory), it is derived in that way. Otherwise the sort of problem that we are trying to eliminate can always occur.

Note also that it is crucial that NP Movement not involve context. If NP Movement could involve context, we could formulate an NP Movement transformation that applies only to degree-1 sentences. Fundamental GR-errors involving failure by the learner to recognize that this transformation had applied could be resolved only with degree-1 data, thereby violating the degree-0 property that we are trying to establish. See Sections 2 and 7.4 for more discussion of this and related points.

As we wish to allow for a certain amount of context for Extended *Wh* Movement in certain languages, we must somehow explain why there is no "Extended NP Movement." Interestingly, the possibility of "Extended NP Movement" does not arise in a lexical theory as there is no rule schema "move α."

7.3. Complex Transparency

It might appear that since the grammatical relations can be established on simple sentences (degree 0), no additional problems would arise on more complex sentences. The same grammatical relations hold for simple and complex sentences, for example. However, something more needs to be said, for two reasons. First of all, it is not logically necessary that the same grammatical relations hold for simple and complex sentences. Second, on complex sentences GR-errors involving binding can cause systematic ambiguities on complex sentences that do not appear on simple sentences.

Consider the first point. Suppose that there is an error that results from the assignment to NP_k of some thematic role determined by V_1 in (37).

(37) $NP_i \; V_1 \; {}_{S'}[NP_j \; V_2 \; NP_k]$

Although the R-structure associated with this sentence would show clearly that the referent of NP_k does not possess any thematic role with respect to V_1, such evidence is available only on a datum of degree 1 or greater. The error would not appear on a datum of degree 0.

To rule out this sort of situation, we must restrict government so that a verb cannot govern the arguments of another verb. More generally, we must constrain the theory of grammar so that it does not allow an NP to bear either a role or a DGR that is associated with a verb in another clause.[65] This restriction on the theory follows from the Locality Condition, relativized to the rules that assign roles and those that express grammatical relations. It is not surprising to note that all variants of the notion of "government" in the literature explicitly incorporate some version of locality.

The grammatical relations must be **intrinsically local**. By this we mean that there cannot be a grammatical relation that **necessarily** requires a complex sentence to be correctly assigned. Consider the following definition: an NP_k is subject$_{i, j}$ of the jth clause in a phrase marker if NP_k is immediately dominated by $S_{i,} \; i > j$. In other words, an NP that is in some level of the phrase marker actually bears a grammatical relation to some verb a specified distance below it in the phrase marker. Presumably, some aspect of the interpretation of the sentence would depend on what the subject$_{i, j}$ refers to. A detectable GR-error could therefore only occur on a phrase marker of degree $i - j$ or greater, in violation of the degree-0

---

[65]This discussion recapitulates in part observations made in Chapter 7 of *FPLA*. There it was observed that the theory of grammar must provide a very restrictive set of possible grammatical relations. Specifically, it cannot in general allow as a grammatical relation a configuration that crucially involves more than one cyclic level of a phrase marker.

property. Thus such grammatical relations cannot exist, except in the limiting case where $i = j$.

Recall the formalism of Chapter 1. The rules for realizing roles are of the form $<\gamma, t>$, where γ is a DGR and t is a role. The rules for realizing DGRs are of the form $<\gamma, \mu>$, where γ is a DGR and μ is a syntactic mechanism defined in terms of a case marker, an agreement marker, or a syntactic configuration.

But this formalism is imprecise in the sense that it does not specify the particular domains over which t, γ, and μ are defined. Thus the rules for realizing roles are more generally of the form $<<\gamma, k>, <t, k'>>$, where k and k' are domains. Similarly, the rules for realizing DGRs are of the form $<<\gamma, k>, <\mu, k'>>$.

In both cases, the rules for assigning roles and DGRs apply quite freely. Unless we make quite explicit the restriction that $k = k'$, it does not follow that the subject of a verb will be assigned a thematic role with respect to the same verb.

Of course, we have selected a formalism that is more expressive than the empirical phenomena demand, in order to illustrate that the actual state of affairs is not the only imaginable state of affairs. In fact, it is only the requirement of degree-0 learnability that explains why the full expressive power of this notation is not utilized by the grammars of natural language. The relevant instantiation of the Locality Condition guarantees degree-0 learnability with respect to these mappings by imposing the condition $k = k'$.

Turning now to the second point, recall that we saw, in Section 5, that movements to COMP could yield detectable GR-errors on simple data. We might suppose that all movements to nonargument positions in complex sentences would result in the same detectable GR-errors because the movement leaves behind a trace which has the correct grammatical relation assigned to it.

This supposition is incorrect, precisely because movements need not be to the COMP of the S in which an argument is assigned a grammatical relation. As we have suggested, a grammatical relation is in fact a pair $<\gamma, k>$, where γ is one of subject, object, and indirect object, and k is the index of the domain in which the argument has a grammatical function. Allowing for movement to other domains, there are at least two sorts of ways in which confusion and errors can arise in the assignment of grammatical relations: (*a*) the learner's grammar cannot assign to an argument a grammatical relation in its proper domain; and (*b*) the learner's grammar is unable to **unambiguously** assign grammatical relations to a set of arguments, all of which have functions in the same domain.

Recall that we have assumed that the learner is capable of constructing a surface structure corresponding to an input string by using the phrase structure rules of the base component. We assume that the learner can identify the presence of traces of certain movement transformations. But we cannot assume that the learner can unerringly assign the correct **index** to every trace. At best, a simple algorithm for assigning indices will work without error when there is only one gap, one fronted argument, and a simple S.[66]

A principle such as the Locality Condition severely restricts the possibilities for relating empty categories and constituents in nonargument position. In fact, for any configuration there is a unique solution, by the definition of relative adjacency. As we observed in Section 5, it is possible for a learner to acquire special rules that violate LC; but such rules must preserve transparency.

The Locality Condition also guarantees that transparency will be preserved in the case of multiple NP movements. Suppose that we have the following deep structure, where $-*$ indicates some designated inflection on the verb.

(38) $[e^a]$ V$-*$ $[e^b]$ $_S[$ NP$_i$ V NP$_j]$

If NP Movement was unconstrained by the Locality Condition, (38) could yield two surface structures:

(39)   a.   NP$_i$ V$-*$ NP$_j$ $_S[\emptyset$ V $\emptyset]$
         b.   NP$_j$ V$-*$ NP$_i$ $_S[\emptyset$ V $\emptyset]$

But these two structures could also be derived from (40).

(40) $[e^a]$ V$-*$ $[e^b]$ $_S[$ NP$_j$ V NP$_i]$

Consequently the grammar is not transparent, as in a sentence like (39a), for example, NP$_i$ and NP$_j$ could always each have one of two grammatical relations. Derivations of the sort illustrated here are ruled out by the Locality Condition, as one NP can never move over another, and could violate that principle only if they involved a special transformation that stipulated the landing sites of the two NPs.[67]

---

[66]There are also configurations with two gaps where correct indexing can be guaranteed (e.g., if one gap is left by an NP and another is left by a PP). However, the algorithm for assigning indices for such a case will be more complicated than the one required when there is only one gap and one fronted argument, and may depend on subcategorization or selectional restrictions of the verb.

[67]A similar problem can be constructed in a lexical framework. In (i), NP$_i$ is related to the object position of the higher verb, while NP$_j$ is related to the object position of the lower verb.

(i) NP$_i$ V$-*$ NP$_j$ V$-*$

A real example would be *John was expected Bill to be arrested* which has the interpretation of "Someone expected John to arrest Bill."

7.4. Eliminating Error-Producing S-Essentiality

In *FPLA* considerable attention is paid to transformations that are S-essential, in that they crucially require embedded Ss for their application. We cannot allow rules of grammar that are crucially S-essential, because errors in learning them will lead to violations of degree-0 learnability.

In Section 6 we showed that raising transformations will not cause degree-1 attachment errors if they are structure preserving as well as context free. As shown in *FPLA* there are other sorts of S-essentiality that must be taken account of. For example, we cannot have any phrasal categories that obligatorily contain S', because rules that involve these categories would never apply on degree-0 phrase markers (see *FPLA*, Principle of S-Optionality). We cannot allow context predicates in transformations or, more importantly, in rules for assigning grammatical relations. If we did, then S' could be a context predicate and thus any rule involving S' would be S-essential.

If all raising transformations are structure preserving, then it might be supposed that they cannot cause any errors at all. This argument fails to take into account the possibility that the transformation is not recognized as such and thus causes a detectable GR-error of a fundamental sort.

Consider the following example: Grammar G contains NP Movement, but [*e*] appears only in subject position in Deep Structure, and only when there is a sentential complement. Suppose that the learner is presented with a surface (or S-) structure of the form in (41).

(41) $NP_i \ V_j \ {}_{S'}[\ V_k \ ]$

The learner will interpret NP_i as being the **theme** of V_j. But since V_j does not take a **theme** (or perhaps the complement S' is its **theme**) there will be a detectable GR-error on such an example. The correct analysis, for which the error provides evidence, is that NP_i replaces an underlying [*e*]. This error will never occur on a degree-0 phrase marker, because there are no [*e*]s in such a phrase marker, by assumption. Thus we have a violation of the degree-0 property.

To rule out this sort of example, we must assume that [*e*] cannot be subcategorized. This appears to be a plausible assumption, one that is consistent with most of the literature in linguistic theory. We thus formulate the following principle:

(42)   ***Principle of Free Dummies:*** *The distribution of empty categories is free.*[68]

---

[68]This principle follows from the reformulation of NP Movement as a lexical relation involving only arguments governed by a verb. As a verb cannot govern the arguments of another verb, a lexical relation cannot involve an NP unless it is an argument of the verb that is morphologically marked for that relation.

The example in (41) brings up an additional important point. In a language where such structures can occur, the failure of the learner to recognize the thematic properties of the idiosyncratic verbs like V_j (i.e., verbs like *seem*) will in fact yield degree-1 errors that do not necessarily also occur on degree-0 structures. We will return to the problem of lexical idiosyncracy in Section 7.6.

7.5. An Informal Proof

Summarizing the preceding discussion, it appears that the principles mentioned will permit a proof of degree-0 learnability. These principles are: Syntactic Uniqueness, structure-preserving movements, Principle of Free Dummies, restricted structural descriptions, and the Locality Condition. The crucial theorem that we want to prove is the following:

(43)   ***Degree-0 Learnability****: If the rules for assigning grammatical relations yield no detectable GR-errors for structures of degree-0, then they will yield no detectable GR-errors for structures of any complexity whatever.*

Sketch of Proof*:* We enumerate the ways in which detectable GR-errors can occur and then show how each is ruled out. One way is if an NP in argument position has been moved to that position by NP Movement, and the learner does not recognize this. A second way is if an NP in nonargument position binds the wrong empty category. A third way is if the learner has misidentified the syntactic device that indicates what grammatical role an NP plays.

1. By the Locality Condition, there cannot be grammatical relations defined on complex phrase markers. Therefore, all grammatical relations involve configurations or inflections that are locally governed.
2. By the Principle of Free Dummies, NP Movement must apply to phrase markers of degree 0 as well as degree i, $i > 0$. So there cannot be a detectable GR-error on a large phrase marker that results from NP Movement without the same error occurring on a simple phrase marker.
3. As all movements are structure preserving and structural descriptions are restricted, transformations do not crucially involve context elements.[69] Therefore, no transformation can mention a

---

[69]Except if there are marked transformations like Extended *Wh* Movement. Such transformations, if they exist, must be explicitly constrained so that they do not produce errors.

context that is necessarily found in degree i structures where $i >$ 0,[70] and thus no new detectable GR-errors can result in this way.

4. By the Locality Condition, movements to both argument and nonargument positions in complex sentences are transparent, and therefore cannot introduce new detectable GR-errors.

This completes the sketch of the proof, because there are no other ways in which detectable GR-errors can be introduced in this restrictive system.

7.6. Problems

Empirical problems with degree-0 learnability involve linguistic phenomena that are necessarily degree-1 phenomena, such as subcategorization of complements and complementizers. For example, the fact that a particular verb takes a sentential complement is a degree-1 fact. Failure on the part of the learner to recognize that a particular subpart of a sentence is a constituent S' can lead to very clear GR-errors. Similarly, if a verb only appears with a sentential complement, and if the learner fails to learn the correct thematic roles governed by this verb, then technically sentences involving this verb will result in detectable GR-errors on only degree-1 or greater phrase markers. (This is because errors become detectable if they are revealed in mismatches between R-structures, which involve thematic roles.)

The distinction between these errors and those considered in previous sections is clear: These involve lexical phenomena, whereas the others involve rules of grammar. The task for the learner is to determine that the errors it is making on particular data are consequences of inadequacies in lexical representations, and not in the rules of the grammar. It is in fact plausible that the selection of a given verb of particular complement types is not strictly speaking a syntactic matter, but is semantic. For example, the fact that the verb *believe* takes a sentential complement is plausibly viewed as a consequence of the fact that belief is a relation that involves a proposition. Thus, when the object of *believe* is an NP we get contrasts such as the following:[71]

(44)   *John believes* $\left\{ \begin{array}{l} \textit{your answer.} \\ \textit{the correctness of your actions.} \\ \textit{*your shoe.} \end{array} \right\}$

Similar facts hold for extraposition, as in (45).

---

[70]For example, move B to A in the context X A Y B S' Z.

[71]Examples similar to these are also discussed in Chapter 3, Section 3.3.3.

(45)   *It is amazing* $\left\{ \begin{array}{l} \textit{what John says.} \\ \textit{that John is still here.} \\ \textit{the things John says.} \\ \textit{the answers he gives.} \\ \textit{the shoes he wears.} \\ \textit{*your shoe.} \end{array} \right\}$

Another important difference between the "lexical degree-1 errors" and grammatical errors is that the lexical errors are not systematic. Suppose, then, that the learner has an equal probability, given a detectable degree-1 GR-error, of changing the thematic structure determined by a verb or of changing the grammatical rules. If the error is caused by a misconstrual of the lexical item and the grammatical rules are changed, many more errors will occur, given that the grammatical rules were correct in the first place. Eventually the learner will change the lexical item, and the particular error will be eliminated. As there is a finite number of lexical items that might cause the sorts of errors we are considering, eventually all of the lexical items will be correctly learned and the grammatical rules will be correct as well.

The other sorts of errors mentioned that crucially involve degree-1 structures are subcategorization of complementizers. Following Chomsky (1981), we might hypothesize that in the unmarked case the full range of complementizers may appear after a given verb; what is then degree 1 is the set of marked exceptions to this generalization.

As we have not defined the notion "detectable GR-error" for subcategorization of morphological phenomena like complementizers, it is not obvious that degree-0 learnability is seriously affected by this complication. The question arises as to whether there can be a detectable **GR**-error on a degree-1 phrase marker involving the subcategorization of complementizers.

To investigate this matter, consider first the following question: If complementizers are free in "core grammar," as Chomsky (1981) suggests, how can the learner determine the idiosyncratic properties of certain verbs with certain complementizers? Subcategorization of NP arguments does not present a problem if the subcategorization follows from the assignment of thematic roles, because the latter is universal and entails the former. But subcategorization of arbitrary markers like complementizers (assuming for the moment that they are arbitrary) presents quite a different learning problem: **Unless they are learned one by one from positive data, the assignment of arbitrary markers cannot be correctly learned**.

The last point follows from three assumptions: that the data presented to the learner involve only grammatical strings, that the complementizers in the unmarked case are free, and that the exceptions to free assignment of complementizers, that is, the subcategorization facts, are arbitrary and unpredictable idiosyncracies. If the learner assumes the unmarked case, that all complementizers are possible in all contexts, then no positive data, consisting only of grammatical sentences, will falsify this hypothesis. Every grammatical sentence will be consistent with the learner's hypothesis.

We must therefore give up at least one of these three assumptions. The easiest to give up is that the complementizers are free, as "positive data only" forms part of the foundation for the learnability theory, and as no comprehensive semantic theory of the distribution of complementizers currently exists. Assuming, therefore, that complementizers are associated with verbs only on the basis of positive evidence, we arrive at a situation in which degree-1 data is required for learning, but in which there is no possibility of error. We will call this type of learnability **degree-0+ learnability**.

Note the distinction between the degree-1 and degree-0+ phenomena. The former are extensions of core rules that are exceptional in certain well-defined ways. The latter are true degree-1 phenomena that do not allow for degree-1 detectable errors. We hypothesize that the only kinds of degree-0+ phenomena that can occur are subcategorizations of the sort we have been discussing, that is, arbitrary syntactic and morphological marking that is not predictable from semantic considerations.

Suppose that we assume that true syntactic subcategorization is restricted to the specification of unpredictable terminal elements. The "subcategorization" of arguments governed by a verb is, we assume, determined by thematic requirements of the verb (see Chapter 3). All degree-0+ phenomena, such as the selection of complementizers, will be local, since such phenomena will occur in the Θ-governed arguments, and the assignment of thematic roles is local.[72] From these assumptions it follows that no error in the acquisition of a subcategorization fact can yield a detectable GR-error, as detectable GR-errors always involve arguments NPs, never terminal elements.

8. Implications of Degree-0 Learnability

In this concluding section we discuss a variety of implications (and problems) of the preceding material.

---

[72]Siegel (1977) observed that morphological selection is subject to an "Adjacency Condition": The selection of a member of a class of morphemes to attach to an element of the category α in deriving an element of the category β depends on the "outermost" adjacent constituents of α. We would expect that the selection of complementizers would properly fall under a theory of morphology, from which a condition of locality could follow.

8.1. Stylistic Transformations Are Structure Preserving

The stylistic transformations that appear to be non-structure-preserving are those that move constituents to the right. All movements to the left, in English at least, are movements into COMP or TOPIC or into argument position.[73] The movements to the right that are possibly problematic are those illustrated in (46) below.

(46) a. *I gave 0 to Bill a beautiful painting of Mozart.*
      b. *Down the stairs 0 came a pair of angry lions.*
      c. *A man 0 came into the room who was looking for the ticket office.*
      d. *A man 0 is sitting in the next room from Internal Revenue.*
      e. *It bothers me that there is no adequate management in this place.*
      f. *There arose in the neighboring apartment a clamor such as we had never heard before.*

These examples illustrate, in order, Complex NP Shift, Stylistic Inversion, Extraposition of Relative Clause, Extraposition of PP (and of Relative Clause), Extraposition, and Stylistic *There* Insertion (see Rochemont 1978).

An interesting problem that arises in connection with rules of this sort in the classical transformational framework is that of specifying the landing site of the moved constituents. Suppose that there is no empty position to which Extraposition of PP, for example, moves a PP. Together, Examples (47) and (46d) show that Extraposition of PP applies to NPs both in subject and in object position.

(47)   *I'm meeting a man 0 tomorrow from Internal Revenue.*

Because of the fact that the subject NP and the direct object are not at the same level in the phrase marker, the two applications of Extraposition of PP differ in certain structural respects, the precise nature of which depends on the theoretical framework in which the transformation is expressed. Suppose, for instance, that the statement of Extraposition of PP

---

[73]See Ross (1967). Certain movements of adverbs might not be structure preserving, for example, attachment to V as in (i).

(i) *John will [completely rewrite] this document.*

See Jackendoff (1972) for arguments that there is no adverb movement per se, but base generation of adverbs. Culicover (1980) suggests that adverbs are transformationally moved, and that attachments as in (i) are non-structure-preserving. To the extent that the arguments in Culicover (1980) are valid, they constitute counterevidence to the position that we are developing in the text.

is as follows, and that it Chomsky-adjoins the PP to the right of the variable over which the PP moves.

(48)   ***Extraposition of PP***: $X_{\mathrm{NP}}[Y\ PP]\ Z$
         $\qquad 1 \quad 2 \quad 3 \quad 4 \Rightarrow 1\ 2\ \emptyset\ 4 + 3$

In (46d) the variable Z is the entire VP *is sitting in the next room*, whereas in (47) it is a portion of the VP, *tomorrow*. Suppose that for empirical reasons we wish to Chomsky-adjoin the moved constituent to VP in either case. In fact there is no evidence that the attachments are different in the two cases.[74] In order to state the transformation in its simplest form, we require a definition of "landing site" that will yield precisely the results that we want, illustrated in (49)–(50).

(49)

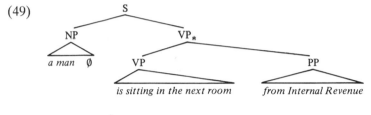

(50)

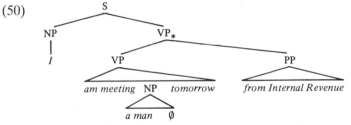

If we proceed along these lines, we run into another problem, however. Notice that the PP in (49) does not c-command the position from which it was moved, whereas the PP in (50) does. It is conceivable that for "stylistic rules," at least, the Surface Structure relationship between a

---

[74]The alternative that we will consider in what follows is that there are different landing sites depending on whether extraposition is from subject or from object. Presumably, extraposition from the higher subject would put the PP further to the right, in particular to the right of constituents of S. But all extraposed constituents go to the left of putative S constituents like result clauses (see Williams 1975), as shown in (i)–(ii).

(i)   a. *So many pictures of John were shown that I felt sick.*
      b. *So many pictures were shown of John that I felt sick.*
      c.**So many pictures were shown that I felt sick of John.*
(ii) a. *I saw so many pictures of John there that I felt sick.*
      b. *I saw so many pictures there of John that I felt sick.*
      c.**I saw so many pictures there that I felt sick of John.*

moved constituent and its original position is irrelevant, but the difference
here at least suggests that we look more deeply into the matter.

Another approach to Extraposition of PP will yield another sort of difference between extraposition from subject position and object position.
Suppose that the theory computes the landing site in terms of the minimal
structure necessary for the rule to apply, so that a moved constituent is
attached to the lowest node that dominates everything in the structural
description. For example, if extraposition is from subject, the PP will be
attached to S, as S is the lowest node that dominates NP, PP, and the
variable Z over which PP is moved. If extraposition is from object, on the
other hand, PP will be attached to VP. The consequence of this approach
will be output structures as follows.

(51)

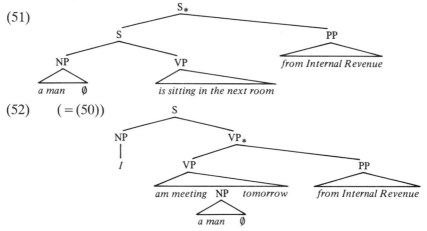

(52)   (= (50))

In such an approach, the computation of where the moved constituent
goes is relatively straightforward, and the extraposed constituent always
c-commands its original position. On the other hand, the surface structures
are quite different.

The problems noted here can be avoided if we assume the following:
(a) there is a designated position in VP to which constituents are moved
when they are moved to the right;[75] and (b) this position is associated with
a standard rule of interpretation that overrides the c-command requirement. Assumption (a) guarantees a uniform output structure for rightward
movement rules and renders them structure preserving. Assumption (b)

---

[75]In Baltin's (1981) account, it is possible to specify the position to which a particular rule
moves an extraposed constituent. On such an approach, it would be irrelevant what the
underlying position of the extraposed constituent was. The analysis that we are moving
toward here is a variant of Baltin's, in which the "landing site" for the extraposed constituent
is in fact a COMP-like position with specific semantic consequences.

gets us around the problem that certain movements to this position will not satisfy the c-command requirement.

What is this designated position? Rochemont (1978) has observed that the apparently non-structure-preserving movement transformations are "stylistic rules" in his sense, which means precisely that they affect the **focus** properties of sentences to which they apply.[76] Horvath (1981) has shown that there is a pre-verbal position in the VP in Hungarian to which focus constituents are moved. Let us suppose, in contrast, that English has a VP-final focus position in VP, which we will call FOCUS, and that the apparently non-structure-preserving rightward movement transformations are in fact movements into FOCUS.[77]

In Horvath's analysis, the FOCUS is a sister of V, as shown in the structure (53).

(53)

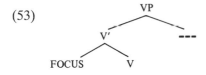

In English, however, we want FOCUS to be the rightmost constituent in VP, so it cannot be a sister of V.[78]

(54)

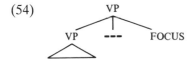

[76]And they do not affect logical form.

[77]As there is also a VP-final focus position in Hungarian, the theory must actually allow two FOCUS positions in VP. See Footnote 78.

[78]See Rochemont (in press) for arguments that both positions must exist in Universal Grammar, and that in fact they both exist in English. The VP-final position is the one to which extraposed constituents move, whereas the position adjacent to the verb is the position of focus in the cleft construction. Briefly, the difference between English and Hungarian is that in English the post-V FOCUS position is an argument position. Any NP in this position will therefore be assigned a thematic role by the verb that governs it, if the verb in fact assigns roles. If the main verb is *be*, no thematic role will be assigned to this position, and thus the object of *be* must bind an empty NP that does have a role assigned to it in order for the interpretation to be well formed. In Hungarian, on the other hand, the pre-V position is not an argument position. So in Hungarian, the FOCUS position can be used even when the main verb assigns thematic roles to its arguments.

It is crucial for this analysis that FOCUS can be a nonargument position, that is, one that does not receive a thematic role. Rochemont also argues that the two positions differ in interpretation: VP-final position is "presentational" focus whereas focus within the VP is "contrastive," in the sense of Culicover and Rochemont (1983).

Supposing that (54) is the correct structure, it will turn out that in Surface Structure PPs extraposed from subject position will not c-command their original position. However, Assumption (*b*) allows us to avoid this problem. Following the analysis of focus in Culicover and Rochemont (1983), let us suppose that there is a rule of Focus Interpretation that necessarily gives wide scope to a constituent marked as focus. The rule of Focus Interpretation in Culicover and Rochemont (1983) is formulated for stress focus; to derive "focus-structure," the focus constituent is moved to the left and an appropriate variable is left behind. Extending the analysis to "constructional focus" (see Rochemont 1978), let us say that FOCUS is moved to the left **without leaving a variable in focus-structure**. As a consequence, the focus-structure for constructional focus will be the same as stress focus.

Example (55) shows the result of Focus Interpretation when focus is stress focus; (56) illustrates a constructional focus interpretation.

(55)   a.   *John sold a picture of MOZART to Mary.*
         b.   *[A picture of Mozart]$_i$ John sold t$_i$ to Mary.*

(56)   a.   *John sold t$_i$ to Mary* $_{FOCUS}$*[a picture of Mozart]$_i$.*
         b.   *[A picture of Mozart]$_i$ John sold t$_i$ to Mary.*

The important point here is that the trace of the moved constituent in (56a) defines the position that will be occupied by the variable in focus structure; in (55) this position is defined by the rule of Focus Interpretation itself.

Assuming that this analysis is on the right track, it can be generalized in a natural way to account for most of the rightward movements illustrated in (46). Complex NP Shift [(46a)] is a movement into FOCUS, as is Extraposition of PP and Extraposition of Relative Clause.

For Stylistic *There* Insertion, we can adopt a similar analysis. In this construction, the subject NP moves into VP-final position. In contrast, in the nonstylistic *There* Insertion construction, the subject NP appears as a Deep Structure complement of the verb. The contrast is revealed when we apply a rule like *Wh* Movement to the moved subject NP. In the nonstylistic case, *Wh* Movement may apply, but it is blocked in the stylistic construction.[79]

(57)   a.   *There was a picture of Nixon on the wall.*
         b.   *Who was there a picture of 0 on the wall?*

___

[79]For a full discussion of differences between these two constructions, see Rochemont (1978) and Milsark (1977).

(58)   a. *There was on the wall a picture of Nixon.*
        b. **Who was there on the wall a picture of 0?*

The example in (57) does not involve movement into FOCUS, whereas that in (58) does. The difference in (57) and (58) may then plausibly be attributed to a general restriction against extraction from a focus constituent; such a restriction is proposed on independent grounds in Culicover and Rochemont (1983). An additional interesting point is the observation in Culicover and Wexler (1977) that extraction is impossible from an NP that has undergone Complex NP Shift. Thus we get differences like the following.

(59)   a. *John gave Mary a picture of Nixon.*
        b. *Who did John give Mary a picture of 0?*

(60)   a. *John gave to Mary a picture of Nixon.*
        b. **Who did John give to Mary a picture of 0?*

The rightmost NP in (60) is moved into FOCUS, whereas that in (59) is in its underlying position. The distinction illustrated here was attributed to the Freezing Principle in earlier work. If we develop a new theory in which this constraint does not follow, it is still necessary to explain the data.[80] It is therefore interesting to see that the account of rightward movement that we are led to in the degree-0 theory has the consequence of accounting for this difference also.[81]

Finally, let us consider the rule of Stylistic Inversion in English. Like *There* Insertion, this rule appears to move the subject NP into an empty position in VP corresponding to NP complements of V. Logically, there are several alternative approaches to this construction:

1. Base generation of the "subject" in VP with
   (*a*) the fronted constituent in COMP or
   (*b*) the fronted constituent in subject position
2. Movement of the subject into VP with
   (*a*) fronting into COMP or
   (*b*) fronting into the vacated subject position

---

[80]See Culicover (to appear) where this point in connection with the Freezing Principle is elaborated in some detail.

[81]The distinction suggested in this paragraph allows for the possibility that the stylistic *there* construction is derived from the nonstylistic one by Complex NP Shift. On such an analysis, the first relevant stage in the derivation is (57a), and (58a) is derived from it. See Rochemont (1978) and Milsark (1977) for arguments that there is in fact a separate rule. Nothing crucial for us rests on whether there are two rules or one.

3. Movement of the subject into FOCUS with
   (*a*) fronting into COMP or
   (*b*) fronting into the vacated subject position

In all three cases, stylistic inversion could be derived from stylistic *There* insertion by deletion of *there*.

In our approach we can rule out Case (1*a*), because it presumes an empty subject at the point of thematic interpretation. Consider the following examples, in which the subject position is not filled.

(61)   a. *[e] was hanging a picture of Nixon [on the wall].
        b. *[e] was a picture of Nixon [hanging on the wall].

We have already discussed the Binding Condition *[e] (a consequence of the Completeness requirement) as a means of ruling out such structures. However, the Binding Condition presumably derives from conditions on interpretations, which are assigned before rules like Stylistic Inversion apply. So while the examples in (61) will be ruled out, they cannot underlie the corresponding grammatical sentences in which the PP has been moved into initial position.[82]

We can rule out all of the (a) alternatives by showing that the fronted constituent is a subject in this construction. In fact this is not easy to show, although Stowell (1981) has explicitly argued that the fronted constituent in Stylistic Inversion is a subject. Consider (62)–(63).

(62)   [On the wall] was hanging a picture of Nixon.

(63)   [Hanging on the wall] was a picture of Nixon.

There is, of course, considerable implausibility to the notion that the bracketed constituents in (62)–(63) are subjects, mainly because they are not NPs. Unlike NP subjects, they do not undergo Subject–Aux Inversion, nor do they appear as subjects in infinitival constructions.

(64)   a. *Was hanging on the wall a picture of Nixon?
        b. *Was on the wall hanging a picture of Nixon?

(65)   a. *It is necessary for on the wall to be hanging a picture of Nixon.
        b. *John believes on the wall to be hanging a picture of Nixon.

[82]The object position is always available for the subject in Deep Structure, because verbs do not syntactically subcategorize their complements, but select them on the basis of thematic considerations. Therefore, the grammar will automatically assign the correct interpretation to the single argument of a verb that takes only one argument regardless of what the grammatical function of the argument might be.

The examples in (64) could be ruled out if we assumed, following Emonds (1976), that strictly local rules must be stated in terms of constants; thus, Subject–Aux Inversion crucially involves NP and AUX, and cannot apply to ADV, VP, etc. Those in (65) can be ruled out in the following way. Following up on a suggestion made in Chapter 2, suppose that the base rules for English require only that subject position be filled by a maximal phrase of some category. There is some evidence for this assumption, based on examples like the following:

(66)   a.   *In my opinion, ignorant is better than stupid.*
        b.   *From here to Boston is quite a distance.*
        c.   *That John speaks French is well known.*

We are assuming that in general infinitival constructions are not sentential (see Chapter 2). In particular, those that seem to have surface subjects are not. In examples like those in (67), the "subject" of the infinitive is actually an object NP.

(67)   a.   *It is necessary for a picture of Nixon to be hanging on the wall.*
        b.   *John believes a picture of Nixon to be hanging on the wall.*

It is therefore possible that the fronted constituent in Stylistic Inversion is a subject. The subjects in (67) are not in subject position, in the sense of being immediately dominated by S. The assumption that the subject position is X^{max} while objects of P and V may only be NP would rule out examples like those in (65) given that there is no movement.

Because of the similar logical properties of subjects and of constituents in COMP, it is difficult to show that the fronted constituent is **not** in COMP. Negative and interrogative constituents take sentential scope when they are in subject position, and when they are in COMP position. Given that a constituent taking sentential scope can be in subject position, assuming that it is avoids the potential problem with the Binding Condition discussed earlier.

Consider next the question of whether the logical subject of the stylistic inversion construction is a complement of V or in VP-final focus position [as in (62) and (63)]. On prima facie grounds it might appear that VP-final position is in fact the correct one. It should be possible to extract from an "object" NP, as in general extraction from objects is permissible in English. As the following examples show, the VP-final constituent in Stylistic Inversion functions like a postposed focus, not as an object.

(68)   a.   *John says that on the wall was hanging a picture of Nixon.*
        b.   **Who did John say that on the wall was hanging a picture of?*

> c. *Who did John say that Mary saw a picture of?*
> d. **Who did John say that Mary gave to Fred a picture of?*

Consider, however, the proposal of Rochemont (in press) that an NP complement of V that is not directly assigned a thematic role by the verb is a focus.[83] In the English cleft construction, for example, the focus constituent forms a VP with the verb *be*, but as it does not receive a thematic role from *be*, it has a focus interpretation. We can imagine a similar analysis for Stylistic Inversion in which the superficial object of *be*, *be hanging*, *arise*, and so on, has the status of a focus. Thus the deep structure of (68b) could be the following.

(69)   . . . $_{S'}$[COMP [*on the wall*] $_{VP}$[*was hanging a picture of who*]]

The general restriction against extraction from focus would still rule out (68b).

Notice that if the fronted constituent is a subject, then the logical subject could not inherit its thematic role by binding [*e*]; there is no [*e*] in subject position. Therefore, the correct analysis of Stylistic Inversion must rely on an alternative device for assigning the thematic role to the logical subject. If the logical subject is in VP-final FOCUS position, an auxiliary device must be presumed. However, if the logical subject is in an argument position, then it will automatically be assigned **theme**. By Role Assignment, **theme** is not assigned by reference to a particular verb or the grammatical function of the NP, but is simply assigned to some NP. Other thematic roles associated with the NP in such cases can be made dependent on the prior assignment of **theme**.

To summarize, then, we have shown how Stylistic Inversion is not a counterexample to the claim that all movement transformations are structure preserving. We in fact concluded that there is no need for a transformational analysis of this construction, so that it does not constitute positive evidence for this hypothesis either.

A nonmovement analysis of Stylistic Inversion raises the question of why agreement treats the NP in the direct object position as the subject. A similar problem arises for the *there* construction. For concreteness we may assume that the non-NP subject "binds" the NP in the VP for the purposes of agreement, at least. See Borer (1983) for discussion of such a mechanism in a somewhat different approach.

What we have argued here is that all movement transformations may plausibly be analyzed as structure preserving, even the so-called stylistic

---

[83]It must, of course, be assigned thematic role, by binding an [*e*] that is assigned a thematic role.

transformations. In order to maintain this conclusion, we must define "structure preserving" in such a way that movement to FOCUS, as well as movement to COMP, is "structure preserving." In fact, these movements are "weakly" structure preserving. Movement to COMP moves a [+WH] to a [+WH] generated by the base and is not sensitive to a matching of categories. Movement to FOCUS also fills a position generated by the base component, and what is moved into this position is **nondistinct** from it with respect to category (as it does not specify category).

Besides reducing considerably the class of possible transformations, the constraint that all movement transformations be (at least weakly) structure preserving plays a crucial role in ensuring that the degree-0 property holds for the class of grammars. Although there are of course many potential counterexamples, the structure-preserving constraint seems both plausible and desirable.[84]

8.2. TOPIC and FOCUS

In our discussion of *Wh* Movement we did not include Topicalization, since the latter cannot be formulated as a movement of SPEC. It must be considered a movement of X^n to some designated position. Movement to FOCUS is such a movement, also. The designated empty category FOCUS discussed in the preceding section may thus be generalized with the TOPIC position.

Let us suppose that TOPIC is in fact FOCUS. The base rules introducing FOCUS will then be the following.

(70) $S' \rightarrow$ FOCUS S'

(71) $V'' \rightarrow V''$ FOCUS

Since S' is the maximal projection of M, which is $[+v, +M]$, and V'' is the maximal projection of V, which is $[+v, -M]$, (70)–(71) reduces to (72), if we ignore order of constituents.

(72) $[+v]'' \rightarrow \{[+v]'',$ FOCUS$\}$

To derive the correct order of constituents, we must first assume that a FOCUS cannot be in a position such that it can be construed as a constituent of a higher phrase. Consider the configurations in (73).

(73)   a.   [NP AUX $_{V''}$[FOCUS V'']]

[84]Weak structure-preservation is viable only if the distribution of FOCUS is severely constrained by the theory. We pursue this matter in the next section.

b. [NP AUX $_{V''}$[V'' FOCUS]]
c. [FOCUS $_{S'}$[S']]
d. [$_{S'}$[S'] FOCUS]

A configuration like (d) may be ruled out on the grounds that in a language that also has (b), there is no way to distinguish the two. Therefore (b) and (c), (a) and (d), or (a) and (c) are the possible orders. If there is a pragmatic constraint requiring sentence FOCUS to be in initial position, then the combination of (a) and (d) is ruled out. If V'' FOCUS is to be distinguished from V FOCUS, as suggested by Rochemont (in press) for Hungarian, then we would expect that for a language with right-branching VP structure, like English and Hungarian, the preverbal FOCUS would have to be V FOCUS, and V'' FOCUS would have to be on the right. Otherwise there would be no way to tell the two apart. Thus we tentatively assume that configuration (a) is not an option for such languages, either, leaving only the combination (b) and (c).

8.3. NP Movement Does Not Leave a Trace

Elsewhere in this book we have assumed that movement of NP does not leave a trace, whereas movement of *wh* does leave a trace. Often, the trace of *wh* can be shown to have phonological consequences, whereas no superficial evidence for the existence of a trace of NP exists.[85] It appears plausible that whether or not a movement transformation leaves a trace may be determined by whether it moves a constituent into an argument position or into a nonargument position.

In the learnability framework that we have developed in this chapter, NP Movement cannot leave a trace but *wh* must leave a trace. Consider the following surface structure inputs to the learner.

(74)   Surface Structure
        a. wh_i $_S$[. . . $[e]_k$ . . .]
        b. wh_i $_S$[. . .]
        c. $_S$[NP$_i$ . . . $[e]_k$ . . .]
        d. $_S$[NP$_i$ . . .]

Imagine that the learner does not have any transformations at the point at which each of these is encountered for the first time. In (75) we give the R-structures that the learner will assign to each input. We use "*" to indicate that no interpretation is assigned to a given NP.

---

[85]See Culicover and Rochemont (1983), Jaeggli (1980) and references cited there.

(75)   *R-Structure*
         a. $\{<wh_i, *, *>, <[e]_k, t', j>\}$
         b. $\{<wh_i, *, *>\}$
         c. $\{<NP_i, t, j>, <[e]_k, t', j>\}$
         d. $\{<NP_i, t, j>\}$

In (74a), wh_i c-commands and hence can bind $[e]$. An $[e]$ must be bound. Therefore the learner can conclude that wh has been fronted, by a chain of inference that we outlined in Section 5. Thus (75a) can be replaced by the representation in (76).

(76) $\{<wh_i, t', j>\}$

However, in (74b) there is no trace of wh. No thematic role can be assigned to wh_i because it is not an argument of the verb. Hence (75b) cannot be resolved into a representation that satisfies the requirements (Completeness and Distributedness) on well-formed R-structures.

In (75c) we see that both NPs have been assigned a thematic role. As $[e]$ must be bound, NP_i must bind it. Therefore the set of individuals referred to by NP_i has two thematic roles assigned by the same verb, which is a violation of Distributedness. The learner can draw the inference that NP_i is not assigned a thematic role by the verb but as the verb is not an idiosyncratic verb (like *seem*) this hypothesis cannot be sustained in the general case.

The data do not allow the inference that NP Movement has applied and left a trace. As long as NP_i has some thematic role, the learner cannot hypothesize that there is a stage at which it does not have a thematic role. Only if NP_i lacks a thematic role can the learner seek a trace with a thematic role that NP_i can bind.

In (75d), by assumption NP_i has been moved and the learner does not know this. NP_i is assigned the thematic role corresponding to the wrong position, and therefore the learner will hypothesize that NP Movement has applied, as we outlined in Section 5.

In summary, given the assumptions that we have made, a learner can acquire a movement rule to a nonargument position, and the movement must leave a trace. But under these same assumptions, structure-preserving movement to an argument position cannot leave a trace, as if it did, systematic violations of the well-formedness conditions on R-structures, in particular Distributedness, would result.

8.4. There Can Be No Movement to COMP in Nonconfigurational Languages

This view of the relationship between $[e]$ and movement to nonargument position has interesting consequences also for the analysis of case marking languages. Suppose that we have a language that uses the device of case-marking to mark grammatical relations. The association between a case-marker and a verb is plausibly one of government; we may say that V "κ-governs" a given case mark κ if V is a sister of the NP on which the case mark is expressed. By this definition, all the NP arguments are sisters to the verb, and the basic phrase structure rule of the language is (77).

(77)   S → V NP*   (or S → NP* V)

Consider next the role of COMP in such a language. It is plausible that universally COMP is a sister of S. Suppose that in a case-marking language of the sort expressed in (77) there could be sentences in which a constituent is moved to COMP position. The learner would then be presented with the following sort of datum, where k is a case mark.

(78) NP_i-k_1 $_S$[V NP*]
         (or NP_i-k_1 $_S$[NP* V])

By the definition of κ-government, k_1 is not governed in (78). Therefore, NP_i will not be assigned a grammatical relation or a thematic role with respect to V. As in a language that marks grammatical relations by hierarchy and constituent order, NP_i must bind an empty category in Surface Structure.

The problem for the learner now is that in a free word order language there is no mechanism for determining the location of empty categories in Surface Structure. Putting the matter more formally, let us say that an NP is "γ-governed" if it is assigned a grammatical relation by virtue of being a right- or left-sister of a V or P in a phrase V^1 or P^1, respectively. It follows from this definition that in order for the learner to determine that there is an [e] in the surface structure of a sentence, [e] must be γ-governed.[86] In contrast, [e] cannot be κ-governed, since it cannot have a morphological case mark. Therefore a language that has κ-government cannot have movement to COMP. Thus we correctly predict the syntax of questions and relative clauses in a language like Japanese, which in fact is strictly case marked and does not have movement to COMP.

---

[86]In *FPLA* Chapter 7 it was suggested that the context-free rules of the base component could be used to perform this function. Informally, a rough procedure for inducing traces is the following.

Parsing for traces:
    i. Verb V_i governs thematic role t
    ii. Verb V_i assigns t to γ
    iii. γ is expressed by configuration μ
    iv. No NP in this sentence bears the grammatical relation γ
    v. There is a fronted *wh* with no thematic relation
    vi. Therefore there must be an [e] that bears relation γ

Procedures such as these can be found in the parsing literature. See Fodor (1978), for example. We will come back to this point in the next section.

To recapitulate, in order for a sentence involving *Wh* Movement to be correctly understood by the learner, there must be a trace of *wh*. For there to be a trace of *wh* the learner must be able to determine where the trace is located in Surface Structure. We might expect, therefore, that there would not be "long" *Wh* Movement in languages that do not mark grammatical relations configurationally. In such languages, as there is free constituent order, a *wh* phrase could be ordered in initial position without movement to COMP. In the absence of substantial cross-linguistic work on *Wh* Movement we are not presently in a position to determine the empirical plausibility of this prediction.

8.5. Learnability and Parsing Are Subject to Some of the Same Computational Constraints

The preceding section points to the similarity, in our framework, between learning and comprehension. As noted in Section 4, a plausible learning procedure would assign a surface structure to an input and then assign an interpretation to it; the interpretation is then matched against the real world. In order for the learner to assign a structure, the learner must have developed a parsing procedure. Thus in this theory (but not in the degree-2 theory), the following holds: **A rule of grammar cannot be learned if it applies only on a structure that cannot be correctly parsed.**

Specifically, the learner must be able to locate surface structure traces in order to learn a rule like *Wh* Movement. There is no reason to believe that the procedure that the learner uses to determine the location of a trace is a different procedure from the one that the adult uses to determine the location of a trace.

In the framework that we are assuming, the parsing procedure that the learner uses for finding traces makes crucial use of phrase structure information in a configurational language. We should be able to make predictions about adult parsing from a consideration of the parsing procedure that must be assumed for the learner, and vice versa. Suppose, for example, that the procedure is essentially as we have outlined it here. Then it follows immediately that the first stage of parsing for an example like (79) will be one of the three structures in (80).

(79)   *Who did you give the book?*

(80)   a.   *Who [you $_{VP}$[give the book $_{NP}$[e]]]?*
        b.   *Who [you $_{VP}$[give the book $_{PP}$[e]]]?*
        c.   *Who [you $_{VP}$[give $_{NP}$[e] the book]]?*

If (80a) is selected, the interpretation must be that *the book* is the **goal** and *who* is the **patient**, as this is the interpretaton of the double object construction. If (80b) is selected, then no interpretation is possible at all, because *who* cannot leave behind a PP trace. We can rule out (80c) by assuming that parsing is "local" in a sense related to the principles suggested by Fodor (1978); as V NP can form a constituent, the parser does not attempt to insert an empty NP.

Suppose for example that the theory of parsing incorporates a Locality Condition, perhaps along the lines of the principles suggested by Frazier and Fodor (1978). Such a principle would require that if A and B are adjacent and there is a base rule C → A B, then A B form a parsing unit C.

Notice that the definition of γ-government given earlier provides us with an alternate basis for ruling out (80c). Suppose that the double object construction is base generated, and suppose that the indirect object position in this construction is not a γ-governed position: The sequence V NP does not form a phrase of category V^1 here.[87] Then the learner/parser cannot project [*e*] into this position. We thus derive the locality result from the definition of γ-government.

Ordering the phrase structure parse before the search for traces thus explains the ungrammaticality of well-known examples like (79). It also explains how traces can be found in the first place, given that they are not always phonologically marked.[88]

In Culicover (to appear) it is argued that other things being equal the Freezing Principle explanation of examples like (79) is superior to a parsing analysis if the principles that the parser obeys are not given some theoretical foundation. This does not mean that the Freezing Principle analysis is necessarily correct, nor that no conceivable parsing account can be right. In fact, we have suggested a revised learnability framework in which the Freezing Principle of earlier work is not motivated.

Moreover, the revised framework makes crucial use of a parsing mechanism that seeks Surface Structure empty nodes. Even so, nothing follows from this about the particular configurations that mask empty nodes from a parser; the principles of the parser must still be independently established. Crucially, as the parser is a real-time performance mechanism, its inability to make the correct hypothesis about the source of the fronted

---

[87]See Stowell (1981).

[88]See Fodor (1978) for discussion of a wide range of cases in which the interaction between assigning constituent structure and determining the presence of Surface Structure gaps is considered in some detail.

constituent in (79) should be explicable in terms of independently established performance limitations.

Berwick and Wexler (1982) show that the c-command condition on binding reduces computational complexity. It is plausible that the requirement that the parser compute only γ-governed ⌊e⌋s has comparable or even stronger computational consequences. Suppose that we in fact allow movement of nonarguments to the right in the case of extraposition, etc. For every NP in a sentence, projection of an $_{PP}[e]$ trace of a possible extraposed PP, or of an $_{S'}[e]$ trace of a possible extraposed relative clause, triples the number of hypotheses for that NP.

A sentence with two NPs thus has nine alternative parsing paths before the end of the VP is reached. Let us presume that complexity of parsing is a function in part of the number of alternative parses that must be sustained over the entire input string.[89] Let us also assume that a reasonable condition on a natural language parser is that the complexity measure is bounded from above regardless of the length of the sentence. Then a constraint on the parser that it hypothesize [e] only when it is γ-governed rules out the situation in which the complexity of sentences in general is a linear function of the length of the sentence.

8.6. Language Learnability and Language Acquisition

A common criticism of learnability theory is that it does not explain very much about the actual linguistic development of the child.[90] The degree-2 theory, for example, would incorrectly predict that children would make misattachment errors (a prediction not made by the degree-0 theory).

We would like to suggest that in principle learnability theory cannot, and therefore should not, make predictions about the course of language acquisition. Recall that we are viewing the input data to the learner as being of the form $(R, |S|)$, where R is a set of thematic roles and $|S|$ a surface structure. An idealization of the learning process places no limitations on the learner with respect to processing these two types of information. An account of language acquisition would presumably draw not only on linguistic theory, but also on theories of development that would account for development in the learner's ability to perform the following

[89]To explain why parsing complexity is measured in this way we would have to determine the organizational principles of the parser. To our knowledge these principles have yet to be formalized, although there are informal proposals in the literature.

[90]Suppes (1983), for example.

tasks: (*a*) process the morphological information of the input,[91] (*b*) perceive the thematic roles of objects in the environment,[92] and (*c*) construct well-formed interpretations of sentences and of what is going on in the environment. Just as a linguistic theory must be tied to theories of perception, action, and cognition, so must a theory of linguistic development be tied to corresponding theories of development.[93] It follows, therefore, that a learnability theory will fail to predict precisely those aspects of language acquisition that depend not on the learner's prior linguistic development, but on its development in other domains. To us this seems to be a perfectly natural and quite acceptable state of affairs.

9. Conclusion

In this book we have treated the learnability issue in terms of recent developments in linguistic theory. We have given particular attention to a modification in the assumptions of learnability theory with respect to the data that the learner is presented with, and with respect to the type of hypotheses and errors the learner makes. Central to our investigation has been the attempt to make feasible a demonstration of degree-0 learnability. This final chapter shows that the assumption of a general locality requirement on syntactic and thematic operations provides a plausible basis for a learnability proof. As such a locality condition would be of little interest if it had no implications for grammatical theory, we have shown that there is an interesting theory of syntax and thematic relations which incorporates just such a requirement of locality, the Locality Condition.

In the LC framework all grammatical rules and relations are subject to a relativization of the generalization that "all rules are local." Our theory,

[91]See Slobin (1966, 1973) for a discussion of the extent to which language learners are capable of extracting inflectional information from the linguistic data.

[92]See Brown (1973) and Slobin (1973) for close observations of developing linguistic perception and cognition.

[93]We therefore believe, following Wexler and Culicover (1980), that a theory of language learnability cannot be in itself a theory of language development. Nor can a linguistic theory be such a theory. A theory of language learnability makes use of a linguistic theory to determine the conditions under which a learning procedure will be successful. The sequence of hypotheses actually made by a learner will depend only in part on linguistic theory and will not be predicted by the theory of learnability; it will also be determined by the development in the learner of analytical abilities, exposure to particular contexts, and perhaps even maturational factors.

including the LC, has certain important consequences. Linguistic theory need not include the abstract, phonologically null element PRO nor a system of abstract case. All major rules, including movement to COMP and FOCUS, are structure preserving. And perhaps most significantly, in both the theory of grammar and the theory of learnability, the assignment of thematic roles plays a central role.

References

Akmajian, Adrian (1977) "The Complement Structure of Perception Verbs in an Autonomous Syntax Framework," in P. W. Culicover, T. Wasow, and A. Akmajian, eds., *Formal Syntax*, Academic Press, New York.

Anderson, Stephen R. (1977) "Comments on the Paper by Wasow," in P. W. Culicover, T. Wasow, and A. Akmajian, eds., *Formal Syntax*, Academic Press, New York.

Bach, Emmon (1979) "Control in Montague Grammar," *Linguistic Inquiry* 10, 515–532.

Bach, Emmon and George G. Horn (1977) "Remarks on Conditions on Transformations," *Linguistic Inquiry* 7, 265–299.

Baker, C. L. (1977) "Comments on the Paper by Culicover and Wexler," in P. W. Culicover, T. Wasow, and A. Akmajian, eds., *Formal Syntax*, Academic Press, New York.

Baker, C. L. (1979) "Syntactic Theory and the Projection Problem," *Linguistic Inquiry* 10, 533–581.

Baltin, Mark (1978) *Towards a Theory of Movement Rules*, doctoral dissertation, Massachusetts Institute of Technology.

Baltin, Mark (1981) "A Landing Site Theory of Movement Rules," *Linguistic Inquiry* 13, 1–38.

Berwick, Robert and Kenneth Wexler (1982) "Parsing Efficiency, Binding and C-Command," in *Proceedings of the First West Coast Conference on Formal Linguistics*, Stanford University.

Bever, Thomas G. (1970) "The Cognitive Basis for Linguistic Structures," in J. Hayes, ed., *Cognition and the Development of Language*, Wiley, New York.

Bird, Charles and Timothy Shopen (1979) "Maninka Structure," in T. Shopen, ed., *Languages and Their Speakers*, Winthrop Publishers, Cambridge, Mass.

Bordelois, Ivonne (1982) "Transparency," *Linguistic Analysis* 9, 161–203.

Borer, Hagit (1983) "I-subjects," unpublished paper, University of California, Irvine.

Bowers, John (1976) "On Surface Structure Grammatical Relations and the Structure Preserving Hypothesis," *Linguistic Analysis* 2, 225–242.

Brame, Michael (1978) *Base Generated Syntax*, Noit Amrofer, Seattle, Washington.

Bresnan, Joan (1971) "Contraction and the Transformational Cycle," unpublished paper, Massachusetts Institute of Technology.

Bresnan, Joan (1976a) "On the Form and Functioning of Transformations," *Linguistic Inquiry* 2, 3–40.

Bresnan, Joan (1976b) "Evidence for a Theory of Unbounded Transformations," *Linguistic Analysis* 2, 353–393.

Bresnan, Joan (1977) "Variables in the Theory of Transformations," in P. W. Culicover, T. Wasow, and A. Akmajian, eds., *Formal Syntax*, Academic Press, New York.

Bresnan, Joan (1978) "A Realistic Model of Transformational Grammar," in M. Halle, J. Bresnan, and G. Miller, eds., *Linguistic Theory and Psychological Reality*, MIT Press, Cambridge Massachusetts.

Bresnan, Joan (1982) "The Passive in Grammatical Theory," in J. Bresnan, ed., *The Mental Representation of Grammatical Relations*, MIT Press, Cambridge, Mass.

Bresnan, Joan and Jane Grimshaw (1978) "The Syntax of Free Relatives in English," *Linguistic Inquiry* 9, 331–391.

Bresnan, Joan and Ronald Kaplan (1982) "Lexical Functional Grammar: A Formal System for Grammatical Representations," in J. Bresnan, ed., *The Mental Representation of Grammatical Relations*, MIT Press, Cambridge, Mass.

Brown, Roger (1973) *A First Language*, Harvard University Press, Cambridge, Mass.

Burzio, Luigi (1981) *Intransitive Verbs and Italian Auxiliaries*, doctoral dissertation, Massachusetts Institute of Technology.

Chomsky, Carol (1969) *The Acquisition of Syntax in Children from 5 to 10*, MIT Press, Cambridge, Mass.

Chomsky, Noam (1957) *Syntactic Structures*, Mouton, The Hague.

Chomsky, Noam (1964) *Current Issues in Linguistic Theory*, Mouton, The Hague.

Chomsky, Noam (1965) *Aspects of the Theory of Syntax*, MIT Press, Cambridge, Mass.

Chomsky, Noam (1970) "Remarks on Nominalizations," in R. Jacobs and P. Rosenbaum, eds., *Readings in English Transformational Grammar*, Ginn, Waltham, Mass.

Chomsky, Noam (1972) *Language and Mind,* Harcourt Brace Jovanovich, New York.

Chomsky, Noam (1973) "Conditions on Transformations," in S. Anderson and P. Kiparsky, eds., *Festschrift for Morris Halle*, Holt, Rinehart and Winston, New York.

Chomsky, Noam (1975) *Reflections on Language*, Pantheon, New York.

Chomsky, Noam (1977) "On Wh Movement," in P. W. Culicover, T. Wasow, and A. Akmajian, eds., *Formal Syntax*, Academic Press, New York.

Chomsky, Noam (1981) *Lectures on Government and Binding*, Foris Publications, Dordrecht, Holland.

Chomsky, Noam and Howard Lasnik (1977) "Filters and Control," *Linguistic Inquiry* 8, 425–504.

Culicover, Peter W. (1976a) "A Constraint on Coreferentiality," *Foundations of Language* 12, 53–62.

Culicover, Peter W. (1976b) *Syntax*, Academic Press, New York.

Culicover, Peter W. (1977) "Some Observations Concerning Pseudo- clefts," *Linguistic Analysis* 3, 347–375.

Culicover, Peter W. (1980) "Adverbial Movement and Stylistic Inversion," *Social Sciences Working Papers* 77, University of California, Irvine.

Culicover, Peter W. (1981) *Negative Curiosities*, Indiana University Linguistics Club, Bloomington, Indiana.

Culicover, Peter W. (to appear) "Learnability Explanations and Processing Explanations," *Natural Language and Linguistic Theory* 1.

Culicover, Peter W. and Michael Rochemont (1983) "Stress and Focus in English," *Language* 59, 123–165.

Culicover, Peter W. and Kenneth Wexler (1974) "The Invariance Principle and Universals of Grammar," *Social Sciences Working Papers* 55, University of California, Irvine.

Culicover, Peter W. and Kenneth Wexler (1977) "Some Syntactic Implications of a Theory of Language Learnability," in P. W. Culicover, T. Wasow, and A. Akmajian, eds., *Formal Syntax*, Academic Press, New York.

Dean, Janet (1967) "Noun Phrase Complementation in English and German," unpublished paper, Massachusetts Institute of Technology.

Delahunty, Gerald P. (1981) *Topics in the Syntax and Semantics of English Cleft Sentences*, doctoral dissertation, University of California, Irvine.

Delahunty, Gerald P. (1983) "But Subject Sentences Do Exist," *Linguistic Analysis* 12, 379–398.

Delorme, E. and Ray Dougherty (1972) "Appositive NP Constructions," *Foundations of Language* 9, 1–28.

Emonds, Joseph (1970) *Root and Structure Preserving Transformations*, Indiana University Linguistics Club, Bloomington, Indiana.

Emonds, Joseph (1976) *A Transformational Approach to English Syntax*, Academic Press, New York.

Emonds, Joseph (1979) "Appositive Relatives Have No Properties," *Linguistic Inquiry* 10, 211–243.

Emonds, Joseph (1981) "Generalized NP–α Inversion: Hallmark of English," unpublished paper, University of Washington, Seattle.

Engdahl, Elizabeth (1980) *The Syntax and Semantics of Questions in Swedish*, doctoral dissertation, University of Massachusetts, Amherst.

Erteschik, Nomi (1973) *On the Nature of Island Constraints*, doctoral dissertation, Massachusetts Institute of Technology.

Fodor, Janet D. (1978) "Parsing Strategies and Constraints on Transformations," *Linguistic Inquiry* 9, 427–473.

Frazier, Lynn and Janet D. Fodor (1978) "The Sausage Machine: A New Two-Stage Parsing Model," *Cognition* 6, 291–325.

Gazdar, Gerald (1981) "Unbounded Dependencies and Coordinate Structure," *Linguistic Inquiry* 12, 155–184.

Gold, E. Mark (1967) "Language Identification in the Limit," *Information and Control* 10, 447–474.

Grimshaw, Jane (1977) *English Wh Constructions and the Theory of Grammar*, doctoral dissertation, University of Massachusetts, Amherst.

Grimshaw, Jane (1979a) "Complement Selection and the Lexicon," *Linguistic Inquiry* 10, 279–326.

Grimshaw, Jane (1979b) "The Structure-Preserving Constraint: A Review of A Transformational Approach to English Syntax, by J.E. Emonds," *Linguistic Analysis* 5, 313–343.

Gruber, Jeffrey (1965) *Studies in Lexical Relations*, doctoral dissertation, Massachusetts Institute of Technology.

Haan, Ger de (1979) *Conditions on Rules*, Foris Publications, Dordrecht, Holland.

Hale, Kenneth (1973) "Person Marking in Walbiri," in S. Anderson and P. Kiparsky, eds., *Festschrift for Morris Halle*, Holt, Rinehart and Winston, New York.

Hamburger, Henry and Kenneth Wexler (1973) "Identifiability of a Class of Transformational Grammars," in J. Hintikka, J. M. E. Moravcsik and P. Suppes, eds., *Approaches to Natural Language*, Reidel, Dordrecht, Holland.

Hamburger, Henry and Kenneth Wexler (1975) "A Mathematical Theory of Learning Transformational Grammar," *Journal of Mathematical Psychology* 12, 137–177.

Hankamer, Jorge (1973) "Unacceptable Ambiguity," *Linguistic Inquiry* 4, 17–68.

Hasegawa, Nobuko (1981) "The VP Complement and Control Phenomena: Beyond Trace Theory," *Linguistic Analysis* 7, 85–120.

Hooper, Joan and Sandra A. Thompson (1973) "On the Applicability of Root Transformations," *Linguistic Inquiry* 4 465–497.

Horn, George G. (1974) *The Noun Phrase Constraint*, doctoral dissertation, University of Massachusetts, Amherst.

Hornstein, Norbert and Amy Weinberg (1981) "On Preposition Stranding," *Linguistic Inquiry* 11, 55–91.

Horvath, Julia (1981) *Aspects of Hungarian Syntax and the Theory of Grammar*, doctoral dissertation, University of California, Los Angeles.

Iwakura, K. (1982) "Government Principles and Trace," *Linguistic Analysis* 10, 275–297.

Jackendoff, Ray S. (1972) *Semantics in Generative Grammar*, MIT Press, Cambridge, Mass.

Jackendoff, Ray S. (1973) "The Base Rules for Prepositional Phrases," in S. Anderson and P. Kiparsky, eds., *Festschrift for Morris Halle*, Holt, Rinehart and Winston, New York.

Jackendoff, Ray S. (1976) "Towards an Explanatory Semantic Representation," *Linguistic Inquiry* 7, 89–150.

Jackendoff, Ray S. (1977) *X-Bar Syntax: A Study of Phrase Structure*, MIT Press, Cambridge, Mass.

Jackendoff, Ray S. (in press) *Semantics and Cognition*. MIT Press, Cambridge, Mass.

Jaeggli, Oswaldo (1980) "Remarks on To Contraction," *Linguistic Inquiry* 11, 239–245.

Johnson, David (1979) *Toward a Relationally Based Grammar*, Garland Press, New York.

Kayne, Richard (1975) *French Syntax*, MIT Press, Cambridge, Mass.

Kayne, Richard (1981a) "On Certain Differences between English and French," *Linguistic Inquiry* 12, 349–371.

Kayne, Richard (1981b) "ECP Extensions," *Linguistic Inquiry* 12, 93–133.

Kayne, Richard (1983) "Connectedness," *Linguistic Inquiry* 14, 223–249.

Keenan, Edward (1976) "Remarkable Subjects in Malagasay," in C. Li, ed., *Subject and Topic*, Academic Press, New York.

Keenan, Edward and Elinor Ochs (1981) "Becoming a Competent Speaker of Malagasay," in T. Shopen, ed., *Languages and Their Speakers*, Winthrop Publishers, Cambridge, Mass.

Klein, Sharon (1981) *Syntactic Theory and the Developing Grammar*, doctoral dissertation, University of California, Los Angeles.

Klima, Edward (1969) "Relatedness Between Grammatical Systems," in D. Reibel and S. Schane, eds., *Modern Studies in English*, Prentice-Hall, Englewood Cliffs, N.J.

Klima, Edward and Ursula Bellugi (1966) "Syntactic Regularities in the Speech of Children," in J. Lyons and R. Wales, eds., *Psycholinguistic Papers*, University of Edinburgh Press, Edinburgh.

Koster, Jan (1978a) "Why Subject Sentences Don't Exist," in S. J. Keyser, ed., *Recent Studies in Transformational Grammars of European Languages*, MIT Press, Cambridge, Mass.

Koster, Jan (1978b) *Locality Principles in Syntax*, Foris Publications, Dordrecht, Holland.

Koster, Jan (1980) "Configurational Grammer," in R. May and J. Koster, eds., *Levels of Syntactic Representation*, Foris Publications, Dordrecht, Holland.

Koster, Jan and Robert May (1982) "On the Constituency of Infinitives," *Language* 58, 116–143.

Langendoen, D. Terence (1979) "More on Locative-Inversion and the Structure-Preserving Hypothesis," *Linguistic Analysis* 5, 421–438.

Lapointe, Stephen (1979) *A Theory of Grammatical Agreement*, doctoral dissertation, University of Massachusetts, Amherst.

Lapointe, Stephen (1980) "A Lexical Analysis of the English Auxiliary System," in T. Hoekstra, H. van der Hulst, and M. Moorgat, eds., *Lexical Grammar*, Foris Publications, Dordrecht, Holland.

Lasnik, Howard (1981) "Learnability Restrictiveness, and the Evaluation Metric," in C. L. Baker and J. McCarthy, eds., *The Logical Problem of Language Acquisition*, MIT Press, Cambridge, Mass.

Lasnik, Howard and Robert Fiengo (1974) "Complement Object Deletion," *Linguistic Inquiry* 5, 535–571.

Lasnik, Howard and Joseph Kupin (1977) "A Restrictive Theory of Transformational Grammer," *Theoretical Linguistics* 4, 173–196.

Marantz, Alec (1981) *On the Nature of Grammatical Relations*, doctoral dissertation, Massachusetts Institute of Technology.

Milsark, Gary (1977) "Toward an Explanation of Certain Peculiarities of the Existential Construction in English," *Linguistic Analysis* 3, 1–29.

Nanni, Deborah (1978) *The Easy Class of Adjectives in English*, doctoral dissertation, University of Massachusetts, Amherst.

Oehrle, Richard (1975) *The Grammatical Status of the English Dative Alternation*, doctoral dissertation, Massachusetts Institute of Technology.

Perlmutter, David (1969) "On the Article in English," in M. Bierwisch and K. E. Heidolph, eds., *Recent Developments in Linguistics*, Mouton, The Hague.

Perlmutter, David and Paul Postal (1978) "Some Proposed Laws of Basic Clause Structure," in D. Perlmutter, ed., *Studies in Relational Grammar* 1, University of Chicago Press, Chicago, Ill.

Pinker, Stephen (1982) "A Theory of the Acquisition of Lexical Interpretive Grammars," in J. Bresnan, ed., *The Mental Representation of Grammatical Relations*, MIT Press, Cambridge, Mass.

Plank, Frans, ed. (1979) *Ergativity*, Academic Press, New York.

Postal, Paul (1972) "On Some Rules That Are Not Successive Cyclic," *Linguistic Inquiry* 3, 211–222.

Postal, Paul (1974) *On Raising*, MIT Press, Cambridge, Mass.

Riemsdijk, Henk van (1978) *A Case Study in Syntactic Markedness*, Foris Publications, Dordrecht, Holland.

Riemsdijk, Henk van and Edwin Williams (1982) "NP Structure," *The Linguistic Review* 1, 171–217.

Rochemont, Michael (1978) *A Theory of Stylistic Rules in English*, doctoral dissertation, University of Massachusetts, Amherst.

Rochemont, Michael (in press) *Focus in Generative Grammar*, E. Storia-Scientia, Ghent, Belgium.

Rosenbaum, Peter (1967) *The Grammar of English Predicate Complement Constructions*, MIT Press, Cambridge, Mass.

Rosenbaum, Peter (1970) "A Principle Governing Deletion in English Sentential Complementation," in R. Jacobs and P. Rosenbaum, eds., *Readings in English Transformational Grammar*, Ginn, Waltham, Mass.

Ross, John R. (1967) *Constraints on Variables in Syntax*, doctoral dissertation, Massachusetts Institute of Technology.

Ross, John R. (1969) "Guess Who," in *Papers from the Fifth Regional Meeting of the Chicago Linguistics Society*, University of Chicago.

Ruwet, Nicolas (1982) *Grammaire des Insultes et Autres Etudes*, Seuil, Paris.

Selkirk, Elizabeth (1977) "Some Remarks on Noun Phrase Structure," in P. W. Culicover, T. Wasow, and A. Akmajian, eds., *Formal Syntax*, Academic Press, New York.

Siegel, Dorothy (1977) "The Adjacency Condition and the Theory of Morphology," in *Proceedings of the Eighth Annual Meeting of the North Eastern Linguistics Society*, University of Massachusetts, Amherst.

Slobin, Dan (1966) "Acquisition of Russian as a Native Language," in W. Smith and G. Miller, eds., *The Genesis of Language*, MIT Press, Cambridge, Mass.

Slobin, Dan (1973) "Cognitive Prerequisites for the Development of Grammar," in C. Ferguson and D. Slobin, eds., *Studies in Child Language Development,* Holt, Rinehart and Winston, New York.

Stillings, Justine (1975) "The Formulation of Gapping in English as Evidence for Variable Types in Syntactic Transformations," *Linguistic Analysis* 1, 247–274.

Stockwell, Robert, Paul Schachter, and Barbara Partee (1973) *The Major Syntactic Structures of English,* Holt, Rinehart and Winston, New York.

Stowell, Timothy (1981) *Origins of Phrase Structure,* doctoral dissertation, Massachusetts Institute of Technology.

Suppes, Pat (1983) "Review of *Formal Principles of Language Acquisition,* by Kenneth Wexler and Peter W. Culicover," *Psychology Review.*

Visser, F. (1963) *An Historical Syntax of the English Language,* E. J. Brill, Leiden, Holland.

Wasow, Thomas (1977) "Transformations and the Lexicon," in P. W. Culicover, T. Wasow, and A. Akmajian, eds., *Formal Syntax,* Academic Press, New York.

Wasow, Thomas (1979) *Anaphora in Generative Grammar.* E. Story-Scientia, Ghent, Belgium.

Wasow, Thomas (1980) "Major and Minor Rules in Lexical Grammar," in T. Hoekstra, H. Hulst, and M. Moortgat, eds., *Lexical Grammar,* Foris Publications, Dordrecht, Holland.

Wexler, Kenneth (1980) "Transformational Grammars are Learnable from Degree Less Than or Equal To 2," *Social Sciences Working Papers* 129, University of California, Irvine.

Wexler, Kenneth (1981) "Some Issues in the Theory of Learnability," in C. L. Baker and J. McCarthy, eds., *The Logical Problem of Language Acquisition,* MIT Press, Cambridge, Mass.

Wexler, Kenneth (1982) "Some Empirical Issues in the Theory of Language Acquisition," in L. Gleitman and E. Wanner, eds., *Language Acquisition: The State of the Art,* Cambridge University Press, Cambridge.

Wexler, Kenneth and Peter W. Culicover (1974) "The Semantic Basis for Language Acquisition," *Social Sciences Working Paper* 50, University of California, Irvine.

Wexler, Kenneth and Peter W. Culicover (1980) *Formal Principles of Language Acquisition,* MIT Press, Cambridge, Mass.

Wexler, Kenneth and Henry Hamburger (1973) "On the Insufficiency of Surface Data for the Learning of Transformation," in J. Hintikka, J. M. E. Moravcsik, and P. Suppes, eds., *Approaches to Natural Language,* Reidel, Dordrecht, Holland.

Wilkins, Wendy (1977) *The Variable Interpretation Convention,* doctoral dissertation, University of California, Los Angeles.

Wilkins, Wendy (1980a) "Adjacency and Variables in Syntactic Transformations," *Linguistic Inquiry* 11, 709–758.

Wilkins, Wendy (1980b) "Constraints on Rule Form—The Implications for Degree-2 Learnability," *Social Sciences Research Reports* 67, University of California, Irvine.

Wilkins, Wendy (1981a) "On the Non-necessity of the Locality Principle—A Review of Chapter 3 of *Locality Principles in Syntax,* by Jan Koster," *Linguistic Analysis* 8, 111–144.

Wilkins, Wendy (1981b) "Deep Structure Predication," *Social Sciences Research Reports* R89, University of California, Irvine.

Williams, Edwin (1975) "Small Clauses in English," in J. Kimball, ed., *Syntax and Semantics* 4, Academic Press, New York.

Williams, Edwin (1977) "Discourse and Logical Form," *Linguistic Inquiry* 8, 101–104.

Williams, Edwin (1978) "Across the Board Application," *Linguistic Inquiry* 9, 31–43.

Williams, Edwin (1980) "Predication," *Linguistic Inquiry* 11, 203–238.

Williams, Edwin (1981) "A Readjustment in the Learnability Assumptions," in C. L. Baker and J. McCarthy, eds., *The Logical Problem of Language Acquisition,* MIT Press, Cambridge, Mass.

Williams, Edwin (1982) "Argument Structure and Morphology," *The Linguistic Review* 1, 81–114.

Index